A Beautiful Shame

A Beautiful Shame

One Team's Fight for Survival in a New Era of College Sports

Ryan Swanson

BLOOMSBURY ACADEMIC
NEW YORK • LONDON • OXFORD • NEW DELHI • SYDNEY

BLOOMSBURY ACADEMIC
Bloomsbury Publishing Inc, 1385 Broadway, New York, NY 10018, USA
Bloomsbury Publishing Plc, 50 Bedford Square, London, WC1B 3DP, UK
Bloomsbury Publishing Ireland, 29 Earlsfort Terrace, Dublin 2, D02 AY28, Ireland

BLOOMSBURY, BLOOMSBURY ACADEMIC and the Diana logo are trademarks of
Bloomsbury Publishing Plc

First published in the United States of America 2025

Copyright © Ryan Swanson, 2025

Cover images: Actionshots Photos

All rights reserved. No part of this publication may be: i) reproduced or transmitted in any form, electronic or mechanical, including photocopying, recording or by means of any information storage or retrieval system without prior permission in writing from the publishers; or ii) used or reproduced in any way for the training, development or operation of artificial intelligence (AI) technologies, including generative AI technologies. The rights holders expressly reserve this publication from the text and data mining exception as per Article 4(3) of the Digital Single Market Directive (EU) 2019/790.

Bloomsbury Publishing Inc does not have any control over, or responsibility for, any third-party websites referred to or in this book. All internet addresses given in this book were correct at the time of going to press. The author and publisher regret any inconvenience caused if addresses have changed or sites have ceased to exist, but can accept no responsibility for any such changes.

A catalog record for this book is available from the Library of Congress.

ISBN: PB: 978-1-5381-9526-0
ePDF: 979-8-7651-5408-3
eBook: 978-1-5381-9527-7

Typeset by Deanta Global Publishing Services, Chennai, India
Printed and bound in the United States of America

For product safety related questions contact productsafety@bloomsbury.com.

To find out more about our authors and books visit www.bloomsbury.com and sign up for our newsletters.

The book is dedicated to the players and coaches of the Lobo men's soccer program. Thanks for, as Fish would say, playing your nuts off.

Contents

The Cast of Characters ix
Prologue: The Gadfly xvii

Chapter 1: Welcome Back? 1
Chapter 2: The Last First Game 19
Chapter 3: Home-Bred and Chile-Fed 35
Chapter 4: Forty Balls 51
Chapter 5: The Shame of College Soccer 65
Chapter 6: $605,630 81
Chapter 7: A Red Card for Pandering 97
Chapter 8: Two Big, Bold, Ballsy Moves 111
Chapter 9: Gallo 127
Chapter 10: Can We Stay If We Call It Fútbol? 139
Chapter 11: The Backs-Against-the-Wall Effect 155
Chapter 12: Is This Purgatory? No, It's Charlotte 169
Chapter 13: Saved by the Bill 183

Afterword 199
Acknowledgments 211
Notes 213
Index 231
About the Author 235

The Cast of Characters

Coaching Staff

Jeremy Fishbein, Head Coach, Seventeenth Season (Eighteenth Overall at University of New Mexico [UNM])
Fishbein took over the UNM soccer program in 2002. Since that time, the Lobos have won 70 percent of their games and appeared in eleven NCAA tournament appearances. He has been named Conference Coach of the Year five times. Fifty-three years old at the start of the 2018 season, Fish is married with two teenage daughters. He is an institution in New Mexico soccer circles.
Preferred name: Fish

Mike Graczyk, Associate Head Coach, Fifth Season
Mike is a Lobo legend, having played goalkeeper for Fish's teams from 2004 to 2007, including the one that reached the NCAA championship game. A native of Albuquerque and a graduate of La Cueva High School, Mike is the lead technical coach for the Lobos. After a short Major League Soccer (MLS) career and before returning to UNM, Mike coached at Harvard and Stanford.
Preferred name: Mike

Kelly Altman, Assistant Coach, Second Season
An Albuquerque native, Kelly came home for what he calls "the dream job." After playing for Division III Trinity College in San Antonio, Texas, and coaching at High Point and Valparaiso, Kelly now leads recruiting and logistical efforts for the Lobos. He is a graduate of Albuquerque Academy.
Preferred name: Kelly

The Cast of Characters

Lucas Champenois, Volunteer Assistant/Goalkeeping Coach, Third Season
Lucas is a volunteer coach in name only. He is at the complex all day, every day. He coaches for the Rio Rapids Soccer Club to make ends meet. A graduate of Saint Mary's College of California, where he was a goalkeeper and team captain, Champenois not only coaches the Lobos' keepers but is responsible for the crucial task of arranging team meals.
Preferred name: Champ

Joe Sorce, Trainer, Graduate Assistant, First Season
Joe arrived at the University of New Mexico just in time to find out that his primary assignment—the Lobos men's soccer team—was on the chopping block. Unfazed, Joe jumped right in. After two years as a training intern with the Dallas Cowboys, Joe is excited to have his own team. Also, as Joe confesses, he knows almost nothing about soccer.
Preferred name: Joe

Returning Players (Thirteen)
Nick Barreiro, Sophomore, Defender, El Paso, Texas
A product of the Real Salt Lake (RSL) Academy, Barreiro brings a quiet intensity to the pitch. A part-time starter and Conference USA (CUSA) All-Freshman player in 2017, Barreiro is looking to play a much bigger role in 2018.
Preferred name: Barreiro

Shamach Broussard, Red Shirt (RS) Freshman, Midfielder, Albuquerque, New Mexico
Shamach joined the Lobos in 2017 after playing at Sandia High School. A quiet presence in the locker room, Broussard has spurts of inspired play in practice. After redshirting throughout his first year, he is intent on finding the field in 2018.
Preferred name: Shamach

The Cast of Characters

Matt Dorsey, RS Senior, Defender, Spring, Texas
At six-feet-four, Matt towers—literally—over most of his teammates. He's a product of the Houston Dynamo Academy. A fifth-year senior who is back for one more season of high-level soccer, Dorsey is working on an MBA.
Preferred name: Dorsey

Grayson Dupont, RS Sophomore, Midfielder, Birmingham, Alabama
After redshirting his freshman year and playing in just a handful of games in 2017, Grayson is poised to take on a more significant role. The only true southerner on the team, Grayson clarifies that "his" Birmingham (AL) is the best Birmingham.
Preferred name: Grayson

Billy Jones, RS Sophomore, Midfielder, Auckland, New Zealand
Billy started every game last season and made the CUSA All-Freshman team. The New Zealander is steady, with a sarcastic sense of humor. He is comfortable in multiple positions on the field.
Preferred name: Billy

Bailey Letherman, RS Freshman, Midfielder, Sammamish, Washington
Bailey is a product of the Crossfire Premier Club in Washington, where his father, Troy, coached. A versatile and creative player, he redshirted in 2017 but is confident that he is ready to contribute in his second year in Albuquerque.
Preferred name: Bailey

Ford Parker, RS Junior, Goalkeeper, Albuquerque, New Mexico
Ford has been waiting for the starting keeper position for three long years. Parker attended Lobos games and camps as a child. Ford's aunt is on the faculty at UNM; his parents never miss a game. The elder statesman on the team, Ford helps set the team duties for the freshman.
Preferred name: Ford

The Cast of Characters

Aaron Scott, Junior, Midfielder, Edinburgh, Scotland
A cocaptain, Scott is understated and professional. He advanced through Scotland's highest levels of soccer, competing for the renowned Heart of Midlothian Club. In 2017, Scott started all eighteen of the Lobos' games.
Preferred name: Scotty

Tom Smart, RS Junior, Defender, Birmingham, England
The most decorated returner on the squad, Tom has been named to the CUSA All-Conference Preseason team. Known for his devastating slide tackles and pointed counterattacks, Tom controls the left side of UNM's defense. He's a cocaptain.
Preferred name: Tom

Simon Spangenberg, Senior, Midfielder, Brussels, Belgium
Simon is the team's academic superstar. After playing for two professional clubs in Europe, he is now in the United States to get an education and wind down his career as a soccer player. Simon chose New Mexico because he wanted a radical change of scenery.
Preferred name: Simon

Michael Sprauer, RS Freshman, Midfielder, Albuquerque, New Mexico
A local, Sprauer made just one appearance during his freshman year. He is an engineering major and a tutoring help for guys struggling with math-related courses. Sprauer went to Eldorado High School.
Preferred name: Mikey

Antoine Vial, Senior, Forward, Sète, France
Antoine moved from France to Springfield, Missouri, to play college soccer for Division II Drury University. He transferred to UNM at the start of his junior season. An honors student and one of the team's feistier players, Antoine is anxious to make an impact during his senior year.
Preferred name: Antoine

The Cast of Characters

Nick Taylor, Sophomore, Forward, Coppell, Texas
Nick came in and made a significant contribution as a freshman. A gifted dribbler of the soccer ball, Taylor is skilled at creating his own offensive opportunities. Though slight, Taylor is hard to miss—his mop of brown hair gives him a distinctive flair on the field.
Preferred name: Taylor

DEVELOPMENT ACADEMY RECRUITS (EIGHT)
Peter Chang, Forward, Parker, Colorado
Chang came up through Real Colorado's Development Academy (DA). Fishbein characterizes Chang as "a dynamic and athletic attacking player." Chang, unfortunately, will spend much of the 2018 season shagging balls, as he arrived on campus with a broken foot.
Preferred name: Chang

Alex Fetterly, Goalkeeper, The Woodlands, Texas
Alex is a supreme talent who has struggled with injuries. After high school, he took a gap year. He played with the Houston Dynamo and Texas Rush Development Academies and was called to camp with the US Under-18 Men's (U18) National Team.
Preferred name: Fetterly

Omar Grey, Forward, Seattle, Washington
Born in Jamaica, Omar looks taller than his six feet due to his Mohawk afro. Omar developed his skills with the Crossfire Premier Club and lettered in basketball, football, and soccer in high school. "[He's the] best athlete on the team," says Fish. Omar, for all his talents and charms, has a problem with being late.
Preferred name: Omar

Miguel Maynez Jr., Forward/Midfielder, El Paso, Texas
Miguel is an attacking player with a strong sense of the game. During high school he spent time with FC Dallas's El Paso club team—the same club Nick Barreiro trained with before coming to New Mexico.
Preferred name: Miguel

The Cast of Characters

Glademir Mendoza, Defender, Phoenix, Arizona
Mendoza is the Lobos' highest-ranked recruit for 2018. An alum of the RSL Development Academy, the wafer-thin Mendoza has competed with the US National Team at the U18 and U20 levels. Unfortunately, Mendoza arrives in Albuquerque with a recently torn ACL.
Preferred name: Pichu (something to do with Pokémon, but I'm too old to get it)

Ben Shepherd, Midfielder, Highlands Ranch, Colorado
Perhaps the most confident of the freshman, Ben was Chang's teammate at the Real Colorado's DA. He earned a top-25 ranking as a recruit from the Southwest region. "He is as driven as any player we've brought into this program," Fish says.
Preferred name: Ben

Erik Virgen, Midfielder, Tucson, Arizona
Virgen, like Pichu, came through the RSL Academy. He'd explored all his professional options before deciding to go the college route. Upon signing, he said, "The coaches at UNM have always been good to me, and it has always been a dream of mine to go to college."
Preferred name: Gallo (pronounced Guy-oh)

Elijah White, Midfielder, Portland, Oregon
White knows Fish the best of all the recruits, having attended UNM camps for years. An alum of the Portland Timbers' DA, Elijah is a versatile player ("can play any attacking position," according to Fish) and has the uncanny ability to always say what everyone is thinking but knows better than to say aloud.
Preferred name: Elijah

Albuquerque Recruits (Four)
Julian Garcia, Forward, Albuquerque, New Mexico
"Julian is one of the most prolific scorers in recent New Mexico history," Fish says the day Julian is signed. Julian competed at St. Pius X Catholic

High School, in the city. For Julian, choosing the Lobos was the culmination of his lifelong dream.
Preferred name: Julian

Carlos Gutierrez, Forward/Midfielder, Albuquerque, New Mexico
"A quiet warrior," Gutierrez waterbugs around the field with a rare blend of grace and power. According to the state's director of youth soccer, Carlos is *the* New Mexico kid to watch, even though he is among the smallest players on the squad. He played for Albuquerque High School.
Preferred name: Carlos

Anthony Munoz, Goalkeeper, Albuquerque, New Mexico
Although quiet, Munoz has a fierce work rate. Anthony comes to UNM from La Cueva High School, the same school Mike Graczyk attended. Because of this, there is a loyal—and loud—La Cueva rooting section at most home games. Anthony's father never misses a home game.
Preferred name: Anthony

Nick Williams, Defender/Midfielder, Albuquerque, New Mexico
Nick comes to UNM from Albuquerque Academy. His father, Greg Williams, is the lawyer leading the challenge to the Board of Regents' decision. In addition to being an all-state baseball player, Williams is a powerful, confident soccer player. His unflappable demeanor serves him well.
Preferred name: Nick Williams

INTERNATIONAL RECRUITS (1)
Maliek Howell, Defender, Kingston, Jamaica
Maliek is as decorated an international recruit as Fishbein has ever landed. He has played with the U17 and U20 Jamaican Teams. Unfortunately, the process of securing Maliek's NCAA eligibility is a complicated one. And so, Maliek is forced to sit and watch for the 2018 season.
Preferred name: Maliek

Transfers (1)
Matt Puig, Forward, Tulsa, Oklahoma
Matt Puig comes to New Mexico from Tulsa University, where, as a freshman in 2016, he started fifteen games, led the team in scoring, and earned second-team all-conference status. After sitting out the 2017 season, Matt has come to Albuquerque looking for a fresh start and, as always, to score some goals.
Preferred name: Puig

Prologue

The Gadfly

I'm still an outsider.

I mean, I've only lived here for a decade and some change. That's nothing in the Land of Enchantment. The people that reside here, in one of the nation's largest and most rural states, tend to have been here for a while.[1]

Maybe it's because of my relative newness that this place—the state of New Mexico and, more specifically, the city of Albuquerque (ABQ)—still catches me by surprise. It seems that weekly, if not daily, I find myself shaking my head and saying, "Only here." Oftentimes, the headshake comes from a place of wonderment, although I'll admit there are days when it's more from frustration.

Regardless, New Mexico is home. In 2013 our family of five relocated here from the East Coast. My three kids grew up here. It's here that my wife Rachael and I learned that, yes, green chile can go on almost everything. I teach at the state's flagship university. I feel a strange thrill whenever New Mexico is mentioned in the national press. *Let's go, New Mexico!* And when I see a fellow New Mexican, so identified by a shirt or hat or tattoo somewhere out in the wild, I have a compulsion to go greet them. *Hey, look at us. We're out here doing stuff.*

Perhaps it's also due to my relative newness, but I'm deeply troubled by something as well. This place has a corrosive mix of pride and shame. Yes, there is an ardent, fierce pride. New Mexicans take pride in their hardiness, diversity, independence, and, of course, their green chile. But this pride is often undermined by a crippling shame. During my job interview at UNM, one hiring official offhandedly said, "You should know, there's a deep sense a self-loathing here."

Partly, it's due to the lists. As the *Albuquerque Journal* editorialized recently, "NM is leading all right, on the lists of bad things." New Mexicans are acutely aware of these lists. They know—and will bring it up before you do—that the state ranks poorly on matters such as education, income, jobs, livability, health care, and child well-being.[2]

Recently, one financial company (Okay, it was WalletHub. What do they know anyhow?) ranked New Mexico as the second-worst place to live in the United States. Ouch. Headlines like this one—"New Mexico Remains Near the Bottom of US News' 2024 'Best States' Rankings"—are typical in New Mexico publications. New Mexicans certainly know that poverty is pervasive in the state. Thus, there's a scarcity mindset here, which creates competition for opportunities rather than a focus on creating a new, bigger pie to split up.[3]

Former Governor Gary Johnson saw the shame every day in his travels throughout the state. "I got it constantly," he tells me. "This is such a sucky place to live," he'd hear. "No, it's not!" he'd reply.[4]

If insiders are conflicted about the place, outsiders seem oblivious: "Wait, New Mexico? Do you need a passport to go there? Albu . . . how do you spell that?"

To outsiders, Albuquerque is as much a vague idea as it is an actual destination. It's the city on the sign post that the Road Runner and Wile E. Coyote race past in *Looney Tunes*. It's the lunar environ that gave rise to a high school teacher turned drug lord in *Breaking Bad*. It's the urban chase zone that appeared over and over again in the TV show *COPS* in the 1990s.

Yes, for most Americans, Albuquerque is a place that is somewhere, well, *way out there*. The three megacities in the west—Phoenix, Denver, and Dallas—each hold Albuquerque at arm's length, maintaining a buffer of several hundred miles. Albuquerque lacks many of the jewels that big cities prize. Albuquerque doesn't have any of the big four (MLB, NBA, NFL, and NHL) professional sports franchises. It has zero Fortune 500 company headquarters. Perhaps most devastatingly, In-N-Out, the beloved Southern California burger chain, cruelly skipped over New Mexico for years, even as it expanded into Arizona, Colorado, and Texas.[5]

What New Mexico does have, on the other hand, is WIPP, the Waste Isolation Pilot Plant. WIPP is the nation's only "deep geologic repository for nuclear waste." Translation: the federal government moves its most dangerous waste—some 185,000 containers thus far—from all around the country to New Mexico. Once here, the waste is deposited in a hole, albeit a very deep and expensive hole, for, well, forever.[6]

Above ground, too, much of the infrastructure is less than inspiring. Major interstates, I-25 and I-40, crisscross near downtown. Strip malls abound. A humble, four-building skyline butts up against Old Town. Weed-filled medians and stark, dusty parks connect the neighborhoods. The Kirtland Air Force Base, Sandia National Laboratory, and the Albuquerque International Sunport conglomeration bookend the city's southern limits. The Santa Ana Pueblo, with its beckoning casino, halts the city's sprawl to the north. Stuccoed, flat-roof homes fill the city. Trees are scarce, although pinon pines and cottonwoods dot the landscape here and there.

But for those who look closer, beyond the slights and the lists, there is a surprising, intoxicating landscape. Albuquerque, the Duke City, is bisected by the Rio Grande River. It is bounded by the ten thousand–foot Sandia Mountains to the east and the West Mesa on its Arizona side. A four-season climate is a haven for outdoor enthusiasts. Endless vistas and breathtaking sunsets are a Tuesday here.

The sun rarely hides in ABQ. At 5,312 feet above sea level, the air is noticeably thin. Each fall, hundreds of thousands of tourists descend upon the city for the annual International Balloon Fiesta, which is, according to its benefactors, "the largest ballooning event on earth, the most photographed event on earth, and the largest annual international event held in the United States." This seems like a hopeful declaration, but perhaps it's true.[7]

Then there are the people. Nearly one million people live in the Albuquerque metro area. The state as a whole is home to double that number. While it's not nearly as simple as the tricultural myth (Latinos, Native Americans, and Whites) that is often trotted out, there is a dynamic mixing of people here. Together, New Mexicans forge a distinct identity. V. B. Price, an artist and writer who has lived in and written about New Mexico for the past sixty years, describes the mindset of those who truly embrace living in the state's largest city, of those who truly get it:[8]

> *I don't find it offensive that the* New Yorker *would run a cartoon with a line that reads "obscure chess moves: queen's pawn to Albuquerque," I find it reassuring. I like living in a city that's the commercial capital of the most foreign state in the union. I like living in the outback, on the far frontier, in a city that everyone else thinks might as well be at the end of the world. It has its psychological advantages if you're part recluse, part romantic.*[9]

Part recluse, part romantic indeed.

***

Daniel Libit, the man who would go on to give the University of New Mexico's athletic department a journalistic colonoscopy, grew up in Albuquerque in the 1980s and 1990s. The only child of a clinical social worker (mom) and lawyer (dad), Libit attended Albuquerque Academy, the city's most exclusive private school for the wealthy and ambitious.

Like many Burqueños, Libit closely followed his hometown team, the University of New Mexico Lobos. With no major professional team, New Mexico's biggest big time was a Saturday night tip-off at The Pit, the University of New Mexico's basketball arena. Libit came of age, rooting for the basketball teams led by Coach Fran Frascilla. His interest "bordered on obsession," recalls one friend. While many years later, Libit would feel the need to clarify that he was not "in love with Fraschilla," something about the coach seemed to spark Libit's deep interest.[10]

Libit started writing early. Beginning in 2000, as a high school student, he interned at *Albuquerque Tribune*, the city's declining afternoon newspaper, where he covered recruiting and college sports. In the fall of 2001, Libit left Albuquerque to attend the University of Wisconsin. After his time in Badgerland, Libit put out his own writing shingle.

The still-emerging news industry of the World Wide Web became his temp agency. Libit pieces appeared in the *Milwaukee Magazine*, *Politico*, *CNBC*, *New Republic*, *National Journal*, and the *Washington Post*.

When he could, Libit worked the state of New Mexico into the national political conversation. He wrote an exposé of New Mexico Governor Susana Martinez when it appeared she might be a pick for vice president. Libit editorialized on the fact that in 2013, New Mexico was the only state to have avoided taking a position on gay marriage. He also wrote sporadically on college athletics.[11]

As he wrote feverishly to build a career, Libit also nursed a latent, half-baked idea—one he had briefly experimented with before. On November 5, 2006, at 10:20 p.m., Libit posted an opening blog post on *LoboAuditor*. "We begin. I'm here to provide a context by which to view the news you gather on Lobo basketball," he explained. "My interest is didactic." Libit then promised to dig deeper into Lobo sports *and* the journalists who covered the Lobo beat. At twenty-three years old, he would be the journalistic equivalent of a lawyer who sued other lawyers for malpractice. "And so, I present to you," Libit closed, "Lobo Audit. In operation until I get bored."[12]

Apparently, Libit got bored a week later. After seven posts that elicited zero comments, Lobo Audit went silent. It joined the deep ranks of mothballed blogs.

But the idea of bird-dogging, of gadflying, the Lobos persisted.

A decade later, almost to the day, Daniel Libit launched *NMFishbowl*. Fresh off of covering the 2016 campaign between Hilary Clinton and Donald Trump, Libit was a seasoned investigator. And he was not a Lobos fan anymore. "The scales had fallen from my eyes," he says. Both of his parents had recently passed away. Armed with an inheritance that gave him some financial wiggle room, Libit took to his new blog as a brawling, sarcastic truth teller.[13]

In his opening post, which called into question the legitimacy of the $10 million naming rights deal for The Pit ("Did UNM Ever Really Believe in WisePies?"), Libit described his new venture as "an independent website dedicated to providing a circumspect look at the University of New Mexico and its athletics department."[14] The description was one of the few understated components of the endeavor.

The timing was interesting. As Libit turned his full attention toward the New Mexico Lobos (beginning in late 2016 and lasting through 2018), a monumental change was simultaneously occurring in college sports.

In 2018 the NCAA was a boulder teetering on the edge of a cliff. Massive changes were looming, with the forces behind these shifts coming from all directions. The resulting uncertainty spread everywhere. Mark Emmert, president of the NCAA, felt the ground shifting. So, too, in a more granular way, did Paul Krebs, the University of New Mexico's longtime athletic director (AD).

At the time, the ramifications of the *O'Bannon v. NCAA* case were hitting campuses across the country. Ed O'Bannon had been a star player on the 1995 title-winning basketball team at the University of California, Los Angeles (UCLA). He was a lanky, smooth lefty. After UCLA, O'Bannon moved on to a short professional career in the NBA. Then he went to work for Findlay Toyota in Henderson, Nevada. It was at that point that O'Bannon realized just how much he had lost in potential earnings: On seeing his image in an *EA Sports* video game, O'Bannon joined forces with Sonny Vaccaro and filed a lawsuit.[15]

Ultimately, in 2015, the Court of Appeals for the Ninth Circuit had decided (mostly) in favor of O'Bannon. The ruling cracked open the door to providing college athletes with new levels of compensation. Before O'Bannon, athletic departments were restricted by the NCAA to paying athletes' tuition, books, and board. But that changed with the court decision, which attacked the NCAA on both pragmatic and antitrust grounds.[16]

Seeing the writing on the wall, a handful of state legislatures began pushing for further changes. In California, Nancy Skinner, a state senator from Berkeley, started working on a bill that would build upon the O'Bannon legal victory. Skinner drafted the legislation that would eventually become SB 208. This bill, upon its passage, would protect college athletes' rights to profit from their name, image, and likeness (NIL). If an athlete could get, say, LifeWallet to pay her to post something on social media, so be it. Such activity represented not a threat to sports but rather an embrace of American entrepreneurship.[17]

Even more dire, at least from the NCAA establishment's perspective, was the proliferation of cases involving direct athlete compensation. They would eventually coalesce into *NCAA v. Alston*. This Alston case, bundling multiple similar complaints and riding off of the high of O'Bannon's success, made a full-throated, unapologetic case for direct athlete compensation. Full cost of attendance and NIL were one thing; Alston was about grown-up compensation: salaries for college athletes.[18]

Perhaps reading the room for once, NCAA explored ancillary changes even as it waited for the courts' impending judgments. An NCAA committee began working on athletes' right to move institutions. Why, for example, were coaches free to move from school to school without penalty while athletes were not? The NCAA had no good answer. Thus, they went to work on a transfer portal. Gone, hopefully, would be the days of a scorned coach or administrator holding up the transfer process of an athlete. Team and school switching would be easier than it had been at any point in the past.[19]

Additionally, as always, there was Title IX. Since its adoption in 1972, the policy had fundamentally reshaped college athletics, adding millions of opportunities for female participants. The policy also served as an ever-escalating friction point in college athletics. As it approached its fifty-year anniversary, schools saw compliance with the gender equity statutes becoming increasingly fraudulent. As a GAO report would make clear, *most* universities were out of compliance with Title IX when it came to athletics. Many school had resorted to, according to a *USA Today* investigation, simply "rigging the numbers."[20]

Athletes brought claims of Title IX failure at Eastern Michigan University, among other places, to court in 2018. Commenting on the case, Peter Lake, a leading higher-education litigator, suggested the floodgates were about to open. As university demographics tilted increasingly female, athletic departments found themselves massively behind in their athletic offerings. A cottage industry of Title IX consults, including Lake, emerged to help universities position themselves in compliance with the law's technicalities and spirit.[21]

All of these changes—impending and realized, litigation and legislation, cost of attendance, NIL, transfers, Title IX, and whatever else was sure to be coming down the pike—left even the strongest, most successful, most well-funded athletic departments scrambling for cover in 2018.

The University of New Mexico got all of this tumult, plus the full, undivided attention of its very own gadfly, Daniel Libit.

Libit's approach with *NMFishbowl* was simple, but innovative. Disregard game scores. Pay no attention to recruiting. Ignore the press conferences and releases orchestrated by the university ("I'm not a stenographer," he says). But otherwise, question everything. "Journalism itself should be adversarial," Libit says. Pay special attention to athletic department administrators. Assume malfeasance on the part of coaches. Rely on inside sources to reveal what is actually happening. "Be skeptical at every turn."

Libit also had clarity about the potential revenue streams from his venture. There were none. "I lost money . . . I made nothing," he says of *NMFishbowl*. "There was no money to be made, like literally . . . take a small market team and then write *critically* about it, then the potential for advertising or any kind of revenue was zilch."

Thus, for Libit, this wasn't about money. It was about something else. It was a journalistic crusade of sorts. Not surprisingly, AD Paul Krebs saw things differently. "I think Daniel had an axe to grind," he says.

Regardless of his motivations, Libit dug in. Over the course of eighteen months, Libit turned his full, undivided attention to UNM's athletic department. He broke stories on a faltering arena naming rights deal. He unearthed serious Lobo athlete complaints through the NCAA-mandated exit interview process. He discovered that the university had been, on the one hand, overpaying two of its coaches by several hundred thousand dollars, while, on the other, failing to collect the dues owed for corporate suites in The Pit.

One scandal after another. Drip, drip, drip.

Libit's weapon of choice was the public records request. He made them by the dozens. Libit seized upon the documents that the UNM Athletic Department wasn't trying to hide exactly but that they didn't necessarily want to broadcast either. "It was abusive . . . he was just fishing," says Krebs. Still, the effect of having someone as relentless and talented as Libit paying attention to their every step dizzied the staff members of the UNM Athletic Department. "There was definitely a sense of paranoia," Krebs says of the Libit era. "Who is this guy? Where is he coming from? Where is he getting this information from?" So, Krebs banned his staff from speaking with Libit. Krebs spent time on leaks and moles. He urged his staff to have conversations in person, instead of requestable emails or texts, whenever possible.

While Libit acted as a lone wolf for nearly a year, eventually, other actors caught the same wave. The *Albuquerque Journal* dug into a story (which had been broken by KRQE's Larry Barker) about a lavish golf fundraiser trip to Scotland. When the money didn't quite check out, the state auditor (Tim Keller) jumped at the opportunity to get involved. Eventually, the attorney general (Hector Balderas) and the Office of Higher Education launched their own investigations as well.

By the time Libit wound down his work on the *NMFishbowl* in late 2018, the University of New Mexico—and especially its athletic department—were reeling. Libit had started a chain reaction. President Robert Franks was ousted. Paul Krebs escaped to retirement. Investigations and audits raged on multiple fronts. In 2019, Attorney General Balderas would bring charges against Krebs, opening up a criminal front to UNM's problems.

It was this mess that welcomed new UNM Athletic Director Eddie Nuñez and new UNM President Garnett Stokes.

And it was in this mess that Lobos' coach Jeremy Fishbein and his powerhouse mens soccer team found themselves fighting for survival.

Regarding that team, about which you're going to learn plenty, let's just start with this: Fishbein's Lobos had won championships, developed players drafted into Major League Soccer (MLS), and produced more Academic All-Americans than any other NCAA soccer team. Just as importantly, the Lobos soccer program had hosted more than twenty thousand children in summer camps over sixteen years. Fishbein and his boys had traveled the state, putting on clinics and promoting youth soccer development. The Lobos *were* New Mexico soccer.

But none of these accomplishments, none of this history, could protect the team from the swirling chaos.

So, in 2018, Fishbein and the University of New Mexico Lobos soccer team faced a season unlike any other. To some involved, it was a long goodbye; to others, a last chance for a miracle. *A Beautiful Shame* tells the story of that season.

Chapter 1

Welcome Back?

Day 1. Tuesday, August 7, 2018.
Albuquerque, New Mexico
"We've got to work our way through the interference," Fish says. "But we're still going to be pretty damn good."

Thus the 2018 season—presumably the last season ever—for the University of New Mexico Lobo soccer team begins with a meeting. Because, although he would tell you otherwise, Jeremy Fishbein loves meetings.

For the first time this year, Fishbein has his whole team in one place: twenty-seven players, four coaches, and a trainer. At the front of the team meeting room, Fishbein roams from side to side, radiating intensity. It's a tight, damp space. The swamp coolers are working overtime. Framed jerseys of Lobos who made it to MLS decorate the walls.

"Welcome back," he says, already halfway through his remarks, perhaps sensing that he's going a hundred miles an hour. "Welcome back."

The players have received a seven-page handout detailing the success of the program of which they are now a part. The short of it is this: the Lobos win—every year. The NCAA tournament is an expectation. So, too, is maintaining at least a 3.0 GPA and getting out into the community. "Excellence, *excellence*!" Fishbein says repeatedly. That's the bar. Yes, the recent decision by the school's Board of Regents to eliminate men's soccer at the university has created new pressures, but the expectations stay the same.

Chapter 1

A pointed discussion of team rules comes next: Go to class. Look sharp. No drugs. Be on time. Show empathy. Be polite. Be engaged and attentive. And on that last note, Fishbein clarifies, "I don't want to see cell phones ever. Ever. Be present!"

A minute later, Miguel's phone rings wildly. It's his mom. As Miguel scrambles in a panic for the mute button, Fish fumes. "Are you fucking kidding me?"

But the moment passes. Fishbein almost smiles. "You New Mexico guys need to wear this gear with a hell of a lot of pride. It's different here," he says. Then, closing, he remarks, "In terms of the future, I'm optimistic."

Day 2. Wednesday, August 8, 2018.
Albuquerque, New Mexico

There are fifteen minutes until practice. Fishbein ambles toward the soccer facility. As always, he has his stiff-brimmed Lobos hat. The Albuquerque sun spares no scalp, especially not shiny bald ones. "Fish," as almost everyone calls him, is walking because his office, like the team meeting room, locker room, and training room, is housed in the Maloof Athletic Office Building, a half mile away.

Through a parking lot, up the sidewalk, between two rows of adolescent cottonwoods, and toward the looming Sandia Mountains—through the University of New Mexico sports complex—Fish walks.

In doing so, he walks past the Tow Diehm Football Building (attached to the south end of Dreamstyle Stadium), where the finishing touches are being put on a $676,000 football locker room remodeling job. Next, on the right, he passes two football practice fields, with white goalposts and painted gridwork. Then comes the massive indoor football facility, then the track and soccer stadium, on his left. Lastly, there is a corridor of grass—never an easy accomplishment in central New Mexico—and some stairs. Fishbein approaches the steps and the overarching sign, "*Robertson Field*, Home of Lobo Soccer."

Just before the first stair, he stops and leans over. Fish grabs some litter. The coach throws it in a nearby, Lobo-emblazoned trash can.

Welcome Back?

With a few minutes to spare before 8:30 a.m., the players congregate in circles, juggling balls back and forth. The guys are dressed in black trunks and gray shirts, everything Nike. A few fire shots off the end line, trying to hook the ball into the net Beckham style. The tenor is loose and easy.

Kelly Altman, a second-season assistant with the Lobos, takes charge. "Alright, on the bands, boys!" he calls. Dutifully, the players pick up the elastic stretching bands and place them around their knees. Then they slide and skip and stretch. Hat pulled down tight, Kelly gets the players loose. For the first twenty minutes or so of each practice, his is the only voice that matters.

After just a few exercises, the goalies—Ford, Fetterly, and Anthony—break off with Champ (Lucas Champenois, a twenty-four-year-old former keeper who is the goalkeeping coach) to do their own thing. To be a goalie is to be part of the team, yes, but it also means these three belong to an entirely different species.

Stretching and then running, the position players limber up. Kelly demands a series of ever-escalating starts and stops, pauses and explosions, in order to prepare for an aggressive practice.

Finally, the balls come out. Cones and pinnies are at the ready. The team transitions in a matter of seconds. "Get a sip," Kelly hollers. The temperature is already in the eighties. The ball work starts with a square passing drill. The goal is to establish a rhythm of quick, crisp deliveries. The ball whips from corner to corner. The chatter of the warm-up echoes off the nearby football building. Given the full sun, everyone is dripping.

The Lobo soccer practice facility is among the finest in the nation. Three full, lush natural grass fields line up in a row. Rolling goals sit at the facility edges, ready for use in this scrimmage or that drill. The fence surrounding the facility is adorned with professionally branded tarps featuring "Lobo Soccer," the program's cherry and silver colors, and the menacing Lobo mascot. At the southern end of the facility is a storage shed filled with all the items necessary for running practices—two-dimensional player mannequins, small goals, flags for the corners, medium goals, and all manner of cones and pinnies.

Chapter 1

"I've had friends who are professional coaches from around the world who come and visit this and are like, 'Man, this is better than what we have,'" Fishbein boasts.[1]

With everyone suitably loose, Kelly turns the team over to Mike Graczyk. As associate head coach, Mike plays the dominant role in practice. It is Mike who stops and starts the drills most frequently. He does most of the correcting. He carries out the day's agenda. Today, at the outset of a long season, Mike focuses on rectifying mistakes. "The minute you lose [the ball], you've got four or five seconds to win it back," he says. He wants intensity and effort, not perfection.

The morning practice last two hours.

The team comes back to the complex at 5:00 p.m. for a second practice. They gather first in the meeting room. They file into the room in socks—no cleats allowed. Fish stresses the importance of pace in practice. "A little bit too slow this morning," he says.

Fish does not mention the news that just came out: New Mexico Attorney General Hector Balderas has concluded that the UNM Board of Regents violated the New Mexico Open Meetings Act with their July 19 meeting. This is the first notable crack in the school's recent decision to cut soccer.

The *Albuquerque Journal* gives the development front-page treatment (right below some happier news: "It's Chile Roasting Time!"), putting the UNM administration on notice. "AG: UNM vote to cut sports unlawful." Balderas is quoted as saying, "I want them to improve their process of evaluation and their process by which they involve community members and the student population they're impacting." The implications of this rather opaque expression of concern become clear in the following days. The attorney general wants the UNM Board of Regents to hold a do-over—another hearing and another vote—on the matter of cutting sports at the university. If the university leaders don't comply, Balderas (who just happens to be up for reelection) warns he will see them in court.[2]

Regardless, the boys head for evening practice with Fish in their ear: "Everybody is working. Everybody is nasty."

Welcome Back?

Day 11. Friday, August 17, 2018.
Colorado Springs, Colorado

Fish is doubled over at midfield, with hands on his knees and shoulders hunched. He has fixed his gaze on the perfectly manicured grass of the United States Air Force Academy at his feet. The New Mexico players flutter back and forth across the pitch while their coach tries to catch his breath on this warm August afternoon.

Partly, it's the physical pain. In his quest to get back into fighting shape ("I was fat last season"), Fishbein recently took a nasty spill on his mountain bike, resulting in bruised ribs and scraped hands and forearms. He's still healing.

But mostly, it's the prospect of losing his program—one that he built over the past two decades—that has literally stopped the bald-headed, old-school coach in his tracks. "I'm angry," Fish says. He slowly stands back up. Then his attention flips back to the task at hand. "Stop fucking complaining. Let's go!" he barks as the guys switch drills. He's stewing, wandering around at his own team's soccer practice, but he's only keeping one eye on the action on the field.

"You hear anything? I'm pretty distracted . . . I don't know what the next steps would be . . ." He trails off.

Wait, does he want me to check my phone?

There are many mantras in the world of Lobo soccer: "Work your nuts off." "Don't let yourself off the hook." "Control the controllables."

There's also this one: "Stay off your phones!" As he'd stated on day one, Fish believes phones should never be seen near a soccer field. *Never.* He holds himself to the same standard, even on a day like this one when he's obviously distracted and badly wants to check in with what's going on beyond the pitch.

What is the big distraction?

As the Lobos practice at the Air Force Academy, a political fight over the program's survival is playing out. Three hundred ninety-three miles south—back down I-25, at the Lobos' home campus in Albuquerque, New Mexico—the UNM Board of Regents has convened a meeting with one agenda item: to cut the men's soccer program (and four other teams) at the university. Again.

Chapter 1

***

Jeremy Fishbein took over as the head coach of the men's soccer program at the University of New Mexico in 2002. He had just finished his first year as an assistant at the school. "I was out recruiting in Arkansas," Fish remembers. "I got a call from one of the athletic directors that Klaus [Weber] had resigned . . . kind of out of the blue." Fish took over in Albuquerque and never looked back.

Fish grew up in Cincinnati, Ohio. A multisport athlete who'd excelled in baseball and basketball, Fish earned all-conference honors as a midfielder while playing soccer for Walnut Hills High School. "I was a tough athlete who liked to compete," Fish says of his playing days. "I wouldn't say I was a great technician."

He played physically and went all out. He didn't necessarily need the ball to do his best work—or, as one of his assistant coaches puts it, "Fish was a bruiser."

Fishbein earned a college scholarship right when NCAA Division I schools had started adding men's soccer programs by the dozens. After considering several schools, Fish signed with the University of Richmond. It was a mistake. His parents wanted a great academic school (Fishbein's father, Harold Fishbein, was a renowned professor of psychology at the University of Cincinnati), but the culture shock was too much. "Not the place for me," he says. "I probably didn't realize how Southern it was . . . and I probably screwed around too much."

Fishbein eventually transferred back to Cincinnati, then to UC Santa Barbara. "In retrospect, it was a disappointing college experience," he shares.

After short stints in professional soccer (in Australia, New Zealand, and California), Fishbein began his coaching career at Fort Lewis College in Durango, Colorado. The college had just begun its Division II men's program and needed someone with the energy and drive to get things cranked up—and someone willing to live in Durango. Fishbein fit the bill.

In short order, Fishbein built a nationally relevant program in remote southern Colorado. "Coach Fishbein created something out of nothing," says Jeremy Gunn, who succeeded Fishbein (and went on to win multiple national championships at Stanford). "He created a tradition of excellence." In 2006 Fort Lewis inducted Fish into its Hall of Fame.[3]

Along the way, Fishbein spent two summers at UNM in Albuquerque, working on a master's degree in sports administration. There Fishbein met UNM tennis player Alicia Meraz. Alicia was on her way to a professional tennis career and two graduate degrees from UNM. She and Fish married shortly thereafter. They now have two teenage daughters.

After a brief stopover at Incarnate Word University, Fish moved to New Mexico. Upon taking over the program, Fish "basically cleaned house," remembers one of his first recruits. New players and coaches flooded in while those from the previous regime mostly left. Any acceptance of complacency was squashed.

"We wanted somebody with a lot of fire and passion," says Rudy Davalos, who was the UNM athletic director at the time. "[Fishbein] was extremely confident in himself, and he was a hard worker. We knew he would be successful if given the proper support."

He was successful indeed.

Year 1 (2002): 18–4
Year 2: 8–9–3 (playing a more national schedule for the first time)
Year 3: 17–1–2
Year 4: 18–2–3

Built on the backs of New Mexico kids, especially those from the Albuquerque Bandidos Club, the Lobos became a big attraction in Albuquerque. Year four (2005) of the Fishbein reign culminated in the Lobos advancing to the NCAA College Cup and then the Division I tournament final. The Lobos fell, 1–0, to Sasho Ciroski's University of Maryland squad.

The winning continued from there. Under Fish, the Lobos won 70 percent of their games, qualified for the NCAA tournament twelve times, made the Sweet 16 five times, and returned to the College Cup in 2013. The Lobos also led the nation in attendance and raised $50,000 for Pat Grange's heartbreaking fight against ALS. The program produced twenty MLS draft selections. Academically, the Lobos were perhaps even more dominant, earning fifteen NSCAA Team Academic Awards

Chapter 1

and producing twenty-two Academic All-Americans under Fishbein's leadership—more than any other NCAA team during that period.

As the University of New Mexico website says, "Fishbein is the program's all-time winningest coach and has built New Mexico into a perennial power in college soccer."[4]

But none of that could offset the budgetary typhoon that had descended upon Lobo Athletics by 2018. Year after year of deficits and red ink. Something had to change.

***

As rumors about cutting the Lobo soccer program surfaced beginning in April, the roster for the 2018 season came together haltingly.

Three of the Lobos who had remaining eligibility bolted to sign professional contracts. Most prominently, Aaron Herrara, a Las Cruces native, inked a homegrown contract with Real Salt Lake. Herrera had led the Lobos in scoring in 2017.

Six other members of the 2017 Lobos with remaining eligibility transferred to other schools. Three players graduated.

It is noteworthy that in 2018, player movement between universities is more rampant in college soccer than in any other sport. According to the NCAA, 18.1 percent of the average Division I soccer roster is comprised of players who competed at another university first. Unlike college baseball, basketball, football, and hockey players in 2018, college soccer players have the blessing of the NCAA to transfer and play immediately.

On average, the Lobos have been turning over about a third of their roster each year. However, in 2018, the tumult is much more significant. The Lobos, for the first time in recent memory, will have fewer returning players than new ones. Thus, the Lobos have an abundance of freshmen. Everywhere you look, there are freshmen doing freshmen things. On gear day, on being instructed to write his name in his team-issued Nike swag, one freshman does so with gusto. Now his name shows through the back of his shirts.

The fourteen newcomers can be separated into four basic groups: United States Soccer Development Academy (USSDA) recruits, Albuquerque recruits, transfers, and foreign recruits.

Welcome Back?

The USSDA recruits arrive in Albuquerque from all over the United States. They're guys like Omar Grey. Born in Jamaica, Omar looks taller than his six-foot frame due to his Mohawk afro. Omar developed his game with the Crossfire Premier Club in Seattle, Washington, and unlike many of his generation, he refused to specialize too early. He lettered in basketball, football, and soccer in high school. "A borderline DI basketball player," says Fish.

The four Albuquerque recruits (Anthony, Carlos, Julian, and Nick Williams) know the city and university well. They grew up attending Lobos games and camps. Nick Williams (who, like Christopher Robin, always seems to be called by his first and last names) comes to the Lobos squad from the ritzy Albuquerque Academy. His father, Greg Williams, is the lawyer who is taking the lead in challenging the Board of Regents' decision. Nick Williams is a powerful, compact, confident player.

The one transfer who sticks around for the 2018 season is Matt Puig (several arrive but then make quick departures without ever playing a game for the Lobos). Puig comes to New Mexico from Tulsa University, where, in 2016, he started fifteen games as a freshman, led the team in scoring, and earned second-team all-conference. After sitting out the 2017 season, Matt is coming to New Mexico looking for a fresh start and, always, to score some goals.

The last of the newcomers is Maliek Howell, a six-foot-one defender from Kingston, Jamaica. He is a dominant player, who has played with the U17 and U20 Jamaican teams. Unfortunately for all involved, UNM cannot figure out how to get Maliek eligible for the 2018 season. Thus, he is marooned in ABQ for the fall, with no outlet for his considerable soccer skill set.

These fourteen newcomers join thirteen returning players.

The returnees also include a good number of Development Academy products. Fifth-year senior Matt Dorsey (Houston Dynamo) leads the veterans. Nick Barreiro (Real Salt Lake U18), Grayson Dupont (Birmingham, Alabama), Bailey Letherman (Seattle Crossfire Premier), and Nick Taylor (Dallas Texans Red U99) all expect to play major minutes.

Additionally, there is a tight-knit international contingent among the returnees: Simon Spangenberg (Belgium), Antoine Vial (France), Tom Smart (England), Aaron "Scotty" Scott (Scotland), and Billy Jones (New Zealand).

Certainly, though, it's the locals—Ford, Mikey, and Shamach—among the returnees with the most to lose, particularly Ford Parker.

Ford Parker is the redshirt junior goalkeeper who has been waiting his turn. A product of Albuquerque's Sandia High School, Ford has targeted 2018 as *his* year. Jason Beaulieu, the goalie who is now with the Montreal Impact, has finally—after four years as a starter—vacated the spot between the pipes.

Day 11. Friday, August 17, 2018.
Albuquerque, New Mexico

At the front of the large ballroom sits the Board of Regents and the university's most senior administrators. A few minutes before 1:00 p.m., President Garnett Stokes enters the room. She greets and chats as she makes her way to the center of the u-shaped table, to the center of a maelstrom that began gathering forces years and years before she'd arrived.

Stokes has a whole host of concerns to tackle for her new university. She's been on the job for less than six months. But athletics tend to draw more public interest than issues surrounding the university's new hospital project or the institution's declining enrollment. As Stokes says with a wry smile, "Athletics is always going to get more scrutiny than, say, the budget for the history department."

Stokes knows well the burdens of Division I athletics and their accompanying scandals. During her time as the interim president at Florida State University, Stokes had to deal with Jameis Winston, the Seminoles' star quarterback. Stokes suspended Winston for a key game after a series of incidents (including shoplifting and lewd behavior) crescendoed. At the University of Missouri, she'd navigated the tumult following the Ferguson riots, when the school's football team threatened to quit.[5]

So, Stokes knows about the power of football, but none of her previous institutions—Georgia, Florida State, or Missouri—even fielded a men's soccer team.

Rob Doughty, chairman of the Board of Regents and a personal injury lawyer by trade, calls the meeting to order at 1:05 p.m. He starts by stating the obvious: This is a do-over. The Board had already made this decision on July 19, and they are only revisiting it because the state's attorney general determined that the original proceedings violated New Mexico's open meetings statute.

Nearly four hundred people jam the ballroom. The seats are full; dozens of additional spectators stand along the outer walls of the space. A high school student wearing a Lobo soccer summer camp shirt holds a sign that reads, "Can we stay if we call it fútbol?"

"Our student athletes are talented, dedicated young men and women, and their accomplishments are a point of pride," Stokes begins, reading from prepared remarks. "Athletic programs are vital to who we are as an institution and a community."

But then it's on to the problems.

The New Mexico Department of Higher Education has placed UNM under its "enhanced financial oversight program" due, in large part, to the recurring issues in the athletic department.

From this sobering reality, Stokes moves on to a point that she emphasizes repeatedly, perhaps because it is among the most simple, powerful arguments at her disposal: The university simply has too many teams. If the University of Texas, for example, with its behemoth $220 million budget, supports the NCAA minimum of sixteen athletic teams, how can UNM (with a quarter of the budget) have twenty-two?

Too many teams. Not enough money.

Stokes's argument wins over few, if any, in the crowd. No one's really here to change sides. But if nothing else, Stokes conveys the real angst over the decision she feels. It's a "painful, painful process," she says. "Obviously no one does this unless they think they absolutely have to."

After Stokes, the athletic director, Eddie Nuñez, takes over. He's been at New Mexico just a few months more than Stokes. He's inherited an athletic department that's under intense scrutiny. Like the president, he came to UNM from a Southeastern Conference (SEC) school—Louisiana State University. There for fourteen years, Nuñez helped to literally build the Tigers program. He oversaw more than $400 million in construction improvements to LSU's gleaming, sprawling athletic facilities complex. Now he's in New Mexico. With a budget crisis. In front of an audience enraged over a soccer cut (LSU does not field a men's soccer team either), and he is tasked with presenting—again—the case for downsizing.

Nuñez articulates the three main criteria used to determine which teams got cut.

First, the athletics department needed to find real financial relief. The cuts only mattered if they could put a significant dent in the recurring budget deficit of nearly $2 million.

Second, the changes had to bring the university into compliance with Title IX law.

Third, the team chosen cannot affect the school's relationship with the Mountain West Conference. The University of New Mexico helped found the Mountain West Conference in 1999 (as a breakaway from the unwieldy Western Athletic Conference [WAC]). The school has no desire to jeopardize that relationship with the conference in 2018. The men's soccer team competes in Conference USA, as the Mountain West does not offer the sport.[6]

***

Fifty-three people have signed up to speak. Every single one is against the cuts. Grim-faced, Doughty calls up the first speaker.

Patricia "Patty" Lundstrom steps to the podium amid applause.

Lundstrom, the chair of the legislature's Appropriations and Finance Committee, puts her reading glasses on the tip of her nose. The sixty-year-old political brawler has served in the New Mexico legislature since 2001. She represents a district in Gallup, a city of twenty thousand that sits on the western edge of the state and is adjacent to the Navajo Nation.[7]

Lundstrom is among the most powerful politicians in the state. She heads the committee that controls the state's purse strings. And right now, she's a bit perturbed.

After starting with a few benign compliments, Lundstrom demands a stay of execution. "Today the legislature is in a stronger position," she says. The oil boom going on in southern New Mexico's Permian Basin has changed the state's situation considerably.

Lundstrom has made the two-hour drive to Albuquerque today, at least in part, because Fishbein has made the trip in the opposite direction so many times. Fish has traveled regularly throughout New Mexico, including to out-of-the-way places like Gallup, to spread the gospel of Lobo soccer. In fact, Fish had taken Eddie, shortly after the AD's arrival, to a meet and greet in Gallup just a few months prior. Such forays were deeply appreciated by Lundstrom and other New Mexicans living in remote outposts. As the *Gallup Journey* editorialized, "Coach Jeremy Fishbein has always been willing to come to Gallup and conduct soccer clinics for coaches and players. Many Gallup supporters in turn have supported his efforts to build up UNM into a national contender."[8]

Lundstrom continues. The state will find the money. For once, there is money to spend. Her applause line is this: "My request of you today is to slow down, postpone your decision, and work with me and the legislature to define a path to solve this problem." With this, the audience erupts in cheers.

Time! Time!

Doughty cuts Lundstrom off, just as she is saying, "You know, Title IX is a good thing . . ."

"Time. Time. Thank you, Representative, the time's up. We've got to get through everybody today."

Stunned, Lundstrom stares at the Board in disbelief. She is offering more funding for Lobos athletics than ever before. The crowd boos and taunts.

"Let her speak!"

"This is stupid."

"Oh, come on!"

"She's an official of the state. Let her speak!"

Chapter 1

Several people shout out offers to give Lundstrom their allotted time. But the Board does not budge from its three-minutes-per-person standard. Slowly, maintaining eye contact with the people at the u-shaped table, Lundstrom gathers up her papers. She lets the moment hang and draw out. Then she backs away from the microphone.

Thus, the embers of political war gain a powerful dose of oxygen.

After Lundstrom, four other Democrat politicians take their three minutes to rail against the Board's decision. Their criticisms range from a call to cut football and a complaint about why more in-state athletes are not on scholarship to points about coaching salaries and the university's proclivity for "golden parachutes."

Rep. Moe Maestras closes with a cultural plea. Albuquerque is a soccer city. "Don't cut soccer in a city where 65 percent of our first graders are Latino; it just doesn't make sense," he concludes.

The parade of speakers in favor of keeping UNM's soccer program continues for more than four hours. "The team can't be here. They're in Colorado getting ready for a game," says Tom Parker, Ford's father. So others talk for them. Students. Alums. Economists. Lawyers. Coaches.

They all have basically the same message: *While we understand the budget challenges, please don't do this.*

Finally, the Board of Regents retakes control of the conversation. The group enters into a forced, awkward, faux debate on the matter.

What had the university requested from the legislature in the past? How important is the Mountain West Conference, really? Should the university just forgive the athletics department's debt? How many New Mexicans are on each of the discussed teams? (This is always a favorite.)

When the group lands back on the topic of Title IX, it becomes clear that the Board of Regents does not really understand the intricacies of the law as they apply to college athletics. One regent begins reading from the statute. He stops. "I wonder if someone could comment on the federal law?" *Can someone explain Title IX?*

"Eddie?"

"I'm the wrong person, I can't comment on federal law," the AD responds, standing halfway before retreating back to his chair.

The members of the Board then ask if the dean of the New Mexico Law School is in the room. Perhaps he could explain the issue. Alas, he is not.

Finally, at 5:25 p.m., Chairman Doughty calls for a vote. Soccer, along with skiing and beach volleyball, remains on the chopping block.

"I move to approve the administration's proposal to eliminate those sports."

"All those in favor say, 'Aye.'"

"Aye."

"All those opposed?"

Silence.

"It passes unanimously. Seven to zero."

The crowd boos but, this time, with a sense of resignation and fatigue. And with that, the Board adjourns. The action portion of the meeting takes less than a minute. It's done. Again.

***

After practice at the Air Force Academy, Fish makes it back to his hotel room in time to watch the last two hours of the Board meeting on Facebook. He is stunned at the result. "Speechless and numb," he says minutes after the final vote.

Later that evening, the team gathers in a frigid conference room at the Baymont Inn and Suites to discuss the situation. Reactions to the news vary. For the New Mexico players especially, the loss of the program is devastating. For those Lobos with just one season left to play, it is disconcerting and confusing. For others, including the foreign guys, it simply means returning to the recruiting treadmill and looking for a new team.

"The distractions are only going to increase," Fish warns the group. Then he sends everyone—two by two, as that's the rooming arrangement—off to bed.

Chapter 1

Day 12. Saturday, August 18, 2018.
Colorado Springs, Colorado

The Lobos play their final exhibition game at noon. The Falcons are a tough, disciplined team; they qualified for the NCAA tournament in 2017.

"It's a pretty sweet test for us," Fish says to the team in the cramped locker room before the game. "Be excited. How good can you be?" And then an odd last-minute reminder: "No cussing."

As the two teams warm up, a cool breeze blows through the foothills. Air Force's soccer stadium consists of a small press building with a set of bleachers on either side. The place would not deserve a second glance if not for the mountains behind the facility. But with the Rampart Range looming over the field, it's one of the most scenic college soccer venues in the country.

As the warm-ups wind down, clouds gather behind the mountains, first providing welcomed shade but then stirring concerns about hail and lighting—a constant issue in Colorado Springs in late summer.

Just minutes before game time, the Air Force coaches jog over to their New Mexico counterparts to confer. With a storm surely approaching, the Air Force officials want to move the game into the school's indoor football facility. It's half a mile away. After a bit of griping, the New Mexico players gather their stuff. The several dozen fans head for their cars. The New Mexico team piles back onto its chartered bus for the short drive across campus.

As it turns out, not even the US Air Force can really predict the weather. By the time everyone arrives at the new game venue, not more than ten minutes after the venue decision has been made, the winds have blown the clouds away. The storm has disappeared.

Walking up the steps in the sunshine, Fish can't help but call out the Air Force. "Army or Navy would have fucking got this right," he jabs at the Falcon's coaches.

Air Force plays to a 1–0 lead during the first forty-five minutes. At halftime, the Air Force contingent comes across the indoor field and issues a mea culpa. "Let's go back outside." The weather is now perfect:

the sun is shining, and a still, cool breeze is blowing. Air Force wants to get back out on its natural grass surface.

After a bit of back and forth, again with some grumbling from his players, Fish gives in. Everybody piles back into their cars to return to the outdoor field for the second half. Several pickup trucks haul the Falcons up the hill, five or six in the back of each.

The second half is played outside. With five minutes left in regulation, the Lobos finally score an equalizer. Bailey takes a penalty kick, and Billy heads in the rebound: 1–1. The game ends tied.

While hardly an ideal exhibition trip, the coaches are generally pleased. Two good teams (the Lobos tied 2–2 at Denver University two nights earlier) and two good efforts. "We're going to be pretty good," Fish says on the field after the Air Force game.

But after a bizarre indoor-outdoor exhibition and two Colorado ties, all while the program is being cut for a second time, who can really know?

Chapter 2

The Last First Game

Day 17. Thursday, August 23, 2018.
Albuquerque, New Mexico
The Pixar movie *Coco* is basically about overcoming death. The film's main character, Miguel, navigates the Land of the Dead to reemerge happier and wiser, with his gifts fully realized. *Coco* is playing this Thursday evening at 8:00 p.m. There must be a message here.

Tomorrow the New Mexico men's soccer team plays its opening regular season game, perhaps the program's last first game. New Mexico is hosting Seattle University, a team ranked no. 22 in the nation that just happens to have an All-American player from Albuquerque. The enemy is led by one who got away.

To get the boys' minds right, Kelly and Champ have arranged for a walk-through on the game field. The players arrive in a trickle, in their usual groups: Simon and Antoine (speaking French); Gallo, Pichu, and Miguel (speaking Spanish); and then Billy, Tom, Ford, Scotty, and Dorsey (speaking English). The rest trickle in just on time. The players walk through the gates, across the track, and slowly toward the center of the soccer field. The only light comes from the scoreboard and the nearly full moon.

The scene would already be too much, too perfect and dripping with sentiment, even without the sounds of *Coco* playing in the background. But it just so happens that the unique architecture of the sports complex at UNM features adjoining football and soccer stadiums. A set of cement bleachers leads up from the soccer field and then plateaus in a walkway before it descends the other side to the east side of the school's Dreamstyle Football Stadium.

And tonight, the UNM Athletic Department is hosting a Movie on the Field night, featuring a free showing of *Coco*. The event started at 7:00 p.m., and thus, by the time the Lobo soccer players arrive on their side of the complex, the Disney movie is in the middle of its Land of the Dead glory. Blankets are strewn across the football field, and families are enjoying their free popcorn. The music of Ernesto de la Cruz hangs over the evening, bridging the divide from football to fútbol.

"Let's get a really big, clear picture," Fish says once everyone is accounted for.

But first, there's a video. For five minutes the players watch from midfield as the season's pregame video is unveiled on the scoreboard. It's Champ's work; he does most of the film editing. This particular footage will be played before home games to ramp up the crowd. It contains montages of each player to be used for their introductions and when a player scores a goal. In other words, it's a pre-orchestrated chance for each player to mug for the camera for ten or so seconds, with the idea that their antics will be shown following a noteworthy play of some sort. Intermixed are montages of previous Lobo glory—shots of great goals and roaring crowds.

If the video's intended effect was to remind this group of twenty-plus twenty-somethings that they are a part of something with a long history, then it's unclear if it hits the mark. But if the point is just to reiterate, before a big game, that these guys rock at soccer, then the mission has been accomplished.

They grin and provide commentary throughout the video, occasionally jabbing at each other and making fun. But they all enjoy it thoroughly.

As it ends, Fish slips off his flip-flops. He walks a small circle barefooted. He scrunches his toes. "How good is this field?" he asks. To be a soccer player or coach is to appreciate great grassmanship. Fish almost always comments on the state of the grass at each field upon which the

Lobos play. But it is rarely better than at home. The Lobo soccer field is perfect. The Bermuda grass is thick and consistent. Most of the guys pull off their shoes. Everyone admires the handiwork of UNM's turf manager.

Then the lights come on. "Go ahead," Fish tells the players. "Walk around and picture what's coming tomorrow night. Get your mind right." They do, some wandering to the far sidelines and nearly around the entire diameter of the field, while others meander just a few yards before circling back. Each does his own mental preparation.

Pichu is present too. He just returned to the team after traveling to his family's home in Phoenix for ACL surgery. He is in pain, but he is present. "I like being involved with the team," he says of his approach to this strange station in which he finds himself. "I go to everything." With his full-leg cast, he can't wander far. "I came here for soccer," he says. "Where I come from," he continues, "no one really cares about [school]." For Pichu, though, this year will be about watching soccer.

After ten minutes of wandering and contemplating, the team reassembles at midfield. "Everyone bring it in," one of the coaches calls out. The team huddles, arms over shoulders. "Enjoy this," Fish says. "In front of this crowd. On this field. With your friends." He finishes. The players put their shoes back on and head for the parking lot. *Coco* is still playing.

***

Kelly and Champ make an evening like Thursday, August 23, possible. While Fish operates as the CEO of the program (raising money, holding a weekly press conference, and providing the overall vision for and assessment of the team) and Mike, as the main teacher of tactics, Kelly and Champ serve as the major connection point between the coaches and the players. They carry out all sorts of off-the-field tasks that an outsider would not expect to be part of a Division I coaching job. They have constant contact with the players.

They do so both as a matter of paying dues and also with the recognition that building a team requires an avalanche of effort. There is always something to do.

Chapter 2

Kelly took the job as an assistant coach at UNM in 2017 because it meant both a step-up in the soccer world and the opportunity to come home. "This is *the* dream job," he says. Kelly grew up in Albuquerque. The son of an orthopedic surgeon, he attended Albuquerque Academy before heading to Trinity University in San Antonio, Texas. There Kelly learned what it means to win—all the time. "That's all we did," he says. At one point, his Trinity squad—Kelly played mostly as a right back—won forty-three straight games. This set an NCAA record. Kelly won an NCAA Division III National Championship in his junior year. He captained the team during his senior year.

Kelly brings a calmness to an otherwise frenetic profession. It might be because, as Kelly often points out, the rest of his family is off (nearly) saving lives. His father is an orthopedic surgeon in Albuquerque. His brothers, Ryan and Kyle, both went to medical school as well. All the Altman men played soccer. Unlike the rest of the men in his family, however, Kelly can't quite shake the game of his youth.

After exhausting his soccer eligibility at Trinity, Kelly played one season of minor league professional soccer for the Charleston Battery (in the equivalent of the USL today). Then he returned to Trinity to complete his degree. He was there, tending bar on the side, when the school's football coach dropped by and convinced him to kick field goals for his team. *Why not?* Kelly thought. He spent a month reorienting his kick prowess toward delivering an oblong ball through uprights. Then he won the starting job. The experience went well enough that a career in professional football seemed like a possibility. There was a tryout in Texas Stadium for an Arena League team and a ten-day trial with the Baltimore Ravens after that. But the call and contract never came. "I had to get a job," he says.

Kelly started his coaching career at his alma mater. He spent six years at Trinity as an assistant coach. From a win-loss perspective, he had a utopian start to a career. His teams won more than 90 percent of their games. Additionally, on the side, Kelly led a San Antonio high school to two state championships.

From Trinity, Kelly made the jump to Division I soccer. He coached his first year of DI at High Point University, then moved on to Valparaiso

University. Along the way, he settled on his own idea of what it means to be an assistant coach. At one point, he and a fellow coach compiled an Excel spreadsheet of all the tasks associated with the assistant coach. When the total reached 341 separate tasks, they stopped counting. In essence, the job boiled down to enabling the head coach to coach and the players to succeed as both athletes and students. It was just as his mentor at Trinity had told Kelly: "Your job is to make me look good."

That task is easier with some head coaches than others. To work for Jeremy Fishbein is an exercise in perseverance and survival. As one coach who previously worked for Fish told Kelly as he contemplated taking the job, "Fish micromanages. . . . If you want to get him off your back, you have to get ahead of the curve." Or, to put it another way, Fish has tremendous energy, an insatiable attention to detail, and a burning desire to win. How all that plays out daily is really understood only by those who have had the chance to work with him.

Just a few days into Kelly's tenure as a UNM assistant coach, he got a telling dose of Fish's intensity. It started when the coaches got an email from an international recruiting agency. The email contained information about an intriguing player, along with some video footage. The player looked promising—really promising. Here's what happened next in Kelly's words: "I received the email; Fish received the email . . . Fish forwarded me the email . . . Fish sent me a third follow-up email saying, 'Can you please look at the email?' Then he calls me on my office phone [the two work in offices separated by a thin wall] . . . and goes, 'Hey, I sent you an email. Did you get my email?'"

This all happened over the course of a few minutes. Kelly grins and grimaces as he tells the story. "I was like, 'Are you kidding me right now? Is this really happening?'" It was.

But perhaps as telling is what happened as a result of this interaction: "And so what I learned," he says, "was, yes, to answer his emails more quickly but also to go above and beyond. To be proactive. I started calling the agencies once a month, asking for their best players," Kelly explains. He started to get footage of the best international players before the email blasts went out to other colleges around the country.

Chapter 2

Because of Fish's dogged persistence, Kelly went on the offensive. He became a more proactive coach and recruiter. He, to put it simply, got better. He had to for his own sanity. "Otherwise," Kelly says, "he'll just keep bugging you."

***

Unbeknownst to the players, the campaign to reverse the Board's decision is entering into a new phase. The attorney general's move to make the university undergo a painful do-over of the cutting-decision meeting ultimately yielded the same result. But the second Board of Regents meeting pushed the matter further, keeping UNM's leadership on the defensive.

Fish is looking for new avenues forward. The goal of the resistance effort at this juncture is basically to maintain pressure, keeping the matter of Lobo soccer's survival in the news. The resistance team, headed by Fish and lawyer Greg Williams, often express that their goal is to find a way to allow the university to reverse its decision while saving face—a tricky balance.

On Wednesday, two days before the regular season opener, Williams sends a letter to the university addressing what he sees as flaws in the Title IX report. He begins, "I am writing to call on UNM to explain to the public how the recently adopted recommendations for [cuts] to the UNM athletic department comply with that portion of Title IX requiring that universities must provide financial assistance for members of each sex in proportion to the numbers of students of each sex participating in intercollegiate athletics."

***

Here is an overview of New Mexico's Title IX situation: UNM, like most universities in the United States, tilts female in terms of enrollment numbers. In 2018 the UNM student body is comprised roughly of 55 percent females to 45 percent males. In terms of student athletes, however, the ratio is basically flipped. Of all of UNM's student athletes, 58 percent (264 out of 455) are male. And when one considers the athletic scholarship numbers, the situation is equally problematic: male student athletes get 58 percent of available athletic aid. Thus, there's not much that is equitable about New Mexico's situation, excepting the fact that the school does not have a gendered version of its mascot. There are no Lady Lobos; everyone is a Lobo.[1]

Like all schools that play Football Bowl Subdivision (FBS) football, the fact that New Mexico awards eighty-five full scholarships every year to football players almost guarantees a male/female equity problem. As a step toward gender equity, New Mexico began supporting a women's beach volleyball team in 2015. This bought the school some time. According to the Title IX audit conducted by an outside reviewer, however, UNM Athletics is again approaching noncompliance.[2]

Schools demonstrate their compliance with Title IX by considering three prongs and meeting their standards: proportionality, finances, and basically everything else. Proportionality, the first prong, is met through one of three tests.

Test 1: "Whether intercollegiate level participation opportunities for male and female students are provided in numbers proportionate to their respective enrollments."[3]

This one is fairly straightforward: If a school has a sixty-to-forty (female-to-male) ratio in its student body, it should correspondingly have 60 percent of its athletic slots filled by females. Division I schools, however, rarely pass this test. The combination of sliding demographics toward women and the eighty-five scholarships that come with football make the first test a pipe dream.

So, there is Test 2.

Test 2: "Where the members of one sex have been and are underrepresented among intercollegiate athletics, whether the institution can show a history and continuing practice of program expansion which is demonstrably responsive to the developing interests and abilities of the members of that sex."[4]

This is where Lobo athletics have lived in recent years. The addition of a beach volleyball program in 2015 (now on the chopping block) allowed New Mexico to claim Title IX compliance by passing the second test—at least for three to five years.

The third test essentially admits defeat.

Test 3: "Where the members of one sex are underrepresented among intercollegiate athletes, and the institution cannot show a continuing practice of program expansion such as that cited above, whether it can be demonstrated that the interests and abilities of the member of that sex have been fully and effectively accommodated by the present program."[5]

For a university to claim Title IX compliance via the third test is an admission that says, "Hey, we're not in Title IX compliance, but we just can't help it." This is not an approach a university the size of the University of New Mexico wants to embrace.

Since New Mexico cannot afford to continue expanding its options for women and stay in compliance through the second test—especially given that they are, in fact, proposing to cut women's ski and beach volleyball—the first test, proportionality, is the new goal. Cut men's soccer and men's ski while radically altering the rosters of men's and women's track and cross-country in order to flip the fifty-five-to-forty-five gender ratio problem.

This will take some creativity. It's often called "roster padding" by experts. Most notably, UNM's proposal calls for creating a forty-three-member women's cross-country team and a sixty-eight-member women's track team. While these huge squads of female runners and jumpers might sound like a boon to female sport, these athletes will be unfunded. The NCAA, in 2018, caps scholarships at eighteen for women's track and cross-country combined. Moreover, while Coach Joe Franklin's squad has won two recent NCAA National Championships in cross-country, he still has to play by the rules. Only five women can score at a cross-country meet.[6]

Williams is arguing then that in its efforts to trim costs, UNM is actually moving itself further away from real, meaningful gender equity—at least according to the financial side of Title IX enforcement.[7]

Hang on here, as this gets complicated and convoluted. You see, where Title IX concerns college athletics (again, Title IX is about much more than just sports), it is adjudicated through proportional participation *but also* a financial assistance component. Whatever the ratio of participation, Title IX requires that an institution spend proportionally on its athletes. New Mexico does not.

By inflating the rosters of women's sports at UNM (primarily in track and cross country) without providing any additional funding and scholarships for all those new athletes (New Mexico already gives out the maximum track and field and cross-country scholarships possible), the financial numbers will only worsen. More female athletes will be at the school, but a much smaller percentage of them will receive athletic aid than their male counterparts.

Williams has found this discrepancy and wants an answer. This he summarizes in bold at the end of a five-page letter: "The main point is clear: Adding significant numbers of female walk-ons without increasing grants-in-aid to females will make UNM significantly less compliant with Title IX than it is now."

Williams requests an answer from the UNM administration within a week. Otherwise, he promises, "I will direct this matter to any proper governing authorities."[8]

Day 15. Tuesday, August 21, 2018.
Albuquerque, New Mexico

The week of practice leading up to the Seattle game is also the first week of classes at the university. The freshmen are now, finally, college student athletes. Perhaps it's the distractions causing a notable downtick in intensity and execution.

Mike stops Tuesday's practice midway through and, in a measured but clearly frustrated tone, demands more. "This is nowhere near the intensity or focus we need," he says. "You have one hour . . . you've got to turn things around."

Chapter 2

The back line remains a concern, particularly with handling deep, attacking balls. Today, Kelly works on something relatively anathema for a soccer-playing team like New Mexico. "Big balls out," he instructs Tom, Barreiro, Bailey, and Billy. "Big height, big contact." After a couple of near shanks, he makes a golf comparison: "Not big swings. Just big contact."

It's not a matter of desire for the back line. They work hard and want to improve ("They take it personally," Kelly confirms), but they simply haven't logged enough hours on the pitch together. The players are still feeling each other out. The connection between a new keeper and a newly assembled back line is bound to cause some problems. During one scrimmage, Ford drills Billy, from point-blank range, directly in the back with a clear-out boot. Billy stays down for several minutes. While Billy lying prone on the field inspires almost no reaction from the coaches, who are well-versed in the soccer player's penchant for faux injuries, his prostration does suggest that the Lobos' defense still has a long way to go.

Another distraction for the coaches is the issue of redshirting. Which of the players, especially the freshmen, are either (1) unlikely to play many minutes and/or (2) interested in preserving their four years of eligibility? Fish meets with the freshmen throughout the week to discuss their roles on the team. Several freshmen—Gallo, Fetterly, Omar, and Miguel—figure they will play significant minutes. So, there is little to decide for them. But for the rest—Elijah, Ben, Nick Williams, Anthony, Julian, and Carlos—a choice looms.

The conversations about whether to stay or go, whether to redshirt or play, linger over the first few weeks of the season. They are exceedingly difficult. Ben, for one, considers it the worst part of the whole fall. "I told Fish," Ben says, "that I wanted to redshirt," then pursue an immediate transfer. For both sides, having that conversation felt like disloyalty when the times were already tough.

"He got a little angry when I told him," says Ben. "He felt semibetrayed that I was going to look at another school." Fish went so far as to question Ben's desire to even stay with the season during the fall. "He was angry and told me to pack my stuff and leave if this was just a distraction." But that was just the spur-of-the-moment reaction. After "his knee-jerk reaction," Ben quickly clarifies, "Fish was very supportive."

Day 16. Wednesday, August 22, 2018.
Albuquerque, New Mexico

To the Albuquerque press, Fish works hard to project a calm and confident demeanor. Today, in his first press conference of the season, the first question is this stinger: "Coach, how hard is it to switch your mentality from this big, long fight that has played out over the summer?"

He answers, "I don't think it's been that difficult . . . you have the ability to compartmentalize things. Collectively, I don't think we've missed a beat."

"What has kind of been the fallout of this whole situation?"

"We've had four guys transfer since May who would have played significant roles on this team. . . . Of course, there have been some effects."

Another reporter asks, "Is your team coming in even more motivated?"

Fish replies, "I don't think it's a motivational tool. Our guys are about this season. What's the final thing? It's not like we're going to die at the end of the season. . . . Time will tell."

After Fish is finished, Simon and Ford take questions. Their responses are clear and cogent. They seem like old pros, even though both are taking on newly prominent roles.

Simon says, "Of course it's a regrettable situation, but we have a job to do."

"What's the morale on the team right now?"

"It's very good. Very good."

"What are you excited about?"

"Our biggest asset is our unity. I'm playing with friends. There's this great atmosphere that exists on the team right now."

The questions continue: "Are you guys approaching this season as, 'We're going to show you?'"

Simon: "Yes and no. We attack every situation."

To Ford Parker comes an ABQ-slanted question: "You've been waiting in the wings as a local kid. Are you ready to start?"

CHAPTER 2

"Growing up in ABQ . . . everyone wants to be a Lobo . . . I don't think we need to prove anything to anyone," he responds.[9]

Day 18. Friday, August 24, 2018.
Albuquerque, New Mexico

The team gathers an hour and ten minutes before game time in the meeting room. By this point they know their Seattle counterparts inside and out. They have watched the film and studied the InStat reports on Seattle. "You guys should be really excited," Fish tells the team. This is the type of game that they came to New Mexico to play. "You're not here to play shitty teams," Fish continues. "It's going to come down to moments, and I think in those moments we're going to be really, really good." And then there's the fact that this is a home game. "You're fit. You're prepared," Fish reminds them. "And you're playing at altitude."

The players make the walk up the hill to the stadium. The place is already full. The women's team, which is at the start of a season that will end with their winning a conference championship, is playing first. Fish leaves the team and ascends to the top of the stadium bleachers. He sits alone as the minutes tick down on the women's game. "I can barely function with all of this," he says to no one in particular.

Warm-ups are followed by introductions and the national anthem, which breaks and crackles through the stadium's sound system. The Lobos wear all white. Ford is wearing turquois. Finally, it's game time.

The starting lineup comes out in a 4–4–2. Ford is in goal; Tom, Billy, Dorsey, and Barreiro are on the back line; Taylor, Scott, Baily, and Simon in the middle; and Puig and Antoine are up front.

There are roughly 2,500 fans in the stands, which makes for a nice but hardly record-setting crowd for a Lobo soccer game. Since the women played before the men and only one ticket was required, the teams split the official attendance for the game.

According to Mike, the key will be "finding the balance against the press." We don't, he tells the guys, "want to play into the hands of Seattle" with too much back passing or too much focus on the center of the field.

For Ford, who has waited for the opportunity to start for his hometown Lobos for more than three years, there's some anxiety to work through. "[I was] *so* nervous for the first twenty-five minutes," he says later. And just four minutes in, there's a near crisis. Reacting late to a relatively benign Seattle delivery from the left side toward the top of New Mexico's box, Ford tries to punch the ball out. But he misses. The stadium holds its breath as the ball bounces toward the goal, just missing outside the right post.

At twenty-four minutes, Puig gets New Mexico going. After a sloppy first touch by a Seattle defender on a short throw-in, Puig pokes the ball away. Then, with three defenders attempting to recover possession, Puig dribbles toward the top of the box, stumbles through an attempted tackle, and delivers a left-footed shot. This caroms off Seattle's final man back, right to Antoine. Antoine deposits it safely in the lower left corner. "Goal, New Mexico!" roars the PA announcer.

Antoine parades toward the corner, arms outstretched and pumping up the roaring crowd. Within seconds, Taylor, Dorsey, Bailey, Tom, Billy, Scotty, Barreiro, and Simon meet him at the flag, each jumping joyfully into the scrum as he arrives. As for Puig, he waits calmly in the box, and when all the jumping around is done, he gives Antoine a high five. "The attacking group is going to be really special," Puig will say at the end of the night. "Antoine and I are doing great up there; we're going to score goals—that's our job."[10]

To make matters even better for the Lobos, one of Seattle's defenders involved in the play—their senior captain, six-foot-four Nathan Aune (who just happens to be the WAC Preseason Defensive Player of the Year and is on the Hermann Trophy watch list)—draws a red card as New Mexico celebrates its first goal of its final season. Seattle will play a man down for the rest of the contest.[11]

Six minutes later, Puig strikes again. This time, Tom surges up from the back to deliver a cross from the left side. Having just checked in for his first regular season action as a college player, Omar heads the ball back into the center, where Puig one times it into the net: "Goal, New Mexico!" This time, the whole team meets in the corner. Antoine piggybacks on Puig and Omar on Dorsey. The score is 2–0.

Yet Seattle, with two goals and one man down, still hangs in. A couple of minutes before halftime, the Seahawks get the game's first corner kick. An outswinger is launched that curves nearly to the top of the eighteen box. There, Seattle's Julian Avila-Good heads a bouncer through a cluster of players, right behind Barreiro's back, and into a narrow door on the right side of the goal. Ford never sees it. Goal: 2–1.

The second half turns into a celebration. Five minutes in, Tom launches a ball from midfield to a streaking Puig. A Seattle defender, filling the gap where Aune would usually knock everything down (Mike's scout on Aune earlier in the week described him as kind of a donkey who likes contact), misplays the ball. Puig cleans it up. "Goal, New Mexico!" roars the PA announcer. This celebration is muted by Puig cramping in the August heat, but 3–1 certainly feels good.

The teams trade goals over the last twenty minutes. Seattle earns several corners in succession and eventually knocks in a goal off a rebound. This tightens the score to 3–2. Ten minutes later, New Mexico responds, essentially ending Seattle's threat. Scotty fires from the top of the box, forcing a diving block by Seattle's keeper. Omar steps ahead of his defender and scores the rebound. "Goal, New Mexico!" Drenched in sweat, Omar races toward the home bench, where he is mobbed by his teammates. Once released, he looks to the sky, offering what seems to be a prayer: 4–2.

The crowd counts down the final seconds until the horn blows. Game over. Lobos win!

After the match, the players and coaches head for the railing that separates the stands from the track (which surrounds the field). Parents, friends, girlfriends, and all other manner of well-wishers are waiting. So, too, are dozens of boys and girls, many of whom are wearing their Lobo Soccer Camp T-shirts. A staffer hands out posters to the kids and Sharpies to the players, and an autograph session ensues.

The sense of relief is palpable. After everything that has transpired, it feels good to think about a game again. "Lots of emotions today," Fish tells a reporter. "It was a hard one to get going, but we've got a confident group. I couldn't be prouder of our guys."[12]

There are plenty of good feelings to go around, but, as always, the guys that score goals get the most credit. Puig's two goals and one assist, as well as Omar's goal and assist, stand out. For Omar, the game had a special meaning. "I'm from Seattle," he says, "So I'm playing against all my friends." Seattle University and UNM were actually Omar's final two choices in the recruiting process. "When I finally got that goal, it was a relief," he says, toweling off after the contest. "It was great because I felt like it welcomed me to my new crowd, to my new home. It was exciting." Indeed, Omar works *his* crowd after the game, smiling and chatting with every child who wants his autograph.

The next day's *Albuquerque Journal* has a picture of Puig and Antoine on the front page. The headline reads, "Fans Give Lobo Soccer a Feel-Good Moment, and Vice Versa." But even with a victory, the possible end still looms. "This could be," the *Journal* reminds its readers, "the last waltz for what has been one of the athletic department's shining lights."[13]

Chapter 3

Home-Bred and Chile-Fed

Whether the locale is Rochester, New York, or Corona, California, the accoutrements are basically the same: minivans, SUVs, collapsible canvas chairs, E-Z Ups, Gatorade water bottles, cones, flags, sunscreen, half-dome goals, hair ribbons, neon jerseys, whistles, and orange slices—oh, and the screaming children and over-caffeinated parents.

This is the kaleidoscope and symphony of American youth soccer. One can experience it on almost any Saturday or Sunday, at any field almost anywhere in the United States. I've been there. I was, at one time, pulled into the American youth soccer vortex with my own children. First, my two boys and then my daughter played on the fields of Virginia and New Mexico. Looking back, I'd say these were happy times for our family—times that seem better and better the more they retreat into the nostalgic past.

But beyond the visual and auditory stimuli of youth soccer—beyond the nostalgia—lies something deep, powerful, and vast. And maybe something that is broken. Consider a handful of numbers.

Of children ages six to seventeen, 3.7 million plus compete in youth soccer annually in the United States.

The average American child "retires" from sports participation at eleven years old.

Youth sports in America are a $20 billion market, and it is growing.

Chapter 3

No fewer than six major organizations are wrestling for control of American youth soccer.

The United States, a country of 330 million citizens, has produced *zero* men's World Cup finalist teams.[1]

These numbers convey what the soccer experts of *FourFourTwo*, the world's premier soccer publication, have resorted to describing with metaphors from the Weather Channel. "Youth soccer [in America] has progressed from a moderate level of chaos to a full-fledged tropical storm mixed with a Nor'easter mixed with Memorial Day beach traffic," journalist Beau Dure writes.[2]

From the United Kingdom, the *Guardian* points to a different, specific problem with the American youth soccer system: "It's only working for the white kids."[3]

While there may be problems, it's not due to a lack of interest. The organizational and financial clout involved in American youth soccer is crushing. The big six groups, ranked by their 2022 annual revenues, are as follows: (1) United States Soccer Federation ($122,296,409); (2) American Youth Soccer Organization (AYSO), ($65,698,852); (3) United States Youth Soccer ($18,633,530); (4) National Association of Competitive Soccer Clubs ($13,161,722); (5) United States Soccer Foundation ($11,207,758); and (6) United Soccer Coaches Association ($5,544,986).

Factoring in regional youth soccer organizations, there are 395 registered tax-exempt, nonprofit soccer groups in the United States that brought in more than $1 million in revenues in 2022—*395!* As the children played, the adults got paid. One organization, the Alexandria (Virginia) Soccer Association, for example, paid its executive director $340,000 to run their 501c3 nonprofit soccer club.[4]

The output resulting from this mass of money spent has been decidedly underwhelming. The most obvious assessment of how the United States is doing at producing talented male soccer players comes every four years at the World Cup. The fact that the United States missed qualifying at all for the FIFA mega-event in 2018 was a damning condemnation.

Of course, it's not the World Cup that motivates most soccer parents. Rather, it's the lure of a college soccer scholarship. The *New York Times* was writing about this holy grail for soccer parents all the way back in 2008. "Heaven is your child receiving a college athletic scholarship," Bill Pennington wrote in the *Times* piece that describes the underwhelming actual prize at the end of the pursuit. Still, "college ID" and "elite camps" annually draw in thousands of hopeful soccer teams, teens, and parents who are looking to connect with college coaches and programs.[5]

There are roughly eight hundred thousand high school–aged boys playing soccer annually on high school, club, and recreational teams. At the NCAA Divisions I, II, and III ranks, just under twenty-seven thousand male soccer players compete annually. About half of these college players (roughly thirteen thousand) play at DI or DII schools, which can offer athletic scholarships. As of 2018, the NCAA has limited the number of scholarships a school can offer in men's soccer to 9.9 at the Division I level and 9 at the Division II level. Therefore, the participating DI and DII schools can collectively offer around 3,900 soccer scholarships annually. Thus goes the funneling of America's male soccer pool: 800,000 to 27,000 to 13,000 to 3,900.[6]

The twenty-seven men of the 2018 Lobos (although several come from abroad, and not all are on athletic scholarship) have defied these statistical odds to continue their soccer-playing days.

***

Back in 2002, Fishbein had been out recruiting on the day he learned of his promotion to head coach. It was an appropriate and early indicator of his intense focus. Fish needed to upgrade the talent in Albuquerque, and the state of New Mexico just happened to have one of its strongest-ever classes of graduating high school soccer players. In particular, one club team in Albuquerque, the FC Bandidos, had groomed a class of potential Lobos who were almost too good to be true.

As club soccer was taking off in the United States—US Club Soccer was incorporated in 2001—it just so happened that a group of New Mexico boys was at the forefront.

CHAPTER 3

As one player, Brandon Moss, remembers it, he showed up to try out for the FC Bandidos at Albuquerque's rolling Arroyo Del Oso Park. He was a nine-year-old looking for someplace to play. He possessed decent skills and a love for the game. He wanted to transition from AYSO soccer to a more competitive environment. The team needed to be serious but fun.

Ricardo Beraun had created just such a team in the Bandidos. The team started as a U10. "The unique thing about that team was that we stayed together all the way through under nineteen," says Moss. Beraun, a native of Peru, kept the Bandidos together by creating a family atmosphere. From the first practice, Beraun had captured his players' hearts. "He's just a grade-A coach," Moss says.

"Soccer is chess on wheels for Ricardo," one team parent told the *Albuquerque Tribune*. "He is amazing with tactics." The Bandidos won ten consecutive state titles and three regional titles, and they advanced deep into the national tournament in 2001 and 2002. To win the Far West region meant a group of New Mexico kids had to defeat the top teams from Colorado, Arizona, and California, among others. The statistical odds—just from a population standpoint, let alone a resources one—said that the Bandidos shouldn't have had a chance. Yet they won.

"Somehow, we were able to compete on the national scene with that group that showed [up] at the park back when we were nine years old," Moss says. The group grew up together. The parents and siblings became friends due to the travel required of club soccer. "Thanksgiving, Christmas, all your three day weekends . . . you were always playing in a tournament," remembers Moss.[7]

In a way, the Bandidos were an antidote to the fragile psyche of New Mexico's athletes and coaches. "This sends a message that there is more than just one or two quality players in New Mexico," said La Cueva High's coach after the Bandidos outscored their opponents, 27–3, in the 2002 West Regional Tournament.[8] There is rarely much protest when New Mexico is left out of something; that is the expectation. But when a group of New Mexico kids succeeds, the community is both surprised and overjoyed. The New Mexico press lavished attention on the Bandidos. "Bandidos make mark for N.M. and loyalty," read one *Albuquerque Tribune* headline toward the end of the run.[9]

"We just want to represent New Mexico well," said Ben Ashwill before the Bandidos headed to one of its final tournaments with the group still together. "The main thing is it's our last solid year together. We didn't expect to stay together so long or to become such good friends."[10]

Finally, after a decade of success together, the Bandidos had to split up and find colleges to attend.

Crickets.

The college soccer powers of the day—Indiana, UCLA, Virginia—ignored the kids from New Mexico despite their long record of success. Moss, in describing how the soccer recruiters did *not* come knocking at his door as he prepared for college, says, "[I was] not as well received of a recruit as maybe I had envisioned myself being. . . . In general, coming from New Mexico, there was always a sense of lower quality . . . less capable, lower quality." The assumption was that even the best kids from this state, those with the most potential, had not been exposed to the same type of competition as a player from a state like California or Arizona. "You were a big fish in a very small pond," he summarizes.

The big-time recruiters never really came. "It just seemed odd that we couldn't attract any more attention from the big schools," says Moss.

Into the void stepped Fishbein. From the time he'd arrived in New Mexico, he had tracked the Bandidos. He attended the team's games and practices. "Man, I recruited the hardest I ever recruited in my life—I went to *every* game," he says. He stalked the players and their families. It was not only the volume of his attention but how he approached the idea of convincing eighteen-year-olds to sign on with his program. "The other thing that was unique about Fishbein was the way that he recruited," Moss says. Fishbein utilized a lot of handwritten notes, in-person meetings, and phone calls. Everything was personalized and passionate. And everything came with an air of confidence: "An unwavering belief in himself and the product that he knew was possible at UNM," remembers one early recruit.

Chapter 3

Seven players from New Mexico formed the core of Fishbein's first recruiting class:

Ben Ashwill (FC Bandidos)
Matt Chavez (FC Bandidos)
Eric Carlson (FC Bandidos—transfer from University of Delaware)
Ricky Francis (FC Bandidos—transfer from University of South Carolina)
Ryan McVay (Hobbs, New Mexico)
Brandon Moss (FC Bandidos)
Jeff Rowland (La Cueva High School, Albuquerque, New Mexico)

The first Bandido to sign on with the hometown Lobos was Ben Ashwill, another of the boys who had shown up at Arroyo del Oso a decade earlier. When Ben chose the Lobos, other local players began to look more closely at their newly revitalized hometown club. His best friend, Brandon Moss, signed on shortly after. "Brandon Moss and Ben Ashwill were the two best kids in New Mexico by a mile," says Jeff Rowland, now a coach at the University of Washington. Eric Carlson and Ricky Francis decided to come back home and play with their old club teammates.

Jeff Rowland, a La Cueva High School player recovering from an ACL tear, walked on and snagged the last spot on the 2002 squad. Fishbein had wavered over allowing Rowland to be on the roster—that is, until the two sat down for a discussion. "I convinced Coach Fishbein that I would work harder than anyone to prove that I could help the team," Rowland says. "And then I begged. Somehow, by the end of that talk, I had talked my way onto the team. At that time I thought I had won the lottery."[11]

Fishbein treated the recruiting process like a cage match. He challenged his recruits to envision a better place for them than New Mexico. Where could they go that would beat what he was offering? "I really don't see what the uncertainty is," he would say, "or what the questions are—UNM is the best place for you. You have everything you could possibly need here!"

He influenced Moss and other players so much that they bent to his view of the college soccer landscape. "Wow, well, I guess there is no alternative," Moss found himself thinking. "He put things in a way . . . where it did not seem like an alternative was a suitable option."

"That recruiting class was the backbone of [an] NCAA finalist," says Fishbein wistfully.

Once his team was on campus, Fish fixated on the details. He started ruffling feathers. "When Fishbein came in, I wasn't sure what to think," says Aaron Day, the strength coach at the time. "He was *intense*, but I was like, 'Whatever, this is the soccer coach.'" Day, who spent fourteen years as a trainer at the school, had often seen coaches (besides those for basketball and football) pay lip service to time in the weight room. They would "give a nod" to the weight room, do a couple of weekly circuit training routines, and call it enough.

"I learned very quickly [that] when [Fish] says he wants something, he wants it done right, he wants it done with excellence. . . . I realized that he was serious and I better be on it, or I'm going to get called on it," Day recalls.

The Lobo soccer team almost immediately took on a different look. During that earlier era, the time before the deluge of Nike gear his players now wear, the pre-Fish soccer team would often show up to the weight room hardly looking like a team at all, all wearing different attire, arriving at different times. Nothing was all that serious or intentional. "Right off the bat, Fishbein was able to do some fund-raising and make sure that all his guys were wearing the same thing," Day remembers. Fish's team would look like a team.

Then there were the workouts. "We just kicked their butts, and we did some stupid stuff that didn't make sense, but we were tougher than everybody else," says Day. Circuit training was meant to push the players far past their limits. Longer sessions, more fatigue, and less rest time were the norm. While most college team plyometric workouts would feature sixty or seventy "touches" throughout an hour-long session, the early Fishbein teams would get in three hundred touches in a half hour. More was more; faster was better.

During the off-season, Fish established Wednesday as the team's track day. Sprints and stairs made the players long for sessions that actually involved a soccer ball. "Ice on the track, and it's fifteen degrees, and we shouldn't have been out there running, but we were going to do it," Day recalls. On other days, trips to the Rio Rancho sand hills were used to prepare for the end of the games.

Fish demanded results and accountability from the training staff, requiring accurate, detailed reports on everyone's progress. "A lot of times when a coach wanted a report like that, he just wanted to hear that the guys were doing OK," says one trainer. In some cases, the coaches were really demanding that the strength coaches assign ever-growing personal bests to every member of their team. The numbers always needed to be going up. All the time. Not Fishbein. "Fish wanted to really know, specifically: What are they doing, and what can they do better? And what do I think is making them tick?" Thus, a report that many coaches might have seen as perfunctory had better be well supported and defensible for the soccer team.

"I think there were a lot of blue-collar kids with a chip on their shoulder for being overlooked," says Rowland of the early years of Fishbein's regime. Fish drove his players ridiculously hard. "Coach Fishbein was a really good motivator . . . he was hard on you . . . he was driven. He asked a lot of us, and he pushed us. And I think that was certainly his greatest strength." Rowland continues, "I feel like he always made us believe that we were the hardest-working team in the nation."

Sometimes, just Fishbein's raw intensity and dogged persistence dominated the practice. "Super intense" is how one of his alums, who went out of his way to dine with the 2018 team on the road, describes him years after the fact. "Very all encompassing," he says of playing for—and going to school—under Fish's oversight. No mistake went undiscussed. Declining grades meant an extra one-on-one meeting with the coaches. There was just nowhere to hide. "I can still hear him yelling, 'For fuck's sake, Carlson!'" says . . . Carlson.

Fish brought intensity laced with profanity, yes, but also an emphasis on discipline, restraint, and academic and athletic excellence—and an aggressive pride in New Mexico.

The relationships between the players and coaches carried the day. "That [first] group brought it pretty quick," says one of the Bandidos. "Fish deemphasized victory. It was the process, then the winning."

That the winning came right away certainly did not hurt. Fishbein took over a team that had not won a single conference game the year before, then created a new team that won its first eight games and went on to 18–4 for the year. The 2002 Lobos won their conference (the Mountain Pacific Sports Federation) and advanced to the NCAA tournament, a feat accomplished only once before in school history.[12]

That this was accomplished with a roster dominated by New Mexicans made it all the more significant to the community. "Home-Bred and Chile-Fed," read one brilliant late-season headline. "We're the only program at this level in the state," said senior starter Javier Carrasco (from tiny Anthony, New Mexico). "Kids look up to us. We're like professionals. We're like role models."

The more the team won, the more the state took notice. "This is the first time that New Mexico has really had an opportunity to field a team that has most of the top players in the state," Fish explained, already on message during his first season in charge.

As the team went to the NCAA tournament, no one compared it to a football team or called it the "other football." This was winning; this was success. "Now, this fresh group of New Mexicans is heading out of state, hoping to make the rest of the soccer world take notice that the state can produce more than just chile," the *Albuquerque Journal* reported.[13]

After a sobering 2003 season where the team took its lumps while playing a much tougher, more national schedule, 2004 and 2005 demonstrated just how high the ceiling could actually be for a team from New Mexico.

The 2004 squad, anchored by New Mexicans Ashwill, Francis, Moss, and Rowland, went 17–1–2 and advanced to the NCAA Sweet 16. Rowland had a transcendent season. He scored forty-five points, averaged a goal per game, and earned first team All-American honors. The program had arrived. "It felt like it meant so much to the community," Rowland recalls, "and it meant so much to us."

But, as always seems to be the case in New Mexico, even achievement came with a dash of disappointment and insult. The team ended the regular season ranked no. 1 in the country. They gathered on a Monday afternoon to watch as the NCAA tournament seeds were announced. This was a team that had defeated the defending NCAA champion, as well as three other NCAA teams during the regular season. It had the nation's best record. What did the national committee think all that was worth? A no. 13 seed. "What had been planned as a selection party quickly turned somber and reflective," reported the *Albuquerque Journal*.[14]

"That's the way it is in the 505," said Francis (originally from Santa Teresa, New Mexico, with a population of 4,258). "It doesn't surprise anybody from New Mexico." Whether this is best described as self-fulfilling fatalism or a rightful objection to being wronged is difficult to say. It's probably some of both. But for residents of a state always at the bottom of rankings (2004 marked the third year in a row that Morgan Quitno had ranked New Mexico the "dumbest state" in the nation), there was always reason to suspect that someone else was laughing at them—or screwing them over.[15]

The draw meant that after a victory over Portland, the Lobos had to face traditional powerhouse University of Virginia. They lost in penalty kicks after playing to a tie in regulation and two overtimes.

The 2005 season started where 2004 ended. Ashwill, Moss, and Rowland were seniors. Another local had also joined the starting lineup: Mike Graczyk. As a sophomore, he won the goalkeeper position. Thus, a decade before he would take a coaching position with Fishbein and UNM, Mike took over between the pipes for a group that expected nothing less than winning all the time.

"Born and raised here in New Mexico," Mike says when asked to describe himself. "I think what's always been great about this program is our program has really reflected the mentality of the city . . . very much a blue-collar, hardworking group." Mike fit the mold precisely: His dad was an Albuquerque police officer, and his mother worked for Budget Rental Car. Mike prepped at La Cueva High School.

The 2005 Lobos ended the regular season with just one loss. They were ranked no. 2 in the country. And the Lobos led the nation in attendance, averaging more than 3,700 fans a game.

When it came time for the NCAA tournament this time, the committee had a bit more respect. It awarded New Mexico a no. 2 seed. Thus, for three games, Fish and his New Mexico-loaded team played in Albuquerque, at altitude. Before raucous home crowds of 4,500 and then 5,000, the Lobos defeated the University of Wisconsin–Milwaukee and California State University, Northridge. This set them up in an Elite 8 game, which was played in Albuquerque versus the University of California Bears on December 2, 2005.

There were not enough tickets to go around. The stadium's 5,600 seats were sold out almost immediately. Not to be dissuaded, hundreds of fans circled the facility's chain-link fence. Many stood on their cars to see the action. The game was a taut, defensive affair—typical of college soccer come tournament time. Neither team had many chances in regulation. Finally, during overtime, everything came together. Brandon Moss played a ball in behind Cal's defense. Ben Ashwill pushed it forward and then delivered a cross into the box. As always, Rowland was there. He delivered the game winner.

The place went crazy. Fans stormed the field. Fishbein was doused in a Gatorade bath, and students tore down the soccer goals (which, given the fact that goals aren't dug into the ground in soccer, is much easier than in football). The *Albuquerque Journal* covered it all on the front page. "Jeff Rowland stood draped in a New Mexico state flag on Friday night, signing autographs as if the University of New Mexico men's soccer team had won just another game," Glen Rosales reported. "But this wasn't just another game. His goal in overtime gave the Lobos their biggest win ever."[16]

Mike remembered the three 2005 NCAA home tournament games as the highlight of his soccer-playing career. "All three of those games were overtime wins. . . . The crowds just got bigger and bigger and bigger," he recalls. Then it was off to Cary, North Carolina, for the College Cup—soccer's version of the Final Four.

"As you were going through it, you didn't recognize how big it was," Mike says, "until you got to the Final Four, and you saw New Mexico on the field." The New Mexico fans who traveled with their team saw the Lobos defeat Clemson University to advance to the NCAA Championship game. In the championship game, the Lobos' dream finally came to an end. They lost in overtime to the University of Maryland.

Still, something had been established. "To play soccer here is something bigger than playing for yourself. You're representing the whole state," Mike summarizes.

Day 21. Monday, August 27, 2018.
Albuquerque, New Mexico

Thirteen years have passed. On this August evening, however, Mike, Fish, and Jeff Rowland are again on the UNM field, preparing for a game. Jeff is in town as the associate head coach for the visiting University of Washington Huskies. He works under Jamie Clark, who was an assistant to Fish during the magical 2005 season.

Tonight, the visiting Huskies are favored. The team is ranked in the top 25. They opened their season by defeating no. 1–ranked Maryland.

In the locker room before the game, Mike reviews the scouting report for the Huskies. This is a strong, experienced team. "Be excited—this is a good test for us," Fish says. Perhaps sensing nerves and distractions in the room, Fish zeroes in on his most productive scorer from Friday's game: "Puig [long pause and intense stare] . . . , work your nuts off tonight."

"Yes, sir."

After warm-ups, Jeff Rowland steps in front of the Lobo faithful. For Rowland, it's a difficult situation. "I've never enjoyed playing against New Mexico if I'm being honest," he says. "I mean, my old head coach is there. . . . My best friend [Mike Graczyk is] on staff, then the program and, obviously, what's happened this past year—it was not a game I was looking forward to." To make matters more awkward, tonight, he's being inducted into the University of New Mexico's Hall of Honor.

Rowland's resume is recounted during a ten-minute ceremony: two-time first team Academic All-American, 2005 consensus All-American, and a finalist for the MAC Hermann Trophy. It's strange—perhaps just a coincidence or perhaps something else—that Rowland received notice of this honor right around the time it was announced that soccer was being discontinued. "The athletic department is inducting you into the Hall of Fame in the same year they decide to cut the program. I thought a lot about that," he says.

Given that Rowland has a game to coach and cannot attend the banquet later in the fall, he has prepared a video statement. Not surprising (for those who know Jeff), it is genuine, heartfelt, and utterly well prepared. He thanks everyone possible. He highlights the on-field success, the leadership training, and the education he received at the university. He mentions just how many New Mexicans have been a part of the program. "UNM gave them an opportunity to play in their home state. In front of their families and their friends. UNM gave them a reason to stay home," he says.

But his graciousness is balanced with a razor-sharp political edge. "I cannot end without addressing the topic on all Lobos hearts and minds," he says. "The best award would be to continue the UNM men's soccer program, to continue its legacy of excellence. And to continue the opportunity it provides to my home state."

He closes with a flourish and a challenge: "I believe the UNM men's soccer program is not done. I believe Lobo soccer has an underdog story to tell. Just as I worked to change a coach's mind through hard work, grit, and determination, we Lobos and New Mexicans must use the same grit and determination—and maybe even some begging—to change some minds in UNM leadership and affect change in Santa Fe."[17]

Eddie, UNM's athletic director, who is sitting high in the stands this August night, can do nothing but applaud politely. His situation is unimaginably awkward and stressful.

Finally, the game begins. The Lobos play in turquoise. The Huskies wear all black. During the first half, neither team can generate many chances. The Lobos maintain more possession but never really threaten Washington's defense. New Mexico seems to pass the ball from side to side; Washington seems content to let them.

The Lobos retreat to the hurdles shed for halftime. Since there are no bathrooms, several make a detour to the fence line. The reserves who haven't played are left to drill on the field—an operational tactic the Lobos hold to, which differs from most programs. It might be due to the small size of the shed. Regardless, the playing Lobos wait for their coaches' recalibration.

"It's going to be a moment," Fish says. Washington is not a team that makes mistakes. Rather, they stay in position and wait for any small crack to appear. "It's going to take something special to score," Fish says, perhaps referencing a couple of the gimmes the Lobos got in three nights earlier, in the game versus Seattle University. "It's not going to be a tap-in."

The game unravels quickly for the Lobos following the break. Less than three minutes in, New Mexico loses possession on a poor throw-in. Washington quickly gets the ball deep into the New Mexico half, nearly to the end line. From there, a pass splits Barreiro and Simon, leaving Washington's Kyle Coffee with a shot from twelve yards. He puts it in the top right corner: 0–1, Washington.

The breakdown on the back line is troubling.

With a one-goal lead, Washington drops further back. The Huskies don't quite "park the bus," but they are content to let the Lobos play around at midfield. The nail in the coffin comes at seventy minutes. Antoine penetrates to just above the box before getting tackled. It looks like a foul. When the whistle does not come, the Lobos—almost in unison—raise their arms in complaint to the referee. Meanwhile, the Huskies are going the other way. The Lobos can't recover, giving Washington time to make several short passes from within the box and to line up a shot: 0–2, Washington.

The loss of composure and the whining are troubling.

"The second half, we came out with a little more aggressiveness and looked out to pressure a little bit more . . . then we ended up scoring a couple of goals, and that [changed] the game," Rowland said, describing the game portion of his strange evening. New Mexico never really challenged Washington's keeper, even though the Husky's keeper was asking for it, dressed in highlighter yellow.

To a certain extent, the letdown for New Mexico isn't surprising after the emotions of Friday. Monday's crowd of just over a thousand fans did not have the same intensity as it had on opening night. Standing on the track, engaging in interviews afterward, the players immediately recognize that they should have given more. "We created chances, we just lacked a little bit of energy," Nick Taylor summarizes. "You could see they were sitting defensively, which made our job a little more difficult offensively. Today we needed a little more energy."[18]

Even with the loss, the scene at the rail is spirited. Plenty of kids still want autographs. The warm, clear evening is perfect, and conversations linger. The team is heading on the road, so this is the last of these gatherings for a few weeks. And certainly, a split with two ranked teams on the opening weekend is not the end of the world. A long season is ahead.

Chapter 4

Forty Balls

Day 23. Wednesday, August 29, 2018.
Albuquerque, New Mexico
After a recovery day (a pool workout with Joe), the team gathers for practice at 8:30 a.m. on Wednesday. The Lobos are facing two weeks of travel—first, to Southern California and then to Tulsa, Oklahoma. With dynamics still so unsettled with this new group, the whole team will be making both trips, even those freshmen who are leaning toward redshirting. Only Chang and Pichu (both still barely mobile after surgery) and Maliek will stay behind. A more efficient travel group will have to wait until later in the season.

The morning is warm and busy at UNM's athletic complex. The women soccer players have beaten their male counterparts onto the field; they're hard at work on the south end of the soccer practice facility. The space is plenty big, but the two teams still represent something of a distraction for each other. In the distance, cross-country runners circle the Lobo track. The sounds of football practice echo from down the hill.

The midweek practice represents the first time this fragile, thin team has gone back to work after a setback. It's their first time responding to a loss, although the UW's rising to no. 3 in the national rankings has softened that blow somewhat. Fish has apologized to the team for his own lack of energy for the Washington game. "It won't happen again," he says.

Today's practice emphasizes handling a pressing defense and counterattacking. Mike works the team in short bursts. Set up the scenario, go hard for thirty to forty seconds, then recap and reset. He likes to see the guys get the ball in the net, even if that's not the primary point of a drill. "If you score, I'll give you a break," he says. "If not, we go again."

Day 24. Thursday, August 30, 2018. Albuquerque, New Mexico

Since the season is just underway, there are still many one-offs to get in order. Today, just before the team heads to the airport, the guys meet with an associate athletic director to go over the NCAA–mandated drug testing protocol. The players ask a couple of quick questions about the randomness of the selection process. Mostly though, they just nod along. No one is particularly excited about being called in to pee in a cup under duress. For his part, Fish is engaged in the presentation, one that he's certainly heard many times before. He asks several pointed questions, then, after the AD leaves, he—as he is wont to do—expounds a bit more. "The drug thing is a minimal thing," he says of the NCAA legalism, "because it's a nonissue with us." The team's policy is much stricter than the NCAA's multistrike approach. Still, these are college students. Fish ends by calling out one player for an alleged marijuana habit. "It's selfish—at some point, you got to be an adult," he says.

Fish has not let go of the season's first loss yet either. He received a call, he says, from an alum who thought the team had not played hard versus Washington. "That hurt," he says.

"Sit up and look at me when I'm talking," he barks. The players, sitting shoulder to shoulder in five rows in the humid team room, collectively straighten. "We let ourselves off the hook on Monday . . . you don't get too many of those opportunities in your life."

Then his tone softens a bit. Fish admits he has his own regrets about his time in college and as a soccer player. Thus, he won't be the coach that lets a player squander this experience. He can't do it. "You guys think I'm on your ass all the time, but someday, you'll leave here, and no one will be on your ass." Indeed, he is right: Not many adults get this kind of attention in their lives.

***

The California trip marks the team's first real travel—the first time these Lobos will walk through airports on official University of New Mexico business together. As such, there are several rules that the newcomers must accept. The first: They must wear suits. The New Mexico men's soccer team, unlike most teams, does not travel in one of the myriad of Nike sweat suits that have been issued. No, everyone wears a jacket, slacks, and a tie in this group because, as Fish reminds them on the same day as the drug talk, "somebody else is paying for this."

As one of the most geographically isolated programs in the United States (New Mexico doesn't have another Division I men's program within 350 miles), the Lobos fly a lot. And when they do, they look good.

In prepping for the trip, it becomes apparent that a couple of the freshmen don't own anything close to a suit. The seniors, especially Antoine, take care of this problem. The Frenchman rounds up extra shirts and pants, making sure that everyone looks presentable. "I have on somebody else's shirt, somebody else's shoes, somebody else's pants, and somebody else's tie," says Omar, one of the previously suitless freshman. "Probably the only thing of mine is my socks. And my underwear."

In the current context, there is no confusion about soccer's role in the athletic budget. "We don't make money," Fishbein clarifies. "So, somebody is paying for you with tax dollars . . . to fly around the country [and play soccer]. You have an obligation to do that at the highest level." What that means to a fifty-something-year-old coach and what it means to teenage soccer players probably differ. But Fish is in charge. So, the players wear suits.

"It's not a democracy," Fishbein explains. And in 2018, no truer statement can be uttered by a Division I head coach. Coaches tell their players when to show up, what to wear, and how to act. The Lobos coaching staff provides advice on academic and social problems, along with a steady torrent of soccer tutelage. Fish, in particular, takes to this power unapologetically yet with caution. "It's not a democracy. Well, that doesn't sound right," he says again. "But you're entrusted with helping them make the right decisions and leading them, at times telling them [what to do]."

In addition to the suit standard, Fish also mandates that the players not walk through the airport with earphones on or their phone in hand. This, of course, is about as enforceable as the fifty-five miles per hour speed limit on Albuquerque's Paseo Del Norte. But the point is that the players should be considerate of those around them. The anti-phone and headphones rule is a longtime Fish statute that is getting more difficult to enforce as every year passes. Still, Fish is holding firm. "I think we maybe give into some of that stuff too much," he says. "If your goal is to develop leaders and impactful people, then you still got to have interpersonal skills." There's some get-off-my-lawn mentality here, but there is a sense of conviction as well. "We need to hold [collegiate athletes] to a much higher standard because, if you're going to spend, to invest in them to the degree that DI athletics departments do, then you need to demand a lot out of them. Otherwise, you're prostituting these kids."

The New Mexico coaching staff as a whole believes that college athletics must prioritize growth. "I hope the guys are better partners and fathers and community members than if they hadn't been here," Fishbein says. Part of that growth process is then preparing the players to move in different circles. "Yeah, your peer group when you're eighteen doesn't care if you're on the phone or headphones . . . or if your pants are hanging down your ass," Fish says. But the day is soon coming for the current Lobos when they will want to be able to operate with community and business leaders.

As Miguel and Gallo board the Southwest flight taking the Lobos from Albuquerque to Los Angeles, they do so looking sharp. Miguel sports a charcoal suit, white shirt, and red tie, while Gallo wears a blue blazer, gray slacks, a light-blue shirt, and dark-blue tie. Given that the age of dressing up to travel has long since passed, the two look better than 99 percent of the passengers they cross paths with this day. And they seem proud of the look. "Business trips," Miguel tweets, along with a picture of the two standing in front of their Southwest Airlines ride.

Day 25. Friday, August 31, 2018.
Northridge, California

The game against the California State University, Northridge (CSUN), Matadors kicks off at 7:00 p.m. CSUN is among the more innovative (or subversive, depending on one's perspective) college soccer teams in the country. The Matadors' head coach, Terry Davila, shuttles players in and out of the action throughout the contest. It's a strategy that takes full advantage of college soccer's liberal substitution rule. "Lots of subbing. It's a weird way to play," Mike says during the pregame scout.

Like with all of their trips, the Lobos get around town in minivans. The team rents four vehicles that Fish, Mike, Kelly, and Joe drive on each trip. The choice of who rides in which van is decided according to seniority, and so, not surprisingly, the oldest players pile into Joe's vehicle. Joe runs a loose ship. He is twenty-seven, a man between the coaches and players. "They're all college kids," he explains. "Sometimes, they act like idiots." The next group, including Champ, loads up with Kelly. Then Mike. Then, for the last of the freshmen, there is a ride with the head coach—always an adventure, always on duty.

Given Southern California's traffic and the long distances that come with traveling between LAX, the team hotel, Northridge, Fullerton, and back to LAX, the trip is a grind. "It feels like we've been here forever," Kelly says as the team takes the field to play against Northridge. These two programs have met nineteen times prior to this game, with UNM winning thirteen times. "They want a broken game," Fish says during the last-minute instructions. "They sub a lot . . . we want a proper game."

The Lobos begin the game with their usual starters. The contest starts at a slow, deliberate pace. New Mexico controls the ball but can produce few viable chances. Northridge is an interesting case study in soccer tactics. Not only do they press and substitute frequently, but they also use almost any throw-in in New Mexico's half as an opportunity to launch the ball into the box, producing a corner-kick effect.

The score at halftime is 0–0. A soccer purist may expound on the tactics, but for almost everyone else watching, it's just boring—except for the players and coaches. And for New Mexico, it marks three consecutive halves without a goal.

To start the second half, Omar and Gallo get the nod. Fish is looking for a spark, and his two most reliable and explosive freshmen offer all sorts of promise.

Chapter 4

Omar immediately alters the complexion of the contest. He is physical and aggressive. For his efforts, he becomes the focus of a small section of vuvuzela-toting Northridge students in the stands. It's "bring your parents to the game" night at CSUN, but there doesn't seem to be much familial supervision of this group. "Welcome to California, Omar," one shouts when Omar gets sideswiped to the ground.

The game's pivotal moment occurs when Barreiro does something that has become part of the fabric of soccer: He milks an "injury" for a few extra seconds. Following a collision, Barreiro stays on the ground, catching his breath and clearing his head. No one is all that worried—that is, except for Joe. As the team trainer, Joe's concern understandably grows the longer his player stays down.

Joe came to New Mexico after working with the Dallas Cowboys for several years. He arrived on campus and learned that the team he was supposed to work with—soccer—might be cut. Nevertheless, he jumped right in. He worked with the team during the summer captains' practices. "The one thing that I was worried about when I got out here was just not knowing much about soccer," he says. But the team brought him along. The players and the coaches appreciated that he wanted to learn the game's strategy. Within a few weeks of the season ("Once they actually trusted that I was going to get [the ball] to them"), Joe was serving as an extra man on the practice field, doing things like kicking balls to Champ as Champ peppered the keepers with shots.

Joe attends most of the team's meetings; he often eats with the team. He is much more than just a trainer.

But now Barreiro is down. When the referee motions toward the sideline, Joe reacts instantly and sprints onto the field. He is worried, given that Barreiro had been bothered by a lower leg injury earlier in the week and so rushes in. "They called me on," he says matter-of-factly.

Unfortunately, Joe's presence isn't really required. As he gets his player up and moving, Barreiro tells Joe what's going on. "Oh, I just needed a break," Barreiro confesses. However, by rule, Barreiro now must be subbed out of the game since the trainer has come on the field. New Mexico scrambles to find a replacement.

The switch occurs at 71:53 into the game. Immediately thereafter, Northridge launches one of its signature long throws into the box. There's a shot and a block by Ford. Unfortunately, however, the rebound goes right to a Matador, who scores a goal: 0–1, CSUN. "Well, great," Joe mutters to himself on the sideline. At 72:02, Barreiro reenters the game.

For the rest of regulation, New Mexico peppers the Northridge keeper with shots. Taylor, Omar, Puig, Billy, and Scotty all get good looks. None can convert. The game ends with the Lobos having controlled the match but lost on the scoreboard.

The locker room after is volatile. "Fish was pissed . . . throwing shit," summarizes one of the guys. As for Joe, he's held at least partly responsible for his reaction to attend to a hurt player. "That was my personal lowlight," he says of the season. "It was just the timing of everything . . . it turned into a mess."

To make matters a bit worse after the loss, the players can't even find the shower room in the Northridge facility. The locker room doesn't have any. Ah, the glories of DI soccer. And so the players wander around in their towels, grumbling and waiting for directions. "No rhythm in the first half," says Antoine. "We can't start that way . . . we're soft," replies Simon. Billy comments on the Lobos' pace. "[It] felt really slow," he says, especially in the first half.

Mike and Kelly are more philosophical. "Guys thought it was going to come easy," Mike says. Kelly points out the obvious: This is not a mature team. "[It's] a lot of guys who haven't played," he says. The team is learning how to travel and how to play together. "I'm glad we have another game right away," Kelly concludes as the players head for the minivans that will take them back to their hotel in Ventura.

In his weekly press conference, Fish finds a bit of perspective too. "Kind of a crazy little deal," he explains. "We had an injury, and our trainer ran onto the field . . . it was at an inopportune time . . . they score right over the guy who just came in." With a smile on his face for the cameras, he concludes, "It was frustrating."

***

Chapter 4

Nick Williams made the California trip despite the fact that he's leaning toward redshirting. He hasn't played yet, but the future is less than clear for him. "We haven't really talked about it," he says. "I've always just been the backup . . . I wasn't expecting that much going into a big-time program," he says. But he's clearly gained some confidence while playing against his teammates in practice.

The program being cut has changed everything. He wants to find another place to play (assuming that the quest, led by his father, fails). "I kind of just stayed optimistic because I needed to get film to give to other schools," he says. So, he has avoided the redshirt conversation with the coaches. That leaves him engaged as a practice player.

Regardless of his redshirt status, Nick Williams has another crucial role in the Lobo ecosystem. He is in charge of the Lobos' forty soccer balls. This position has all the stresses of a CEO position but none of the benefits, perks, or salary. "It gives me anxiety," Nick Williams says.

Everyone on the team has a job. Everyone is in charge of something: cones, jerseys, practice prep, practice cleanup. But nothing compares to the pressure on Omar, Julian, Carlos, and Nick Williams. They are the ones in charge of the soccer balls.

On just the second day of practice, Fish boiled over regarding the ball count, an issue that lingers throughout the season. The problem is multifold.

First, and most basically, college soccer players can kick a soccer ball a long way. With a mere two-step run-up, most of the Lobos can send the ball fifty yards.

Second, soccer players rarely pass up a chance to boot a ball. Almost every time the action in practice stops, any and all stray soccer balls become an opportunity target. Players take the chance to launch the ball at a faraway goal. Or they try to hit the top post (Antoine has been telling me all season that he's going to do it, but I never saw it). Or they target a teammate walking away, minding his own business.

Third, freshmen are inherently irresponsible. As Nick Williams explains it, one member of his team began shirking his ball duties almost as soon as he arrived in Albuquerque. "Omar would *never* take a bag," Nick Williams says.

Thus, the keeping of the forty soccer balls has become a subplot for this team. "We didn't do a very good job at the beginning of the season taking care of the balls," Nick Williams admits with the seriousness of a convicted felon. "We'd already got in trouble for the balls once . . . then one day, Carlos and I were counting them, and we were like, 'Oh, we only have thirty-three—we're like, oh no! *Seven missing balls.* This isn't good."

"Seven, yeah, oh yeah—I don't know how either," Nick Williams says, a bit ashamed. "Of course, that day, [Fishbein] is like, 'This doesn't look like forty balls . . . let's count 'em.'"

So, a count ensues. Since everyone involved can count to thirty-three, the outcome is fairly straightforward. Fish is pissed. Fearing for their futures as part of the New Mexico soccer program, the freshmen set out to find the missing soccer balls. They scour the equipment shed, the outer reaches of the practice fields, and the locker room. "And we found a few . . . so we got back up to thirty-six or something like that."

Then a crucial piece of information emerges. A get-out-of-jail-free card came from one of the assistant coaches. "He comes up to me," Nick Williams remembers of his salvation, "and says, 'Like, don't worry about, we bought, like, seventy balls.'" *Wait what?* "So, we have some extras," the coach tells Nick Williams. "If you just come get them, you can just go put them in the bag and say that you found them."

Encouraged, Nick Williams hatches an extraction plot. "I just do that part by myself," he says. After all, a solo job seems better than four freshmen trying to sneak incognito into the coaches' offices.

"So, I try to sneak into Champ's office because he's the one with the balls," Nick Williams remembers.

The problem is that the coaches' offices are a series of adjoining fishbowls—glass walls everywhere. And as Nick Williams enters, Fishbein just so happens to be in a meeting in his office with one of the ADs. Nick Williams decides to go for it anyway. "I see that Fish is in his office, and I'm like, 'He's not going to ask me what I'm doing in here,'" Nick Williams remembers. There is no way this head coach buried in season prep and a political fight for the survival of his program will have the mental bandwidth to keep track of soccer balls. *Right?*

Wrong. "He knows right away," Nick William says, shaking his head.

There is no meeting on earth that could keep Fish from calling out Nick Williams in this moment, in this predicament. "He stops his meeting in there with all those people, and he starts yelling at me. And he's yelling at me in a joking way, but still in a way that says, 'You screwed up.'"

"You guys are the worst ball crew that we've ever had in the history of this university. How do you lose *seven* balls?" Fish roars.

There are no easy answers. "I'm just like . . . I don't know," Nick Williams says. "And then we had to pay." A debate transpires among the team over how to deal with the debt. On the one hand, it is the freshmen's fault that the balls had gone missing. On the other hand, however, everyone knows that the balls went missing because each of them had launched balls all over the practice facility.

Regardless of who, why, or how, Fish demands accountability—in this case, financial accountability. "So, of course, me, Omar, Julian, and Carlos are the four guys on the balls—they [make] us pay twenty-seven dollars each, covering four or five balls, which is ridiculous," Nick Williams says. "Everybody else [pays] four bucks." The money goes toward replacing the balls. "That is ridiculous," Nick William says again, shaking his head.

However, what happens after this episode is informative. Nick Williams gets better: "So now, every morning, I get into the locker room, take out all the bags, make sure there's ten in all of them. Every day, count that forty. That's what I'm thinking about. We have to have forty, because I don't want to pay that money again."

Nick Williams becomes a bit of a ball dictator himself. To his teammates, he says, "I'm like, '*Double check your bag*, make sure we got it.'"

Still, every day, Fish follows up. "Nick Williams, where are we at with the balls?" the coach questions. So while his father is helping put together the political and legal effort to save the New Mexico soccer program, Nick Williams's dreams are devoted directly to the soccer balls themselves. "Now I'm like, at night, thinking, 'I've got to have forty balls,'" he says.

But Nick Williams is also a cagey young man. He has also gone on the offensive. "I have one ball in my locker that is an extra," he admits. "It's like a rainy-day ball. Just in case."

Day 27. Sunday, September 2, 2018.
Fullerton, California

After a day off, the Lobos face California State University, Fullerton (CSUF). Game day is spent waiting for game time. To pass the time, Kelly goes out for a run. Fish walks the campus. The players try to stay off their feet and kill time. It's still early in the semester, so school work, mostly an afterthought on these trips, is not too pressing.

The pregame meal is at 3:30 p.m. in a stuffy CSUF Marriot conference room. The menu, as always, consists of a mix of protein and pasta: chicken breasts, spaghetti, salad, rolls, and water. Finding the place and getting the food falls to Champ. This time, he's nailed it. "If we start out slow," he says, chewing, "it's because of these rolls." They're too good to resist.

Instead of addressing the team, something he does almost by second nature, Fish simply eats and leaves. He gives his players some space. The guys are loose and relaxed. Oddly, this is not a homecoming trip for any of the players. Not a single member of the Lobos team hails from California, something of an anomaly for a New Mexico collegiate team. Mike moves around as the players finish up their food, showing game clips to groups of players on his MacBook. He's concerned that the volume of information has been too much, too fast, for this new team. And so he wants to show short, pointed clips to the players individually.

As his players finish up, Fish, standing in a nearby hallway, stews over his strange position. He's trying to lead a team, the same as always, but he also carries the burden of the crusade to save the program. At yesterday's meal, he brought up the fight to save the program—the support by politicians and movement among the Board of Regents—and several of the players told him they'd had enough. They don't want to talk about the politics and the future unless they absolutely have to. Thus, for Fish, it's a tough balance. "I wonder if I'm doing the right thing," he says. "Is it better to just let it be dead?" If he did go the dead route, Fish could focus on winning some games, finding the players new schools, and positioning himself for a new job. Instead, he's stuck between.

After two games of scoreless soccer, New Mexico gets on the board quickly against the Titans. They are playing in a cavernous former football stadium that can seat ten thousand. CSUF discontinued intercollegiate football in 1992, but only after setting an NCAA record with seventy-three fumbles in its final campaign. The two soccer squads play in front of about two hundred fans. Less than thirteen minutes into the contest, on this warm Southern California evening, Taylor converts an assist from Antoine: 1–0, New Mexico.

The lead doesn't last for long, however. Ford comes out too far, and a Fullerton player scores on a boot from near midfield. "Deep kick dropped in over goalkeeper's head," describes the scorer of the shocking goal: 1–1. That's how the teams enter halftime. "We scored a nice first goal, then made a big blunder on the equalizer, but I thought we had a good first half," Fish tells a reporter from the *Albuquerque Journal*. "A howler," he calls the Fullerton goal later, "One of those fluke cross/shot on goals."[1]

In the locker room at half, the assessment is succinct: "A pretty fucking great half. Just one mistake." Mike wants a controlled attack. He sees openings on the edges of Fullerton's press. "Nothing frickin' gets us down!" he barks in closing. "Energy!"

Whatever was missing in the last two games is found tonight. Just five minutes into the second half, Puig scores off a Barreiro assist, and then, four minutes later, Antoine converts an offering from Omar: 2–1 and 3–1. Relief is evident on the Lobos bench. The goal has opened back up again—finally.

The coaches substitute liberally as the game winds down. Schumach, a sophomore from Albuquerque, gets his first minutes of the season. So do Mikey and Elijah. Fetterly comes on for Ford, giving the highly touted frosh his first time-in goal during the regular season. Still, the team is not finished. With seventeen minutes left, Taylor scores on a breakaway: 4–1. Just a few minutes later, Omar scores a rebound after Puig drills a shot off the post: 5–1. Victory.

"The forwards played tonight," Fish tells a happy, relieved postgame locker room. Tonight, the team took its chances and converted, something the coaches saw that was missing in the games against Washington and Northridge. And the shots went in. Of the ten shots (and seven on goal), the Lobos converted five. This is not a sustainable shots-to-goals ratio, but for tonight, it works.

Back at the team hotel, Fish sits in the lobby, directing traffic. The low-minute guys are lacing up their shoes to head out with Kelly for some running. The starters and key subs make their way toward the pool for a postgame recovery.

"It's a good group," Fish concludes, wrapping up the team's trip to California.

CHAPTER 5

The Shame of College Soccer

In 2011, Taylor Branch—a Pulitzer Prize–winning historian, renowned for his magisterial trilogy on Martin Luther King Jr.—turned his attention to college sports. At first glance, one might see it as a curious pivot. After all, Branch made chronicling the civil rights movement his career. He had, many moons earlier, turned down a football scholarship to attend Georgia Tech. In the 1990s Branch had also served as a confidant to President Bill Clinton.

Thus, one had to ask, How did sports fit into a portfolio of work based on civil rights and political scandal?

Remarkably well, as it turned out. After conducting more than one hundred interviews and combing through NCAA archives, Branch put forward a powerful case that college sports functioned as a "classic cartel." Even more striking (and damning), Branch noted the "unmistakable whiff of the plantation" within college football and basketball.[1] Branch argued that while the public occasionally became overly excited about an isolated college sports scandal (e.g., an athlete being provided a car by a booster or selling his gear), there was something much more repugnant transpiring. College sports, he contended, was a booming business built on the exploitation of unpaid labor, most of which has been provided by young Black men.

The fourteen thousand–word article appeared as a cover story in the *Atlantic Magazine* in October 2011. Legendary sportswriter Frank

Chapter 5

Deford called the piece "the most important article ever written on college sports." Branch simply titled the cage-rattling opus "The Shame of College Sports."[2]

***

There is shame in college soccer as well, but it is different. In college soccer, it's not a case of resources being withheld from the athletes. It's not about unpaid labor. Nor does this shame concern the diversity (or lack thereof) of Division I male players. Instead, the leaders of college soccer seem obsessed with identifying where their sport fits in the world's broader soccer landscape. And in 2018, they are, quite frankly, embarrassed about it.

The inferiority complex of men's Division I college soccer hangs over the sport like a cloud. I heard it from players throughout the season, especially those who came up through the Development Academy system or who had experiences with US Soccer. "The level of soccer we're playing here is just OK," says one Lobo as the season begins. For the Lobo coaches, every scouting report hints at what the college game has in excess: directness and physicality. At times, it's as if those involved believe they must apologize for the structure in which they participate.

Pushed into a confessional, college coaches would quickly ask for forgiveness for the following soccer sins: *Please forgive us father, college soccer has*

- A short, compressed, fall-only schedule
- A chaotic, free-for-all substitution policy
- Rules allowing reentry in the second half—*reentry!*
- A tendency toward direct, physical play
- A lot of scoreless games

And that's not all. Important soccer people (read: those connected to the MLS or the US Soccer Federation [USSF]) say that (1) the NCAA game no longer produces high-level coaches, (2) college soccer helped the US *not* qualify for the 2018 World Cup, and (3) DI college soccer puts on a bitterly cold and sparsely attended national championship.

Further, some MLS clubs would rather pass than select an NCAA player in the MLS SuperDraft.

These are the sins—at least some of them. This is the shame of college soccer.

And so, to a certain extent, when *College Soccer News* (*CSN*) reported on the cutting of New Mexico's program, they did so with a sense of resignation. Add the Lobos cut to the list of challenges facing college soccer. "The decision to cut a very successful men's soccer program," *CSN* editorialized in July, "is a disappointing and short-sighted approach."[3] But what could be done?

Day 30. Wednesday, September 5, 2018.
Albuquerque, New Mexico

The Lobos have three days between trips. The team had Tuesday off and returns to practice today. In the team meeting room at 8:00 a.m., Fish again addresses the issues swirling around the program. It's as if the circumstances can never quite be put aside to allow the focus just to be on the field. "I'm 100 percent committed to this team going forward," he reiterates before snapping back to the upcoming opponent.

Having reviewed the Fullerton tape, the coaches are happy with the 5–1 victory. They liked the score and outcome, of course, but also the work rate of most of the team. Mike shows footage of several players, especially Simon, making long recovery runs, turning tracks after a mistake, and chasing down the ball forty yards up the field. "Can you be a hard fighting *and* skilled team?" Fish asks. If so, there are good things in store.

On the grass, however, everyone is sluggish. "You had a day and a half off," Mike yells. "You should be fresh." The coaches' tone is all business today. The newness of the season is gone. The results have been mixed. Expectations are still pressing. Mike keeps stopping the action. This annoys several of the more outspoken Lobos. "I'm only stopping it because the energy isn't right," Mike says. "The energy is low," the players mumble, "because you keep stopping the action."

Champ works the goalies, as usual. While the weather is cooling slightly, with highs in the mid-eighties today, Champ, Ford, Fetterly, and Anthony perspire mightily as they work. Champ's concerned with the "one big mistake" pattern Ford seems to be falling into. Ford is brilliant for long stretches but then gives up a positioning goal, like at Fullerton. If this becomes a pattern, the damage done to the Lobos' defense will be both literal and psychological—more goals surrendered, more doubts festering. "The team decides," Champ explains about the keeper slot. "Once they lose confidence, you have to make a decision."

Strangely, Champ is both the keeper-whisperer for the team and a regular practice player. With the team's numbers down, Mike often calls on Champ to grab a pinnie and play in team scrimmages. A former goalie, the twenty-four-year-old assistant coach can still hold his own on the field. In some ways, Champ has as close a beat as any of the coaches on how this team is coming together (or falling apart). He manages the goalies, plays in the team scrimmages, and gets the team's food—no one is more vital.

Day 31. Thursday, September 6, 2018.
Tulsa, Oklahoma

The team departs for Tulsa, Oklahoma, at 12:40 p.m. on Thursday. The team traveled well last weekend, so Fish has only one slight correction. "Black socks!" he emphasizes.

The traveling party is slightly smaller than just a week ago. Having confirmed their desires to redshirt for the season, Carlos, Ben, and Anthony stay home. Nick Williams is the only freshman who makes the Tulsa trip that has not played yet and, thus, could redshirt without any complications.

Day 32. Friday, September 7, 2018.
Tulsa, Oklahoma

The team stays in a nearly deserted Doubletree Hotel in downtown Tulsa. As always, on game day, the hours before the game drag out interminably. The team meets for breakfast at 9:00 a.m. and then watches video on Tulsa's set piece till 10:00 a.m. Then at 11:00 a.m., the team takes over the steamy indoor pool for a shakeout/activation exercise with Joe. The twenty stretching, jogging, and otherwise active Lobos in the pool scare away other guests.

Then there's just the waiting. Fish works out in the hotel weight room. He emerges with sweat glistening on his bald head. Mike and Fetterly appear in the hotel coffee shop before retreating to their respective rooms to rest. Simon finds a tucked-away couch in a hotel corridor on which to complete some schoolwork.

The week itself has been a mix of politics and soccer preparation. Fish has had contact with a handful of politicians—Lundstrum, Maestas, and a member of the Lujan Grisham campaign for governor—during the few days the team was back in Albuquerque. Fish is a man remarkably comfortable with conflict. He keeps pushing. Fish's fight against the cuts has created real unrest among the coaching fraternity at UNM. Coaches who otherwise would sidle up and commiserate with Fish, the longest-tenured Lobo coach, are nowhere to be seen. Fish describes his new social standing as that of a "pariah" and a "dead man walking."

This isolation hurts. So, too, does the obvious fact that his bosses want him gone. There is no playbook here, but in the countdown to taking on Tulsa, sipping a coffee in the hotel lobby, Fish is certain of this: "I don't want to get fired." That would ruin everything. And it would cost him a healthy sum of money. *Continue to advocate, but don't cross the line. This is the goal.*

The team arrives on the Tulsa University (TU) campus an hour and a half before the 7:00 p.m. kickoff. TU is a private university that, taking sports out of the equation, shares little in common with the University of New Mexico. Tulsa has roughly a quarter the number of undergraduate students (four thousand) as UNM but twice the endowment ($1.1 billion). Tuition and room and board at Tulsa total more than $60,000 per year. The campus is small, but it is vibrant and immaculate.

The first player out on the field for warm-ups is Puig. He's an Oklahoma native who knows this lush, dense field well, given that he played on it as a freshman two years ago. As the players test the surface (Puig, Antoine, and Elijah dance and move the ball around a triangle), they finish a conversation that's been going on since they left Albuquerque: "Who would play you if they made a movie about our season?" The players, like most twenty-year-olds, have a surprisingly easy time arriving at a mental place where they can imagine another person devoting such resources to their situation. The players joke about finding an actor with the intensity to play Fish. Who could carry such a role? For his part, Scotty doesn't say much until he's asked which actor would play him.

"Mel Gibson," he says without a moment's hesitation. And that's that.

The Lobos dress in their all-red kits. Somehow, Tom's jersey has gone missing. "That should be a fun conversation," Champ says, glancing toward Fish, who is already amped up for the game.

The players sit knee-to-knee in the small visitor's locker room. They listen and fidget as the coaches provide final instructions. The lineup has been slightly altered. Ford remains in goal, but the back line looks different, running Tom, Billy, Dorsey, and Barreiro from the left side to the right. The midfielders (Antoine, Bailey, Scotty, and Simon) and forwards (Taylor and Puig) remain the same.

In warm-ups Ford looks nervous. He hits a few of his practice boots into the stands. Not a good sign. But when the game starts, he's a brick wall. The Hurricanes get off eight shots in the first eighteen minutes, compared to just one (by Taylor) for the Lobos. At one point in the early barrage, Ford charges a ball at the edge of the box, fails to clear it, and then has to watch as it hits the post. It's a lucky break.

The night is damp and drizzly. The Tulsa soccer field, unlike most the Lobos play in, has no protection over the team benches. Fish sits on the top edge of the bench, hat high on his head, mostly impassive as the first half unwinds. With less than three minutes left in the half, a Tulsa defender wins a tough header in his half and launches a rather benign approach fifty yards in the other direction. The TU forwards control it. The ball advances quickly as Dorsey and Billy retreat. The defense is far too soft. Tulsa exchanges two passes in the box before a left-footed shot finds the top left corner: 0–1, Tulsa. Dorsey throws his arms up in frustration.

When the horn buzzes, signaling halftime, the starters cut back across the field for the locker room. Mike and Fish spend five minutes on the bench, gathering their thoughts. Finally, when they address the team, the coaches focus on creating more opportunities. The action has all been in New Mexico's half. "Pick your moments," Fish urges. Mike wants to push the wingers up further into Tulsa's half. "We're making them look good . . . win tackles, connect passes, and good things will happen," Fish finishes.

For the second half, the freshman duo Gallo and Omar—for the second straight game—come out as starters. The two first-years are becoming more and more integral to the Lobos attack. Right away, both make their presence felt. Off a stoppage, Gallo delivers a long pass across the field to Tom, who serves a ball forty yards into the box. There Omar controls it and shoots. The ball hits the keeper and slowly tumbles into the goal. After being thoroughly outplayed in the first half, the Lobos have tied the game: 1–1.

And that's where the score stays for the rest of the half. Ford makes save after save—eight in total during the second stanza. Meanwhile, the precipitation finally breaks through. A soft sprinkle starts. The coaches put on their rain gear. The temperature drops into the seventies. The ball slides and skips across the field. Finally, with everyone drenched, the game buzzer sounds.

But, unlike almost everywhere else in the soccer world, there is more still to come. In what one coach calls "the most stupidest rule in college sports," college soccer, even for regular season games, has overtime.[4]

***

The day after the US men's national team failed to qualify for the 2018 World Cup, an indignity the country had avoided for thirty years, blame was cast in almost every direction. Not surprisingly, college soccer got pinged. One prominent professional coach pointed directly to college soccer as the culprit. "I honestly believe the system for basketball and American football and maybe baseball is . . . as good a setup as you can have anywhere in the world," Minnesota United coach Adrian Heath postulated before continuing, "It's probably the worst for soccer."[5]

Sasho Cirovski, the head coach at the University of Maryland and one of the most influential proponents of changing college soccer's rules and scheduling, put it even more bluntly: "College soccer is the laughingstock of the soccer world now," he told ESPN in March 2018.[6]

That New Mexico has played ninety minutes with Tulsa on an increasingly spongy field in the humidity of late-summer Oklahoma and is now heading into overtime serves as a fine exhibit for soccer's critics. College soccer is just "a strange bird," says Steven Goff in the *Washington Post*.[7]

Still, the ninety-seven-page NCAA soccer rule book lays out the overtime rules clearly enough. If, at the end of ninety minutes, two teams have a tie score, they shall play a first overtime period with a "sudden victory" mandate. Elsewhere, this is called "sudden death" or "golden goal." The first team to score wins. If the first overtime period expires without a score, the teams proceed to a second overtime. This, too, can end with a "sudden victory" score. Only after two scoreless overtime periods will the game be finalized as a tie (in the regular season) or proceed to penalty kicks (in tournament play).[8]

Nowhere in its ninety-seven-page document—or elsewhere—does the NCAA explain *why* college soccer games cannot end in a tie. Perhaps there is a lofty ideal at stake, something along the lines of what Ted Lasso would say several years later: "If God wanted games to end in a tie, she wouldn't have invented numbers."[9] Or maybe there is a case to be made that the college game should handle the matter very differently than its professional counterparts? Unfortunately, the NCAA doesn't say.

And, of course, scoreless soccer games played all over the world end as ties. In fact, the tie is a relatively accepted part of the sport. On average, about one-third of all English Premier League games end as a draw. Columbia University psychologist James Curley found that in 125 years of English soccer, there have been some 13,475 0–0 ties (or "Nil-Nil Draws").[10] Such is the nature of a relatively low-scoring sport.

The belittling of NCAA Division I soccer by the broader soccer community matters immensely to the sport's college coaches. "We must follow FIFA rules, we are behind the times, and it is embarrassing," says one coach in an anonymous NCAA feedback forum. "If a game is a tie and ends in a tie, no need for overtime after 90 minutes except for the playoffs." Or, as another coach puts it, "[They] need to change the overtime rule in season. A tie is a tie."

In 2014 the University of California, Davis men's soccer team set the NCAA record for the most overtime games in a single season. Fourteen of the Aggies' twenty contests went into extra time. While not setting any records, Fish has plenty of overtime experience as well. During the previous three seasons, New Mexico has played fifteen *double*-overtime games. In eleven of these extra-extra-long games, the score remained tied, even after the additional twenty minutes of play.

The NCAA overtime rule is so jarringly different from the rest of the world that several of New Mexico's foreign-born players did not know about the NCAA extra-time policy until it happened to them for the first time. "I came in blind," Tom says. "I didn't really know what I was getting myself into." The transition to Albuquerque and an American university was one thing, but so, too, was the difference in the US game itself. "I knew it was a bit different, but I didn't know the overtime rule," Tom says. "Frankly, I didn't like it."

Though the overtime rule is the most obvious variance to the casual fan either attending an NCAA game or glancing at scores online, there are a host of other, smaller rule discrepancies that make college soccer different from the game led by FIFA. They are mostly little things. For example, in 2018, in college soccer, the clock winds down from forty-five minutes; in most other leagues, it goes in the opposite direction. Additionally, the referees don't keep the official time in college soccer; the scoreboard operator does instead.[11]

To a certain extent, it's simply a case of the NCAA reacting slowly to changes elsewhere. When, in 2016, FIFA changed its kick-off rule to allow a kick in any direction, American college soccer continued to mandate a go-only-forward approach for two additional seasons.

These things matter mostly to people who deeply care about college soccer, like the coaches working in NCAA programs. When surveyed at the end of 2016 about their concerns for college soccer, NCAA coaches boiled over at the way their game looked compared to everyone else. When asked to provide "additional feedback," the coaches let the NCAA have it: "Kickoff . . . whether it rolls inches forward or backward[,] has zero bearing on the game . . . and a referee enforcing it looks stupid."[12]

Substitution rules serve as a clear demarcation point in terms of substantive differences between college soccer and, say, the United Soccer League (USL) or MLS games. In terms of gameplay itself, the NCAA game's substitution rules make it, in some ways, closer to high school or youth soccer than to any high-level men's league. In a sport where endurance and pacing are so key, the NCAA rulebook for soccer allows college coaches to use their entire rosters—in one game. "Either team may substitute up to eleven players at a time," reads the NCAA rule book.[13]

This means that a player might be substituted out fifteen minutes into the second half for a rest and then reenter the game ten minutes later. Fish does this regularly. Against Tulsa, Omar starts the second half, then comes out at the sixty-minute mark and is replaced by Simon. After catching his breath and conferring with the coaches, Omar checks back in for the final fifteen minutes of regulation. This substitution rule allows soccer players to do, in essence, what their counterparts in hockey do: come in and play a shift (often with a particular task in mind). All-out running, more physical contests for headers, and hustle have thus come to define the game.

And the non-soccerist might ask, What is so wrong with this? Why not substitute and interchange players? After all, isn't soccer an extraordinarily taxing game? And shouldn't playing time be spread around, given that most college squads consist of twenty-five to thirty players?

The answers to such questions depend on one's perspective.

To many soccer purists, the substitution rules allowed by the NCAA fundamentally change the play on the field. The "beautiful game" becomes a disjointed, overly physical contest. The game is ragged and simple. "The game is broken," one of UNM's players repeatedly says of college soccer. This same sentiment is readily heard both from venues that cover college soccer extensively (*Soccer America*, *TopDrawer Soccer*, etc.) and in the results and university-centric coverage that appears in, for example, local newspapers.

"While the MLS has entered an era of genius No. 10s and goalscoring wingers, the college game still largely emphasizes, well, being large," writes one reporter. "There's still a lot of long ball and a lot of running." Such tactics don't produce skilled players. *FourFourTwo* points to "an overemphasis on speed, fitness and physicality" as the key problems in the college game, problems which are caused by the "nearly unlimited substitutions and other significant . . . rulebook quirks compared to the global game."[14]

What if heavy-handed NCAA officials tampered with other sports in such a manner? Some college soccer coaches have begun advocating for imposing equally corrosive alterations on college baseball and softball rules:

> *If we allow [reentry substitution rules] in Division I Men's Soccer, then we need to have a proposal for both Baseball and Softball to allow re-entry in those two sports. We must stay consistent with the laws of the game in all sports. Nowhere in the world of soccer is re-entry allowed for soccer, only in NCAA Soccer. We are in the dark ages in terms of our substitution rules. Let's all vote now for Baseball and Softball in the NCAA to have re-entry just like NCAA Soccer.*[15]

This reaction seems very different than a debate over the difference between the NCAA's three-point line and the NBA's or the differing rules that govern overtime in NCAA football and the NFL.

***

In recent years college soccer seems to be on the precipice of, well, something. Maryland's Sasho Cirovski continues to lead the way. In August 2016 a committee of the National Soccer Coaches Association, led by Sasho, introduced a proposal to radically change the NCAA college season, moving the college game to an academic year season model. The proposal, later known as the twenty-first-century model, shifted the college season from one constrained to the fall semester to a more stretched model. College games would take place between September and November and then between March and May.[16]

The benefits of such a season are numerous. Games would be more spread out, usually taking place on weekends and just once a week. This spacing would cut down on injuries. Additionally, players would miss fewer days of class. During the 2018 season, for example, the Lobos will miss eleven days of class due to their CUSA travel schedule.

In point after point, the committee argued that college soccer would be better for the student athlete (in terms of "ability, ambition, health, safety, and time demands, and to balance personal, academic and other priorities") with the elongated schedule. Buried deep in the FAQ, however, was the illusive development piece. "For elite youth players the proposed model will be very appealing . . . and will offer an improved collegiate development model for collegiate performance, and for those with professional soccer aspirations," the committee argued. "This is very important as an increasing number of youth players are circumventing college and signing speculative professional contracts because college soccer is viewed as an insufficient development environment."[17]

If Sasho's 2016 proposal raised hopes, then the 2017 annual MLS SuperDraft brought college soccer folks right back to earth. Held every January, the MLS draft is modeled after the highly-covered NFL and NBA drafts. And the selection event does, in fact, provide *some* college players with dream-come-true moments. For New Mexico, the selection of Niko Hansen with the ninth overall pick in 2017 was a high watermark for the program—never before had a Lobo gone so high in the draft. But, starting in the third round, the feel-good moments for college soccer in that same 2017 draft soured.

With the tenth pick of the third round (the fifty-fourth overall), New York City FC selected Chris Wingate, a midfielder at University of New Hampshire.

With the eleventh pick, the Philadelphia Union selected Chris Nanco, a forward at Syracuse University.

With the twelfth pick, the Seattle Sounders selected Douglas Goodman, a midfielder at Georgetown University.

This brought the draft to the fifty-seventh selection overall, a choice owned by Real Salt Lake. With the thirteenth pick of the third round, Real Salt Lake . . . passed.

The club was so uninterested in the college talent available that it did not even want to select a player to invite to camp. Although the selection would have cost the club almost nothing, Real Salt Lake simply said to college soccer, "No thanks. We're good."

The 2017 draft started a trend. After seven clubs passed on picks in 2017, clubs passed on eleven picks in the January 2018 draft. By January 2019 the draft seemed to reach a watershed moment. "If you had any doubts about the lack of interest many MLS clubs place on the college game these days," soccer reporter Paul Kennedy wrote just a few months after Fish and New Mexico concluded its 2018 season, "it was evident on Monday when teams passed on 21 of the 48 SuperDraft picks."[18]

For Nathan Aune, the Seattle University player ejected during the Lobos 4–2 season opening victory, the beginning of the 2019 third round went as follows:

Some other player

Me!

Pass

Pass

Some other player[19]

If the college game is supposed to develop professional soccer players—and who says that it should?—then something clearly needs to change.

Day 32. Friday, September 7, 2018.
Tulsa, Oklahoma

"Fans, if you're new to the process, there will be a ten-minute period. If either team scores during that period, the match will be over," the announcer says as Champ walks out to meet Ford at the end of regulation. Overtime looms. Later, during the intermission, the man with the microphone provides more instruction about the mysteries of college soccer:

Chapter 5

"Fans, you may have noticed this year that our clock has been going up, but for the extra time period, it has to go down. Don't let that throw you."

"Guys, we've got to control the ball," Fish exhorts as his team breaks the huddle for extra time.

Both teams get a couple of chances in the overtime. At five minutes Taylor runs down a deep ball on the left side and, twice, cuts back right, then once back left to get a clean look from fifteen feet. His shot is just a little too high. After one hundred minutes, the game remains tied at 1–1.

The teams get just a two-minute break between overtime periods. Champ riles the bench players, sending them out to huddle with their teammates as the struggle continues. Finally, in the 103rd minute of the game, the Lobos earn their first corner kick. Unfortunately, they can't do much with it. The fact that the offense has generated just one of these opportunities speaks to the balance of play during the contest. Although the scoreboard shows a tie, the game has been anything but even.

Still, if the Lobos can hang on for just a couple more minutes, they'll leave Oklahoma with a hard-earned (if ugly) bit of progress.

But no. With 2:30 remaining in the second overtime period, a Tulsa wing delivers a cross in front of the goal. Dorsey pops it up with a header. The ball falls at the feet of Tulsa's Adam Habib, a forward who did not play until the second overtime period. Habib jukes once, scoots around Barreiro, and chips a soft knuckleball into the top right corner: Goal Tulsa. Final score: 1–2, Tulsa Hurricanes. In 108 minutes of competition.

Several of the Lobos on the field simply fall onto their backs in disbelief. Billy argues with the referees. Puig, who had just reentered the game to shouts of "Come on Matt, show 'em what they're missing" from his vocal, local cheering section, walks, stone-faced, back to the Lobos' bench, working his way around a pileup of celebrating Tulsa players. Champ again walks out to meet his keep. He puts an arm around Ford's slumped shoulders.

"What a shit show that was," Taylor seethes as he enters the locker room. Shortly before the winning goal, the sophomore was tripped in what appeared to be a foul. Both teams, in fact, had stopped playing until it became obvious the referees had no plans to blow the whistle. Taylor earned a yellow card for arguing just twenty-eight seconds before the winner hit the back of the net. Taylor's family traveled three hours from Dallas to see the game. They wait as he changes.

Scotty (Mel Gibson) is more reserved. He rarely loses his cool. He tends to burn slowly and steadily. "We put so much into it," he says in his thick Scottish brogue. "That's what makes this so hard." Dorsey, the senior who had a close-up view of the winning goal, can still hardly believe how the game ended. "Wrong foot, top corner," he says with a shake of his head. "You don't expect those to go in."

With the loss, the Lobos fall to 2–3. Still, given Fish's preference for arranging tough schedules at the beginning of seasons, this is not unchartered territory for the program. There's still time to get it right. "We've got a lot of things to fix," Ford says as he heads for the vans. And after his busy night, he has a suggestion. "We play a lot better," he submits, "when we're in their half."

CHAPTER 6

$605,630

Eddie Nuñez began the day on September 8, 2017, in a splendid gray suit. Taking the podium sporting short-cropped brown hair, a silver watch, and a perfectly knotted red tie, Eddie could have been a Wall Street executive. One might have expected him to talk about hedge funds or venture capital rather than the Mountain West Conference and football schedules.

And if he looked good outwardly, Eddie seemed even more so to be all sparkle on the inside. He radiated positivity. He began on this fall Friday—the day he was announced as the University of New Mexico's new AD—teeming with smiles and enthusiasm.

Here, it seemed, was a man with a great suit *and* great expectations. By nightfall he had lost both.

Eddie arrived at UNM from Louisiana State University (LSU). At LSU, over fourteen years, Eddie rose through the ranks of the Tigers' booming athletic department. He played pickup basketball with Nick Saban, built lasting relationships with alums like Shaquille O'Neil, and ascended to be AD Joe Alleva's right-hand man. At LSU Eddie became known as the man who could get things done. He could glad-hand all kinds of people. Partly due to his architecture background, Eddie also had a knack for orchestrating complex construction jobs. As he proudly noted in his bio, Eddie oversaw more than $400 million in building projects for the Tigers. During his last year at the Southeastern Conference school, LSU's annual athletic budget stood at $145 million.[1]

The son of first-generation Cuban-American parents, Eddie grew up in Miami, Florida. He attended Miami Senior High School in the city's Little Havana neighborhood. At Miami Senior, Nuñez played basketball for the legendary Shaky Rodriguez and for future NCAA coach Frank Martin. The school was a powerhouse, winning 90 percent of its games, five state titles, and producing numerous Division I recruits during the 1980s and 1990s. As a six-foot-two guard, Eddie never particularly stood out in the hypercompetitive Stingarees program. The most exciting recruiting calls he received were from Billy Donovan, who, at that time, was an assistant coach at the University of Kentucky. However, the coach was targeting Eddie's friend and teammate, Allen Edwards, not Eddie. But still, Eddie played a fearless and joyful brand of basketball. "Basketball was my love," Eddie says. He flourished in Miami's competitive athletic environment.[2]

After high school, Eddie moved on to Miami Dade Community College. There he made the basketball team and averaged a few points per game over two seasons. He also worked toward a degree in architecture. While other players might have seen this relatively nondescript junior college experience as an end point, Eddie plowed ahead. Remembering the phone calls (that were never actually aimed at him), Nuñez went to see Billy Donovan, who, by this time, had become the head coach at the University of Florida. Standing in the coach's office with a prepared speech, Nuñez asked to walk on to the basketball team. "I'm not asking for a bunch of minutes," Nuñez bargained. "I just want to show you I can help the team." Eventually, Donovan gave in. Nuñez kept playing. During his two years as a Gator, Eddie dove for every loose ball. He led the team in floor burns and high fives. He brought constant energy.[3]

Eddie's rewards for this effort were mostly internal. He appeared in just a handful of Florida games, during which he scored not a single basket. However, as his time wound down, Nuñez knew he had earned his place. He'd certainly earned Donovan's respect. Before a big game with Kentucky, Donovan spoke of Eddie to the local press, saying, "He's as valuable as anybody on our team." This wasn't technically true, of course—at least not unless Donovan cared less about winning basketball games than it seemed. But the statement was coach-speak for "I see you and I appreciate you."[4]

After graduating, Eddie worked as an assistant basketball coach at Marquette. From there he moved on to Vanderbilt, where he transitioned into a role in athletic administration. Then Eddie jumped to LSU.

During his introductory press conference at UNM, Eddie made a speech that was long in both sincerity and platitudes. He recalled his upbringing in Miami and his experiences at Florida and LSU. He promised a commitment to—as almost all new ADs do—academic success and winning championships. During the question-and-answer session, Eddie refused to be brought down by local reporters' questions about the problems facing UNM's athletic department. The first question, asked by *Journal* beat writer Geoff Grammer, brought up the budget shortfalls. The questions that followed pointed out other issues. In response, Eddie was all lemonade. Yes, there were "six or seven" investigations facing the unit. Sure, the budget was limited. Of course, pressure existed to fill the basketball arena to increase revenues. Despite these factors, however, Eddie promised that even better days were ahead. "We are one team," Eddie said at the end of his remarks, "and together we will continue to make things great here."[5]

The bit of ceremony that happened next would have been perfect if Eddie had been a five-foot-nine former basketball player instead of a six-foot-two former basketball player. In keeping with university traditions, President Chauki Abdullah presented Eddie with a cherry red blazer. "You've earned it, Eddie," Abdullah said. Off came Eddie's gray jacket and on went the Lobo red. The only problem was the fit. The sleeves fell several inches too short. "They gave me a red coat that went to my elbows," Eddie remembers, still slightly embarrassed.[6] Eddie spent the rest of the event as a T. rex, constricted at the arms.

Things only got worse from there.

After the press conference, Eddie met with Abdullah at the president's house. Arriving at the seven thousand–square foot, middle-of-the-campus adobe mansion, Eddie took a seat in the kitchen. Then Abdallah, a systems theory engineer by training, began listing the problems facing the athletic department: an attorney general investigation, a state auditor investigation, an internal audit, Title IX concerns, a budget crisis, and the university as a whole being under the watch of the Department of Justice. It was one thing after another. "A lot of scary things were thrown at me that first day," Eddie says. At that point, as he sat in that kitchen, he had buyer's remorse. "I'm just sitting there, thinking to myself," Eddie says, "'Did I sign the contract?'"

Then came the real bomb. "Shortly after that, I was told I would have to cut sports," Eddie remembers. This was the only way to cut the annual deficit being produced by the UNM Athletic Department.[7]

Properly fitting suit jacket? Gone. Optimism? Gone.

***

On the surface, Eddie Nuñez needed to cut sports at the University of New Mexico because of an edict that came down from his bosses. The Board of Regents and university president said sports had to be cut. Thus, for Nuñez, it had to be so.

But there was a deeper, more systemic reason behind the crisis as well. It was a reason and a way of thinking so pervasive in college athletics that few people stopped to question it at all. It was not unique to UNM, and it still persists in college athletics today.

Here it is: an NCAA Division I athletic department is *supposed* to be able to pay for itself. To put it another way, DI athletics *should* bring in enough revenue (through television contracts and ticket sales, among other things) to cover its expenses. This is—and has long been—the sword-in-the-stone premise of big-time college sports.[8]

And, in fact, this idea of self-sufficiency existed as an actual NCAA policy, albeit a completely unenforceable one, from 1978 until 2008. When it became embarrassingly obvious that no one was actually following the policy, however, NCAA membership voted to strike the requirement of "strives to finance its athletics program insofar as possible from revenues generated by the program itself" from the Division I standards. The vote did away with the policy.[9]

$605,630

Still, the allure of self-sufficiency persists. According to Andy Schwarz, a leading antitrust economist who has repeatedly spearheaded the testimony against the NCAA in federal court, self-sufficiency exists today as a faulty ideal at best and a fraudulent one at worst. And to be clear, almost no other unit on campus is held to this self-sufficiency standard.

"This idea that athletic departments are supposed to be self-sufficient," Schwarz says to me on the phone one day, as he's in between trips to the hardware store to pick up paint, "I know it is a . . . [long pause] . . . I know it's a sentence. But it has no truth content to me."

To Schwarz, the idea of an institution with a multibillion-dollar budget making painful programmatic cuts—cuts that result in fewer students attending the university and in fewer young children wearing Lobo soccer camp T-shirts every summer—only to save thousands of dollars is proof that too many "innumerate people" (as he terms them) are making numbers decisions.

Ouch.

To his credit, Andy Schwarz works hard to present his expert economic analysis in a palatable manner. He recognizes the tension between the theorist and the practitioner. Therefore, he trades heavily in self-deprecation. He deflects credit to his partners at the successful OKSR firm. Schwarz is exceedingly generous with his time. He reminds me several times that he didn't actually complete his PhD in economics. He also acknowledges his limited field of vision. "I don't have a ton of spots where I think I know more than most people," Schwarz clarifies, "and not too many that most people care about."

Schwarz readily concedes there are many skills that he just doesn't have. When he describes the characteristics that he sees as the ones that universities prize in their athletic directors ("good at raising money and remembering names and looking people in the eye and having a nice haircut and a good firm handshake"), he says that economists have severe deficiencies. "Economists are dorks," he says.

But Schwarz knows economics. He also knows college athletics. And he's convinced that most everyone else—well, they just don't get it.

It gets particularly interesting to listen to Schwarz and his fellow economists when they are forced to get specific, pointing out specific flaws and naming names. Ask the right questions, and interesting analysis follows. For example, One might ask, In what ways is the NCAA specifically distorting the market? Where are athletic departments making economically indefensible decisions? Or, most pressingly, in 2018, should the University of New Mexico cut sports to balance its athletic department budget?

Schwarz and his colleagues have plenty to say on such matters, but they tend to zero in on a couple of things.

First, the NCAA inflates the cost of an athletic scholarship. This is the NCAA's foundational economic sin.

Through its policies and practices, the NCAA does everything it can to shine a spotlight on the value of an athletic scholarship. It does so because the athletic scholarship has long been the cornerstone of the NCAA's legitimacy. And if, as the NCAA contends, the athletic scholarship is something of extraordinary value (in actual dollars and otherwise), well, that covers up all manner of other injustices and problems.

To highlight the value of these athletic scholarships, the NCAA, among other distortions, creates a picture where an athlete accepting a scholarship to attend a university means that a different student, who would otherwise attend this same university, cannot do so. It's a zero-sum scenario. The perception is created, for example, that if not for the twenty-seven players on the UNM men's soccer team, twenty-seven other deserving students would have the opportunity to attend the school.

But this just isn't accurate, at least not at most universities. While Schwarz points out that at his alma mater, Stanford University, there is indeed a queue of students waiting in line, ready to pay full freight for every slot that may otherwise be taken by an athlete, the University of New Mexico presents an entirely different reality. UNM is underenrolled in 2018. It is down to 24,391 students, representing an enrollment drop of 12.5 percent over the prior five years. But, as Schwarz points out, the buildings are still there, the lights are still on, and the teachers are still teaching. Thus, students (whether on scholarship or not) can be added at a marginal cost to UNM. Each additional student costs the university something much less than the full sticker price.

According to the NCAA, however, it will cost UNM nearly $35,000 annually for every scholarship athlete added to the mix. Period.

"The price is not the cost," Schwarz scolds here. "The price is not the cost!"

Hang with me here, as we have to travel pretty far into the NCAA's bizarro world to truly feel Andy's frustration. But I think it's worth it.

The NCAA propagates a price/cost distortion through the financial reporting form that it requires every athletic department to file annually. This form is basically organized into expenses and revenues. The first line item in the expenses category on the form is "Athletic Student Aid." For 2018, the Lobo athletic department lists an $8,150,932 expense in this category. This number came from the athletic department awarding the equivalent of 235.87 full athletic scholarships at a value of $34,557 per full award for the year. Thus, the university spent more than $8 million to give scholarships to its athletes.

Generous, right? Yes, but not as much as you'd think. Remember, the price is not the cost.

What's more, there is other money actually flowing into the university as a result of this athletic scholarship activity, which, strangely, isn't being counted.

Consider Athlete X:

- Athlete X came to UNM from Colorado as a recruited soccer player.
- There is nearly a 0 percent chance Athlete X would have attended UNM without Soccer.
- Athlete X has an athletic scholarship that covers 50 percent of tuition, room, and board.
- Athlete X lives on campus and buys books and other supplies.

What does Athlete X look like according to the NCAA's financial report? In a word, *expensive*.

CHAPTER 6

The athletic department must account for Athlete X with a -$17,278 under the "Athletic Student Aid" section in its 2018 NCAA financial disclosure. The debit goes against the soccer team's account, so to speak. And that's it.

In filling out the NCAA's report, UNM athletics has no place to provide the revenue side of Athlete X. The soccer program certainly won't get credit for bringing a student to campus who otherwise wouldn't have come to UNM nor a place in its budget to report the tuition that Athlete X actually paid to the university. "It's wrong," Schwarz says of the picture the NCAA paints concerning scholarships. "But it's standard."

The irony here is that many smaller universities in the United States have come to see sports as a way to gain students they would not otherwise draw. It's why, in 2018, as New Mexico is considering cutting soccer, Briar Cliff University—a Franciscan school in Iowa with one thousand students that competes in the National Association of Intercollegiate Athletics (NAIA)—has a forty-two-man soccer roster. It wants as many soccer players as it can get. That's because the vast majority of college athletes in the United States, regardless of their level (NCAA Division I, II, or NAIA), don't receive full, no-money-out-of-pocket scholarships. Thus, smaller schools have come to (seemingly accurately) view athletes as much of a source of revenue as an expense.

Now if we step back even further, this all seems strange. What organization wants to minimize revenues and fluff up expenses? Why would the NCAA inflate the actual cost of a scholarship? Schwarz offers up a comparison: the Mafia. It's an exaggeration, but the Mafia (like the NCAA) does have an incentive to obscure profits, Schwarz points out. "Surprise, surprise," Schwarz says of the NCAA. "They just happen to pick a standard [for accounting for scholarships] that applies to a small number of schools, and . . . they magically settle on the one that shows the highest cost," Schwarz says.

To be clear, this budgetary misdirection by the NCAA makes sense for the mega-athletic departments of the Big Ten and SEC. "They have a strong incentive not to look profitable," Schwarz says. After all, show too much extraneous revenue, and questions about paying athletes and faculty complaints about the size of the athletic department are bound to pop up. The problem is that the Big Ten/SEC mindset has become so universally entrenched that even schools with no extraneous revenue to minimize in the first place (the University of New Mexico) take on the hide-and-seek principles propagated by the NCAA as well.

Thus, universities like UNM forget that they are essentially ignoring certain revenues, and now they're worried about their bottom line. It's as though an obese man had fibbed about his weight for so long (shaving pounds off every time someone asked how much he weighed) that he began to worry he was truly in danger of becoming too thin.

Second, athletic departments are small parts of much, much larger organizations. They should act accordingly.

"If the transaction involves moving the money from your right pocket to your left pocket," Schwarz points out, "your pants have no more money than when you started."

This, of course, is a very economist-type thing to say. It seemingly ignores the need for a big institution, whether a university, company, or hospital, to understand the costs and revenues derived from its smaller parts.

For the UNM Athletic Department, the cost cutting that occurred in 2016 and 2017 looked like the actions of an isolated, scared, small business desperate to keep its doors open. Yes, the unit was under attack from all sides. The New Mexico Office of the State Auditor and Higher Education Department conducted investigations. The *Albuquerque Journal*; Daniel Libit, through his *NM Fishbowl* website; and local reporter Larry Barker all dug into stories about the athletic department's overspending.

Accordingly, the Board of Regents demanded answers from Nuñez and Stokes. This pressure trickled down the ranks. So leadership asked for suggestions at an athletic department staff meeting during the budget crisis. The list produced was earnest, if a bit naive:

Monitor all thermostats.

Cut down on printer usage.

Use fewer charter flights and more bus trips.

Play closer, nonconference games.

Eliminate media guides.

Schedule daytime practices to eliminate turning on field lights at night.

Chapter 6

Reduce men's scholarships.

Limit the number of team uniforms.

Cut insurance for foreign student athletes.

Given that the department's most significant hard cost was staff salaries ($14.5 million) and its biggest NCAA-mandated expenditure was scholarships ($5.8 million internally, or the $8.1 million reported to the NCAA), such nickel-and-dime solutions seemed more about appearance than actually changing the financial position of the unit. But such was the game the athletic department found itself playing. The department needed to, as Daniel Libit describes it, "show some sort of austerity."[10]

There's another piece of the puzzle though. Before Nuñez and Stokes arrived at UNM, the school's athletic department had long treated its budget as something of an elastic, wink-wink document. It wasn't that the budget didn't matter; rather, there was a collective understanding that it was very unlikely everything would turn out as forecasted.

"I was led to believe by several presidents," says former AD Paul Krebs, "'Do what you need to do, and we'll figure out the budget.' And so that's kind of the general mantra that I operated with." If a situation arose, like retaining a successful coach, Krebs did what was necessary. Krebs's superiors told him, "Don't worry about paying the coach more, pay him more. We'll figure it out, and at the end of the year, we'll have a deficit . . . but we'll just keep moving on."

With escalating scrutiny from Libit, the New Mexico Department of Higher Education, and others, this approach no longer worked.

In April 2017, in one of his last major acts as athletic director, Krebs announced that UNM men's and women's ski teams would be discontinued, effective immediately. This was Krebs doing everything he knew to satisfy increasingly intense calls to cut spending in his department. On the surface level, it made some sense. The state of New Mexico itself was facing a budget deficit. Thus, cutting a team filled with athletes from Scandinavia, Steamboat, and Aspen seemed prudent. After all, only ten other NCAA Division I schools sponsored skiing.

The university announced that cutting skiing would result in an annual savings of $600,000. However, the men's and women's programs collectively could be summed up in a handful of numbers: twenty athletes, eight scholarships, two vans, and just over $100,000 in coaches' salaries. "We've looked at many options," Krebs explained, "and unfortunately, our current model isn't sustainable." What the calculations didn't consider, again, was the tuition paid by these wealthy out-of-state and out-of-country students. Additionally, the decision cut off UNM from the support of the New Mexico Tourism Board.[11]

When student protests erupted, and New Mexico's ski industry responded with promises of new funding, the UNM Board of Regents quickly remembered just how small the budgetary impact of such a decision would make. Accordingly, President Abdullah announced a reversal:

> *Several months ago I directed Vice-President Paul Krebs to develop cost saving measures that would bring the Athletic Department's budget into balance. I instructed him to consider any and all legal means to accomplish this objective. As has been widely reported, VP Krebs eliminated a number of positions, has several new donors and eliminated the sport of skiing. All of these actions will lead to a more balanced budget in the department, barring unforeseen problems. With respect to skiing, Mr. Krebs has received relentless, and in my opinion, undeserved criticism for this decision, even though he was following my directions. This is unfortunate. However, substantial good has come from this decision as those who care about this sport have pledged financial assistance for the next year which will allow us to explore long-term financial commitments. So, today I am announcing that we will reinstate skiing for the next year while we seek those solutions. This is indeed a good day to be a Lobo student athlete.*[12]

One has to wonder, Was this exercise in performative belt-tightening worth it? Paul Krebs, dragged through the mud in the process, certainly didn't think so. "I recall this very vividly," he says. "I was walking through the Indy airport on my way to a NCAA meeting, and I got a call, 'We're going to announce today that we're bringing skiing back.'" Years later, he shakes his head at the memory: "Fucking cowards."

Third, the numbers are never quite as definitive as they seem.

Cost accounting has been around for more than 150 years. Jerome Lee Nicholson, a New Yorker who was born during the Civil War and who also happened to teach at Columbia University during one of the school's very rare periods of football success, is considered by many to be the father of cost accounting. The point of his life's work was to figure out, as the name suggests, how much various activities and products cost a company or organization. If, for example, a company makes baseball bats over here and tennis rackets over there, cost accounting aims to show how much it costs to produce each, considering materials, overhead, labor hours, and so forth. Armed with such information, management can then make informed decisions about where to invest and to cut. Up with the bat production; reign in the racket people.

During his lifetime, Nicholson spread his cost-accounting gospel far and wide. He worked with the Pennsylvania Railroad Company during the boom of the Second Industrial Revolution and then with the US Military during its World War I ramp-up. Over the course of his career, Nicholson wrote several thousand pages of instructions about how to break down the costs incurred in an American factory. He formed associations and held conventions. Under Nicholson's guidance, for example, the first meeting of the American Institute of Accountants took place on a Monday and Tuesday in 1919 in Buffalo, New York. By the 1920s cost accounting was widely accepted in American business and credited as part of the fabric of America's rise as an economic power in the twentieth century.

While it's easy to get lost in the details here, Nicholson accomplished something truly transformative and monumental: He gave the American producer a way to understand what it cost to do business.[13]

If only college athletics had its very own Nicholson. For the past twenty years, an academic debate has evolved (in the spirit, if not quite the practice of Nicholson) over the costs of college athletics. People like Andy Schwarz and Kristi Dosh helped bring the debate into the courtrooms and onto sites such as *Deadspin* and SB Nation.[14] But a more esoteric discussion has transpired in academic journals. Scholars such as Brian Goff, Dennis Wilson, Victor Matheson, Debra O'Conner, Andrew Zimbalist, Ellen Staurowsky, and Heather Lawrence have argued back and forth. They have considered price, cost, revenues, subsidies, debt, and all other manner of budgeting constructs. Peer-reviewed pieces in venues such as the *Sports Innovation Journal*, the *Journal for Intercollegiate Athletics*, and the *Journal of Sport Management* have probed deeply into the workings of athletic finances and accounting.[15]

But still, even with a generation of scholarship and a century of NCAA governance on the matter, there remains a widespread conclusion among academics that most university presidents and athletic directors don't actually know how much it costs their university to have athletic teams. On the subject, Lawrence and a team of researchers from Ohio University recently said, "Commonly used accounting methods in intercollege athletics fail to accurately attribute costs to each sport and increase the difficulty for leaders to make informed decisions."[16]

The University of New Mexico, however, has come up with an exact price tag to hang on its men's soccer team: $605,630.

Cutting men's soccer would, it was announced in the summer of 2018, save UNM exactly $605,630 annually. Exactly. What's more, using this number, the school determined that men's soccer had "the second-highest cost per participant" of any Lobo sport.[17]

In an effort to be transparent throughout the process, the UNM President's Office had released more than one thousand pages of documents regarding the decision. Budgets, account ledgers, salary schedules, scenario analyses—they are all there for the public to consider.[18]

En masse, the document dump defies easy comprehension. Pouring through the pages reveals random things like the fact that Fishbein had spearheaded nearly $500,000 in fundraising over the previous five years, that it cost more than $120,000 annually to get the soccer teams to its games in the far-flung Conference USA, and that 150 of 151 soccer program alums were still alive. Ledger lines further reveal that the athletic department had sold off miscellaneous weight equipment in prior years and that the junior-most academic advisor in the Lobo Center for

Student Athlete Success made a salary of just under $36,000 (as compared to Nuñez's $325,000).

But nowhere is it made exactly clear how the number $605,630.00 has become the cost of a soccer team. The calculations on UNM's end seem to involve saved expenses (salaries, scholarships, and program costs) minus some lost revenues (NCAA and Mountain West sports sponsorships and scholarship funding), but the exact line items are difficult to extrapolate.[19] Accordingly, critics of the decision attack the numbers from all sides. "The deficit is not real," writes one editorial to the *Albuquerque Journal*. Then, taking on the matter of scholarships as expenses, the editorializer continues, "This is an internal accounting device that might be valid for accounting types but does not reflect real cost."[20]

And so the $605,630 becomes a balloon floating over the soccer situation. Everyone takes shots, but most noneconomist snipers can't seem to get a direct hit.

It is in the midst of the argument, particularly over scholarships, that a UNM soccer supporter reaches out to Andy Schwarz. And Schwarz, because he is a self-professed Cassandra (the priestess in Greek mythology who knows the truth but is never believed) and someone who "sees it as a mission to make the world slightly less wrong about the facts," produces a counter-analysis almost overnight. He does so for free, then posts the analysis on his blog, *Sports Geekonomics*. He also sends a copy to President Stokes and Eddie Nuñez.

Schwarz's analysis spares no punches. It posits that UNM had badly overstated potential savings. The problem again revolves around the issue of scholarships. "My conclusion is that rather than saving money from cutting scholarships," Schwarz writes on his blog, "UNM is likely losing revenue from these cuts." The lost revenue is lost tuition.[21]

"Under conservative assumptions, I calculate that cutting the scholarships in question [for the four sports] will worsen UNM's financial position by approximately $330,000, rather than achieve the claimed savings of approximately $470,000."[22] As Schwarz tells me much later, the problem was UNM giving the numbers over to nonexperts. "You don't want to learn economics from an associate athletic director," he warns.

$605,630

University administrators respond to Schwarz with more documents. Unfortunately, their counterattack memo, "Sports Reduction Analysis: Cost Savings vs. Lost Revenues," is an embarrassing rejoinder. Perhaps it is an unfair fight, given that Schwarz makes his living working as an economist in exacting litigation spaces. Regardless, UNM produces a handful of weak counterpunches, including these flimsy swings.

Maybe the University of New Mexico was indeed at full capacity in some ways.

It wasn't.

Maybe the roster padding for women's cross-country produce new tuition revenues.

Perhaps, but then why weren't such revenues counted before?

Maybe the dollars saved in athletic scholarships will be used to recruit other new students to the institution.

Hypothetically possible, but unlikely.

Then there was this final sloppy shot. According to the document's final line, the cuts were "minimal to the overall scope of the university" anyway. *Maybe we shouldn't be arguing about this rounding error*, the message seemed to say.

This last salvo managed to offend the athletic purists and the fiscally minded alike.[23]

As for Schwarz, he can't let it go. He responds back to UNM's response. This time, he has even less patience. "It appears that UNM is not fully appreciating the economic arguments I have made," he writes. "Rebutting the assessments of marginal impact with averages is a good example of how perfectly fine accounting can yield incorrect economic answers."[24]

Schwarz closes by again offering his services. And lastly, he warns UNM against playing truly small ball. "Whatever tiny benefit UNM believes these savings provide," Schwarz concludes, "the true answer is half-as-tiny."[25]

Chapter 6

Day 33. Saturday, September 8, 2018.
Albuquerque, New Mexico

The Albuquerque International Sunport (not airport, *Sun*port) is a delight. Though it is small compared to the airports of Phoenix, Denver, and Dallas (the hubs that travelers most frequently connect to from ABQ), the facility fits with its hometown. The Sunport is a pueblo-style building that features a grand, lofty entryway adorned with *vigas* (wooden beams) and southwestern art. It has a viewing deck that overlooks the runways, expanding toward the desert and mountains. The facility is dominated by Southwest Airlines and can be walked, from end (Black Mesa Coffee) to end (Albuquerque Outpost, selling mostly *Breaking Bad* and Zia-adorned merchandise), in less than ten minutes. In short, the city's airport, like the city itself, is distinctive and charming. And, yes, it would benefit from some remodeling and modernizing.

The Lobos arrive back at the Sunport at 2:00 p.m. on Saturday, the day after the Tulsa game. The players go straight from the airport to campus, just a few miles away, where they go through a recovery workout with Joe. Given that there's a Tuesday night game on the horizon, rest is precious, but so, too, is training time for a team still looking to put the pieces together.

On the following day, Sunday, practice does not go well. The team is tired and nonresponsive. "Kept hearing 'Do it again,'" one Lobo says, summing up the session.

The Lobos practice at US Air Force Academy as the UNM Board of Regents vote to cut the program. *Photo by Ryan Swanson*

With *Coco* in the background, Lobos meet before their first game. *Photo by Ryan Swanson*

At the rail, after the first game of the season. *Photo by Ryan Swanson*

Grayson (*left*) and Mike (*right*) share a moment. *Actionshots Photos*

ABQ native Ford, goalkeeper. *Actionshots Photos*

Kelly, deep in thought. *Actionshots Photos*

The Lobo soccer complex. *Photo by Ryan Swanson*

Nick Williams, with one of his forty soccer balls. *Actionshots Photos*

Omar, ready to play. *Actionshots Photos*

Fish at practice. *Actionshots Photos*

Gallo on the move. *Actionshots Photos*

Scotty (*left*) and Tom (*right*), captains. *Actionshots Photos*

Simon, Academic All-American. *Actionshots Photos*

Antoine attacking. *Actionshots Photos*

Dorsey celebrating. *Actionshots Photos*

Chapter 7

A Red Card for Pandering

Day 35. Monday, September 10, 2018.
Albuquerque, New Mexico

The team meets at 8:30 a.m. to start another week. Fish walks in a few minutes late, which is unusual for him, and closes the door. He makes his way slowly to the front of the room. He's not wearing his hat yet because there are no hats allowed inside the team's indoor spaces. Fish is somber and serious. He makes eye contact all around the room before starting.

"Balls are all sorted out," he begins. Nick Williams, who is sitting in the front row with most of the freshman, relaxes a bit. Then Fish launches into a big-picture scout of what's ahead.

"Everything. Is. Quality," he stresses, perhaps feeling the time crunch that comes with multiple games each week. The University of California, Santa Barbara (UCSB), team coming in offers another stiff nonconference test. UCSB plays out of one of the nation's college soccer hotspots. The Gauchos led the nation in game attendance for nine consecutive years, and the school has advanced to the NCAA tournament six times in the past ten years.[1]

Still, the New Mexico coaches see an opportunity for the Lobos. UCSB is talented, yes, but the team is also prone to mistakes. "They work hard, but they don't work smart," says one of the assistants. "This is a team that doesn't know who they are," Fish chimes in. Still, what the Gauchos do have is size along the back line—they go six-foot-three and six-foot-five in the center. Thus, winning balls on corner kicks and set pieces will be challenging. "The common theme," Kelly summarizes as his guys are getting antsy, "is they have *big* guys." The Lobos will have to stay connected and build properly in order to get good goal-scoring chances.

From the team room, the players head up the hill to the practice fields. Despite all the areas of concern for this squad, there are real limitations to what the coaches can hope to accomplish regarding their players' skills on the day before a game. And so, as they do on most days, the coaches have scheduled the "three-team-possession" drill. This is a drill that, as the name implies, splits the position players into three groups. With the teams positioned in a tight field (usually something along the lines of twenty yards by ten yards), one team is placed in the middle. The other teams then attempt to pass the ball among themselves a certain number of times before delivering the ball over or through the middle guys to the other outside group. Then that team will connect a certain number of short passes before sending the ball back.

Three-team possession is competitive, fast-paced, and cathartic. "When you've got games every three days," Scotty says, "you really just want touches and you want to run around and you want it to be short." What the guys want is to feel sharp. Three-team possession works on all these fronts.

What's interesting, given the purposes of the exercise, is just how fixated many of the players are on perceived injustices during the drill.

"Wait, they got the ball first last time."

"That's four touches. We got four."

"Hey, that was on the line."

"He touched it. Did you see that? He touched it!"

Barreiro, Billy, and Puig are particularly vigilant purveyors of blown calls today. They pepper Kelly (the referee ostensibly, although he's much more concerned with simply keeping the action moving) with their complaints. Whether this should be seen as engagement and competitiveness—or simply as whining—remains unclear. Maybe it's just soccer players being soccer players.

Fish looks on from the side. "I used to coach more," he says. In fact, he used to direct everything in practice. "I used to be pretty damn good," he confides. Now Mike, Kelly, and Champ carry out his designs. Fish is the big-picture guy. "This is a good team," he says, observing. "Not a great team, a good team." He's hopeful, though, and with a long record of taking teams deep into November play after challenging games at the beginning of the season, this might again be a gritty New Mexico team that gets stronger as the season progresses.

Day 36. Tuesday, September 11, 2018.
Albuquerque, New Mexico

From the beginning, when it was announced that cuts were on the table back in the spring of 2018, Fishbein recognized the political nature of the crisis. In a state like New Mexico, there is a steady commingling of political, higher education, business, and athletics leaders. Fishbein understands this about his adopted home state. He has been racking up political connections for years. He is friends with former Governor Gary Johnson. The two met skiing. The two also once had dinner, along with their wives, and wore headlamps when a power outage hit while they were breaking bread in Santa Fe. After Johnson, Fishbein got to know Governor Bill Richardson a bit, although there was no skiing or dark dining.

More broadly, Fish has a knack for connecting with people. He has contacts with lawyers, doctors, and bail bondsmen in the state. He counts best-selling author Hampton Sides as a personal friend.

Starting in April 2018, when it became clear that his program was in jeopardy, Fish reached out to everyone in his proverbial Rolodex. He mobilized alums. He orchestrated protests. He granted interviews to local press. Fish did all of this despite the athletic department leadership warning against politicking for one's own program. "Disobeying the direct orders of Nuñez to avoid the media and taking his case public," Will Webber of the *Santa Fe New Mexican* reports, "Fish may have saved soccer, but he may have dinged his own security in the process."[2]

Fish met with Albuquerque Mayor Tim Keller and then with the campaign managers for Michelle Lujan Grisham, the Democratic front-runner for governor. He managed to convince Keller and Lujan Grisham—arguably the two most powerful politicians in the state—to produce a Facebook message in support of saving UNM men's soccer. It appeared on August 16, 2018.[3]

Obviously, the preseason moves to save soccer outright were unsuccessful. So the politics continue as summer gives way to fall.

Today the UNM Board of Regents has again convened in an airy student-union building ballroom. There is much to do at the university, but again, athletics takes up a sizable portion of the agenda. On the table is a motion to OK a request for a much bigger outlay from the state to support the athletic department—$1.5 million more, to be precise. In requesting a total of $4.1 million in direct support from the state for sports, Nuñez also makes clear that any additional funds will not be used to reinstate soccer or any of the other cuts. That matter is done. This new money will be used to increase the overall budget for athletics in order to better serve fewer sports. Without the extra $1.5 million, Nuñez clarifies, more cuts may be necessary. Baseball might be next.

While the possibility of more state funding could have lightened the mood, the political tension only increases on this Tuesday morning. The stress of the situation is evident. Pamela Pyle, the president of the UNM Faculty Senate and an associate professor of piano who studied at Juilliard, gets caught in the cross fire as she gives her usual report to the Board of Regents.

It quickly becomes evident that Regent Tom Clifford has grievances. After mostly dismissing Pyle's report on successful faculty collaboration and new curricular matters, Clifford cuts in and turns the attention back to the athletic cuts.

"I think it's cowardly for the faculty to . . . allow us to take the heat from legislators," Clifford says. "You're basically hanging our new president out to dry on this, and the fact that you won't step up now when it's difficult and difficult choices had to be made, I just think you're not doing your job."

Pyle needs a few seconds to gather herself given this strange turn.

"I rebut your accusation that I don't stand up with courage," Pyle fires back.

A Red Card for Pandering

And from there, the conversation only unravels further. What exactly Clifford, a former state cabinet secretary, wants from this piano professor is unclear. Pyle notes that the university faculty had not been at the table for the athletics decisions. Clifford is unmoved.

Pyle is now steaming.

"Your discontent is noted, but so is your belligerence. Thank you, sir," Pyle says, attempting to extricate herself from the ten-minute exchange.

"So is your name calling," Clifford retorts.

For members of the press forced to sit through the nearly five-hour meeting, the exchange is a godsend. The tiff gets prominent treatment in the next day's news reports. After all, it's not often a piano professor is accused of cowardice because of her stance (or lack thereof) on soccer.[4]

***

Game night on 9/11 is hot. It's eighty-eight degrees when the PA announcer welcomes the smallish crowd to Lobo Field. While Fish aims to keep the fight for Lobo soccer in the news, people are not turning out as the coaches had expected. Perhaps it's simply the mixed results of the team, or maybe it is the negativity surrounding the entire New Mexico athletics program. Regardless, less than one thousand fans show up this Tuesday night. The long streak of the Lobos men's soccer team residing in the top twenty-five in attendance nationally seems in jeopardy. Of course, all streaks for the program are in jeopardy.

One streak that does remain intact, however, is that of technical difficulties occurring during the national anthem and player introductions. The 2018 home games, from a production standpoint, leave much to be desired thus far. Tonight, the microphone cuts in and out during "The Star-Spangled Banner." Several loud cracks break up the introductions.

Even still, the larger scene has a beauty that has nothing to do with technology. Two teams with proud soccer histories take the field. The Lobos program banners touting the team's many NCAA tournament appearances and two trips to the College Cup ripple in the light breeze. The Lobos' field remains a deep, rich green. And the Sandia Mountains are watermelon pink as the sun dips toward the horizon just as the game begins.

Now if the Lobos can find their own bit of beauty.

Things start well. The Gauchos retreat on their heels, and New Mexico gets several good early chances. The large center backs from Santa Barbara are having a tough time keeping track of Puig and Antoine. The Lobos control things. Shot by Taylor, shot by Taylor, shot by Antoine, shot by Antoine—this happens in quick succession. Then the Lobos earn the first corner kick of the game. Then, immediately, they get another. Then Simon gets a shot.

Finally, the flurry of action yields something. At thirty-eight minutes, Miguel, who has begun getting more minutes lately, works with Tom up the left side. Miguel controls a pass and then delivers a ball through a UCSB defender to Tom, who is streaking toward the corner. Tom crosses it to the team's offensive spark plug Omar, who scores: 1–0, New Mexico.

Omar—who grew up with four older sisters—raises his hands, pulls his shirt over his head, and races toward the sideline in celebration. "I'm the energy booster," Omar says of his role. "When I come in, the game gets more lively." Indeed, that seems to be the case so far this season. The half ends with the Lobos holding the lead.

The team retreats to its hurdles shed. The mood is upbeat. "Here's my three things," Fish says. The Lobos need to keep calm and be disciplined. If they do, Fish promises, "They will implode."

As if right on cue, Fish holds up a hand for silence. "Listen." Yes. The noises of some very intense coaching are rising from the visitors' "locker room" (a canopy located across the track). Fish smiles. They're "cussing at each other," he says. While the half has been a decent one for the Lobos, Mike still has his concerns. He doesn't like how the Lobos handled the Gauchos' set pieces and is concerned about transition opportunities.

"The first ten minutes is key," Fish says, wrapping up. "They will come out with energy."

Starting the second half, the Gauchos are a new team. They immediately attack. Retreating, Billy has no choice but to poke the ball across the back line just a minute into the new half, giving UCSB its first corner kick of the game. This is what the Gauchos players, who could be mistaken for NAIA basketball team players walking through an airport (they've got six-foot-two, six-foot-three, six-foot-three, and six-foot-five players in the game at this point), have been waiting for.

The corner delivery finds grass in the middle of the box. A UCSB player makes a play on the ball, which Barreiro meets. Both players go down; the result is a shot and a deflection. And so UCSB earns corner kick number two. But first, UCSB tries to earn a penalty kick. There was, after all, a collision. After pondering it for a few seconds, the Santa Barbara player goes down, holding his ankle. The referees huddle. As they do, the players do a bit of pushing and shoving.

Antoine, never one to back down, approaches the tallest Gaucho of them all—Hunter Ashworth, the six-foot-five center back. The two exchange words, and then, with the officials still huddling to consider whether the situation merits a penalty kick, Ashworth goes down like he's been shot. He writhes for a few seconds. The referees come running and whistling and push the teams apart. Finally, they rule no penalty kicks despite UCSB's protests.

It's been more than two minutes of distraction. Finally, the Gauchos line up for their second corner kick. It's delivered right into the mix where UCSB's height goes to work. Meanwhile, Ford has been pushed down or fallen—it's unclear—leaving the net momentarily unattended. The results of all of this confusion are resoundingly simple. A header goal: 1–1. Santa Barbara has quickly found its equalizer.

The Lobos are rattled. The Gauchos' score seems to have sucked the confidence right from this fragile team. There's a near goal for the visiting team two minutes later. The Gauchos attack repeatedly up the Lobos' right side. Then, at fifty-two minutes, the Gauchos get a transition opportunity. A quick pinpoint pass delivers the ball from the box to midfield. From there, the ball is laid out in front of streaking UCSB player number nine. Dorsey tries to catch up but loses the contest. He falls away, leaving a point-blank shot. Ford has no chance: 1–2, UCSB.

And that's basically the game. After taking the lead, UCSB retreats into a defensive posture. Their size and physicality allow a packed-in

CHAPTER 7

approach. When the Lobos approach, Santa Barbara focuses on simply clearing the ball out rather than connecting to their own offense.

Still, with four minutes left, it looks like Omar might come through again. He narrowly misses a lunging header. His momentum carries him through into the net. Then, in a fitting ending to this game, he can't get out. Omar's cleats are stuck in the netting. The clock winds down. It's over—a deflating loss.

"This was a game you needed to handle," Fishbein tells a reporter after the game. "Two bad mistakes in the first seven minutes of the half. . . . That was a game for the taking. [I'm] pretty disappointed in our performance and maturity." Fish also indicates that the coaches will consider making some lineup changes, given the last two games.

Several Lobos skip the rail and fans altogether tonight. Puig, for one, takes a direct line from the field toward the locker room. Some still stop and sign a few autographs, but the fan side of the gathering is thinner as well. Simon and Antoine stop and talk quietly with their girlfriends. Mike greets the La Cueva contingent. Ford's parents, Tom and Laura, are visibly stressed by the game and season but console their son—or maybe it's the other way around. They're all hurting.

Back in the locker room, Fish lets loose. "Probably a nine out of ten angry," says one Lobo. Fish was particularly incensed because he felt his team was the better on the field tonight. This was a winnable game—and one at home. "He was right." Regardless, the loss stings. "It's as low as we've been as a team since I've been here," says the same upperclassman.

The season seems to be unraveling. The fight to restore the program seems to be stalling.

Day 39. Friday, September 14, 2018.
Albuquerque, New Mexico

Just at the darkest moment, a hint of a Hollywood ending appears.

This hint is conjured up from an unlikely place: a gubernatorial debate hosted by the NAACP at the Sheraton Hotel in Uptown Albuquerque. Democratic candidate Michelle Lujan Grisham is attending, as is the Republican nominee, Steve Pearce. So, too, is Jeremy Fishbein. Fish

A Red Card for Pandering

just happens to be friends with Albuquerque NAACP President Harold Bailey.

The two candidates take the stage at 6:00 p.m. to field questions from NAACP leaders and Delta Sigma Theta Sorority members. Several hundred attendees, most of whom paid $40 to get in, listen as the two answer questions about education, poverty, civil rights, and criminal justice. The discourse is polite and nuanced. Lujan Grisham and Pearce are both seasoned debaters. Then comes a very different kind of question: *What about the decision to cut sports at the University of New Mexico?*

It's a stark pivot from the matters being discussed, but Lujan Grisham is ready.

"It's outrageous. I will work immediately with the Legislature to provide whatever oversight and investment we need to immediately restore those programs and to hold universities like the University of New Mexico accountable."[5]

Wait, what?

Following up a few days later in an email to the *Albuquerque Journal*, Lujan Grisham doubles down. Asked if she would reinstate sports, Lujan Grisham answers, "Absolutely."[6]

"I will," she continues, "work with administration, the Regents, the business community and the Legislature to ensure we have funding for all our sports programs at New Mexico universities and that we are always in compliance with Title IX."[7]

Then, to make it social-media real, she follows up on Twitter: "As governor I'll put our students first and push for transparent budgeting and restore the programs cut at UNM. #NMPol #NMGovDebate"[8]

Lujan Grisham's words are a salve around the soccer facility. Maybe there is a happy ending in sight! While most of the Lobos players haven't had enough political seasoning to parse campaign speeches from actual, actionable promises, the fact that an important person is promising to fix their problem is not at all insignificant. Everyone grabs hold of this new hope—especially Fish.

CHAPTER 7

DAY 40. SATURDAY, SEPTEMBER 15, 2018.
ALBUQUERQUE, NEW MEXICO

Ford is out. Fetterly is in.

After the Santa Barbara loss, Champ pulled Fetterly aside: "Are you ready?"

"Yeah, absolutely," Fetterly answers. "I've taken someone's starting spot before. Yeah, I'm ready to play."

With the team's record standing at an unconscionable (by Lobo standards and anywhere else, really) 2–4 as CUSA play begins, the coaches have decided to make a change at the goalkeeper position. The team is "just bleeding goals," according to Champ. Giving up nearly two goals per game puts far too much pressure on the team's offense. "The one that kind of broke the camel's back was Santa Barbara," says one of the coaches. While Ford, the senior and ABQ native, has been given the benefit of the doubt, Fetterly will now get his shot. He takes over with Old Dominion University (ODU) coming to town.

Ford takes the news hard. "A bullshit decision," he calls it. For two days, Ford is angry and embarrassed. He pouts a bit. Then he does a 180. "Super supportive," say the coaches of his attitude moving forward, although Ford, too, even as one of the oldest players on the team, is not immune to daily ups and downs.

Fetterly, on the other hand, is all confidence. He is nonplussed by the fact that he's taking someone else's spot.

This transition, in fact, is something that Fetterly had been expecting for quite some time. He is a Development Academy product. "Extreme confidence," one Lobo says, describing Fetterly. Perhaps this fearlessness comes from Fetterly's unique upbringing. His family owns ScreamWorld, a Houston area haunted house with attractions that include the Edge of Darkness and Jake's Slaughterhouse. "We really do make a living out of scaring people," says Fetterly's father. In addition to working in the family business, Fetterly has his own entrepreneurial endeavors. He has a thriving online shoe resale business with which he's bought and sold more than $9,000 of sneaker inventory in the past two years.[9]

Fetterly is a ringer, the kind of player that Fish has long managed to lure to the University of New Mexico, beating out schools with more academic prestige and bigger budgets. Fetterly played for the U20 national team and was recruited by all the major soccer powers. Injuries, however, have complicated the process. Fetterly suffered several concussions (at least three "official" ones, he says) over the past couple of seasons. But now, in mid-September and with the season nearly off the rails completely, he's ready to go.

The keeper position is a strange one. A team either has one undisputed goalkeeper—a trusted commander of the defense, the organizer of the team's shape, and the distributor of balls to begin mounting attack—or it has none at all. "It's a confidence thing," Champ says. "It's a lot of trust that goes into the position and a lot of relationship between center backs and the goalkeeper." This trust tends to sort itself out. "It's almost the players [who] decide who the starting goalkeepers are. The team has the most trust in a guy and that's . . . how it's picked."

Now it has picked Fetterly.

Leading up to the game, Fish continues to push and prod and extol. For him, grinding takes on a decidedly verbal character. Fish has something to say to everyone and about everything.

On reports of slipping grades, he says, "If you don't start taking care of business, we'll go football style—scheduling every minute of your day."

On the guys' hijinks and general tomfoolery, he comments, "I'm expecting you to be fully functioning *young* adults. Not actual adults, but young adults."

On his role at this juncture, he explains, "My job isn't to be a dick. But I want everyone to be able to say, 'I've got 10 games left, and I've done everything I can do.' Are we doing everything we can do?"

On the pathway forward, he says, "To be special, you've got to have guys taking care of themselves and others," *and* "My belief is that we will win the conference," *and* "It's a great challenge; that's the beauty of this thing."

On game day the team meets at the Johnson Center pool at 11:00 a.m. for activation with Joe. Then at 3:00 p.m., everyone goes over set pieces once more with Kelly. At 3:30 p.m., it's time for dinner. At 5:50

p.m., the team sits, dressed, in the team room, ready for its 7:00 p.m. game with Old Dominion.

Ford slips into the team room quietly. He is dressed as usual, but he is fully aware that he won't need his goalie gloves on this night unless something drastic happens. His first game as a backup is, for him, a disappointment. "Goalkeeper is a tough position," Ford says. "There's one spot on the field . . . and I got benched for, I don't know, for . . . reasons."

"You should be excited because you're prepared," Fish says to the guys as he wraps up his pregame remarks. The team leaves the room and heads for the field. Mike, Fish, and Kelly linger behind. They all recognize that this is a team on the brink. The team has a chip on their shoulder, but it's difficult to tell if that's made them feisty or scared—or just discouraged. "A shutout would help," Kelly says quietly. "It's hard to lose then." The coaches head for the field.

It's warm again—still in the high eighties at game time. Drake and J. Cole boom from the speakers as the teams warm up. The Lobos wear their turquoise kits with red socks. For the keepers, the warm-up situation is a radical shift. As Champ warms up Fetterly, Ford and Anthony pass back and forth. Then the two backups come in to warm up the new number one. It's insult added to injury for Ford, but he handles it coolly.

The stadium is buzzing. Nearly 1,500 fans have showed up to support the team. Their enthusiasm, however, is thwarted right away.

Less than two minutes into the game, ODU gets their first goal: 0–1.

Halfway through the first half, Fetterly comes out of the box to challenge a breakaway. He loses in the exchange: 0–2. "He came out of the goal, and he whiffed the ball," Champ remembers, wincing.

"It was a mistake," Fetterly says flatly.

Still, the faithful don't give up. Chants of "We want Omar" start up in the stands. Fish sends in the freshman, who almost immediately responds, on a long pass from Tom, with a goal: 1–2.

The tone in the halftime hurdles shed is positive but urgent. "This is our game if we fucking take it," Fish says. Mike makes some technical adjustments. Then Fish jumps back in. "Where is Scotty?" he barks. "Where are you?" Scotty just happens to be in the front row, right in front of Fish. Scotty raises his hand, wearily. "Right," Fish says, and he's off with more instruction and ideas. One can't help but wonder if this old coach perhaps wants it much, much more than his young guys. That can't be good.

Regardless, the second half is a parking lot. Neither team can manage much flow or movement. Mutual frustration takes over. The game ends with the halftime score (1–2) intact. It's the Lobos' third loss in a row.

To the *Albuquerque Journal* after the game, Fish is emotional. He can't help but bring up the big picture. "We're just missing a little bit of something," Fish says. "We're just missing some little piece of our hearts. I don't know what to say. I haven't referred to this the whole year, but I just feel like they've taken a little bit of our heart. They've taken a little bit of my heart."[10]

In the days following, the *Albuquerque Journal* editorial board piles on. While the newspaper has covered the cutting of the soccer program extensively and has been an outlet for many voices criticizing the decision, the politics of the situation are too much to resist. "Lujan Grisham earns a red card for UNM Pandering," headlines a cutting opinion piece.

"Lujan Grisham," the paper charges, "cut the new president of the state's flagship university, and the head of its athletics programs, off at the knees." Lujan Grisham will, in fact, have the power to follow through on her campaign promise, and she could go a long way toward doing so by replacing most of the members of the Board of Regents. "She appears to be setting the stage to do exactly what our governors have been criticized for, for years—meddling in the policies and personnel decisions at the state's universities." And for this, the candidate deserved "a red card for pandering."[11]

Chapter 8

Two Big, Bold, Ballsy Moves

Day 45. Thursday, September 20, 2018.
Albuquerque, New Mexico
Practice starts at 7:00 a.m. The weather has finally begun dipping toward autumn. A light rain falls. It's sixty-one degrees and cloudy, a welcome departure from the near-constant heat and sun that have enveloped the season so far.

"Yeah, this is soccer weather," Tom, the Brit, says.

"You guys are in hog heaven, right?" Fish shouts toward a group of European-born players.

However, not everyone is so excited about the weather. A few players try to start a move to the indoor football facility. Fish, though, won't hear it. If nothing else, it's a chance to break out the Nike-provided rain gear the team received back in August. It's also a chance to practice under different circumstances.

"Let's get focused, boys," Fish yells. "Come on! *Quality!*"

As the balls skip across the wet grass, Fetterly is finding his voice. "Come on, boys." "Bill, tight . . . good!" "Back post, watch it, Tom." Bailey, who is getting more time on the back line, gets extra attention from Fetterly and the coaches. "I'm embracing it," Bailey says of playing a new position (right back). "I've noticed when I get the ball that I've got a lot more space."

Chapter 8

After an hour, Mike and Kelly transition the practice into a full scrimmage, with two seven-minute halves. When the starters lose the first half, Fish rips into them. His voice echoes across the facility.

Fish is a different coach now than when the team stood at 2–2. He is desperate for a win. He's known few losing streaks during his seventeen years at the university, and he has no patience for one now. Today Fish is equal parts bark and praise, all of it loud and sharp. While Fish mentions the Lujan Grisham promise again at practice today, he's also firmly aware of the negative momentum surrounding his program—both on and off the field. "We just need to win a game to validate what we're doing," he says.

Last night, Fish had Gallo and Pichu, two of the freshmen, over to his house for a pep talk. The coach is aware that the two first-years will be prized recruits when the season ends, assuming there is no reversal to the cuts decision. He wants them to remain in Albuquerque as long as possible.

The session ends with four-minute games on a small field. Winner stays. It's sharp and competitive, lots of touches and service. Puig shines. "I just love shooting," he yells. With that, Mike blows his whistle to conclude the session.

Fish calls everyone in and orders a tight huddle. Everyone goes arms over shoulders.

In a way, the huddle up is a manifestation of the question facing Fish: How does one care for a group of men under such duress? Should he push harder or lay back? Meet and talk more or just play? There is no handbook.

On the surface the coaching staff keeps plugging away. They try to go about business as usual. Mike provides the technical coaching. He breaks down the team's film and its opponents, peppering his sessions with "Does that make sense?"

Kelly starts the practices and leads the warm-ups. A quick whistle, followed by an "OK, on the bands, boys," and everyone gets started. He scouts and coaches set pieces. He stays tightly connected with the players.

And Champ toils away with the keepers. With Fetterly now starting, backed up by Ford and Anthony, the order is a bit different. But the seclusion of the goalies remains. Twenty-four years old and a former all-conference player himself (at St. Mary's College), Champ frequently fills in on the field during practice.

As for Fish, by September, his role is dominated by talking: individual meetings, group meetings, phone calls to supporters and politicians, and impromptu pep talks during breaks in practice. He seems to be trying to will the team toward victory by talking them through the process. He is also doubling down on his attention to detail.

A few days ago, when Omar showed up late—again—Fish made him run laps around the field for an entire practice. "Keeping going, Omar," Fish yells when Omar looks his way. "Keep going."

And so, Fish gathers the team in the middle of the practice field to end today's session. He has things to say. "You're eighteen-to-twenty-three-year-old men," Fish points out. "You've got to act like it."

"It's about moments," he says. In ninety minutes of game time, there are just a handful of moments that decide the outcome. Messing up in the key moments matters. "It'll cost you a game," he says.

And the same goes for life—even more so.

"A DWI? . . . Life ruined."

"Cheat on your wife? . . . Marriage over."

Fish's words find their mark today. The proximity and eye contact are powerful. The rain has stopped, but the whole group is damp. No one really cares. There's still brotherhood here, even in the midst of the strain.

***

As the Lobos prepare for their trip to Florida, President Garnett Stokes continues her first-year listening and speaking tour. She has met, greeted, spoken to, addressed, dined alongside, and convened with dozens and dozens of university and community groups since her arrival. Such is the life of a twenty-first-century university president. On this September afternoon, she is speaking to 150 members of the Economic Forum of Albuquerque.

Chapter 8

None of Stokes's meetings are made easier by the difficult athletics decisions she had to make almost immediately upon stepping onto campus. It isn't the start that she had hoped for.

"Prior to my arrival, I'd been made aware that athletics was dealing with serious budget issues," she says. "I had hoped that they would be taken care of before I arrived. . . . I think Eddie Nuñez also was told they might be taken care of before he arrived." They had not. The problems, which had been festering for more than a decade, awaited UNM's new leadership.

Stokes, however, came to New Mexico, which has been called "something of a graveyard for presidents," uniquely prepared for crisis management. "I'd been watching New Mexico for a long time. . . . This is a fascinating state and a beautiful state," she tells me in her office on a bright January day. Stokes's story is both traditional (in terms of a rise to the top of a university) and extraordinary. On the one hand, Stokes took the ordinary career steps. She earned a PhD in applied psychology at the University of Georgia. Then she secured a tenure-track job at the same university. Her research took off. She studied personnel and hiring decisions, tackling the question of how an entity should use biographical information in job selection and promotion decisions. She also studied leadership training.

Unlike many academics, Stokes attracted attention for her research far beyond academia. She went to work consulting for all manner of organizations, ranging from the US Labor Department to Kraft Foods and the Athens, Georgia, Police Department. To be an expert on finding, training, and retaining the right people means that there is a nearly unlimited pool of organizations interested in your expertise.

The transition from researcher to administrator (or the crossover to "the dark side," as many faculty members call it) made sense for Stokes. It was an extension, at least to a certain extent, of her research. Stokes went from one rung to the next at Georgia: chair of her program, chair of her department, and then dean of the Franklin College of Arts and Science. Then she left the nest, departing Georgia to become the provost at Florida State University (FSU) from 2011 to 2015. Then she became the provost and executive vice chancellor at the University of Missouri.

Two Big, Bold, Ballsy Moves

In November 2017 the Board of Regents at the University of New Mexico announced the hiring of Stokes as president. She became the first female president in the institution's 129-year history.

Stokes knows as well as anyone about the burdens of Division I athletics and their accompanying scandals. During her time as interim president at Florida State, Jameis Winston played the quarterback position for the Seminoles. On the field, Winston gave the program everything it needed. He won football's Heisman Trophy in 2014. Off the field, however, Winston was one problem after another. A fellow FSU student accused Winston of rape just before the start of his Heisman season. In the end, the charges did not stick, but FSU ended up paying a $950,000 settlement due to its handling of the case. Winston also faced charges of shoplifting. For this, he was sentenced to community service. Then, also in 2014, right before FSU's pivotal Atlantic Coast Conference (ACC) contest against Clemson University, Winston stood atop a table in the school's union and shouted profanities. Coach Jimbo Fisher decided that a suspension for one-half of the Clemson game fit for this particular misconduct.

Shortly thereafter, Stokes stepped in and changed the punishment to a full-game suspension. Given Winston's track record, it was hardly a harsh penalty. But, as Stokes remembers from the safety of New Mexico, that did not make it any less controversial. "If we hadn't won the Clemson game once Jameis Winston was suspended, I would have needed police protection." The Seminoles did win, but the experience taught Stokes much about what she calls "the underbelly" of college sports.[1]

As interim chancellor at Missouri, Stokes navigated the tumult following the Ferguson riots, when the school's football team threatened to quit if the racial climate was not addressed. What did she learn from that experience? "The importance of developing relationships," Stokes concludes, "and [of] having difficult conversations."

At UNM she didn't have time to do the former before she had to do the latter. "There were a series of things that just simply got out of hand," she says. "I was working hard in the state of New Mexico and at UNM to establish relationships and get to know this place, but then to be forced into or feel compelled to do something without first having that [relationship] opportunity probably made the difficult circumstances that we have here."

After sharing her prepared remarks at the Economic Forum, Stokes opens the floor for Q and A. The first question (more of a comment, really) raises the matter of Title IX, the debt on The Pit being foisted onto the athletics department, and the actual cost of athletic scholarships. Stokes responds with a long answer regarding the cuts to the athletic department. She defends her team's math while acknowledging that differences of opinion exist over budgeting metrics. She ends with this: "We made a really tough call, a very unpopular decision, but I believe firmly today that the decision we made was in the best interest of the University of New Mexico and the best interest of the future of our athletic department."

The crowd responds with polite applause.

***

There's a lot of talk about testicular fortitude on the soccer field—or, at least, there is at the University of New Mexico when the men's team takes the pitch. "Play your nuts off" is one of Fish's favorite exhortations. The question of who's "got stones" and who doesn't comes up regularly. "Sack up" is another common encouragement.

In keeping with such customs, the following stands as a great compliment in Lobo land: A slight nodding of the head. A purse of the lips. And then a one-word affirmation—*Ballsy.*

When it comes to college athletics then, there have been two significant—ballsy, if you will—attempts at change over the past century. And what's happening at the University of New Mexico is not one of them.

While an element of the decision to end New Mexico men's soccer seems radical—permanently ending a successful program—the reality is that Stokes and the UNM are just nibbling around the edges of change in college athletics. Nothing they are doing here is particularly paradigm-altering.

Two Big, Bold, Ballsy Moves

Stokes is not, for example, proposing to dramatically alter the structure of the athletic department. She is not suggesting that the school drop down to another NCAA division. She is not proposing a massive infusion or cut of student fee money.

Certainly, neither Stokes nor Nuñez is suggesting that the popular men's basketball team be asked to make any sacrifices. They're not touching football.

Likewise, no new funding models are under consideration. Yes, of course, there is the hope that a bit more can be squeezed from television contracts, ticketing, and NCAA subsidies, but this has been the plan (hope?) for decades.

Perhaps what is most troubling is that the administration is not considering any radical new investment strategies to truly bring the university into Title IX alignment. The university will still, come 2019, be spending dramatically more on male athletes (both per student athlete and overall) at a university with a majority-female student body.

No, the changes UNM is going through are painful, but they are pedestrian.

There are, however, two examples of big, bold, ballsy changes made in the 125-year history of college athletics. There are probably more than two, actually, but these two examples were so daring in scope that they still blow back the hair of those who work in sports.

One happened in 1939 at the University of Chicago and the other, in 2003 at Vanderbilt University.

***

First, Chicago.

The University of Chicago opened its doors in 1890. John D. Rockefeller and Silas B. Cobb provided the initial land and financial investments for the university. Rockefeller then selected William Rainey Harper as the institution's first president.

Harper, aged thirty-five at the time of his selection, was a unique mix of intellectual verve and pragmatic business acumen. He was both lofty and fastidious. At a time when Chicago was booming and about to host

CHAPTER 8

more than twenty-seven million visitors for the 1893 World's Fair, one of Harper's foundational tasks was simply to gain attention for his new institution. Harper did so by creating new departments and promising high salaries. He poached away faculty members from rival schools.[2]

He also started a football team.

Here Harper went big. He recruited Amos Alonzo Stagg, then at the powerful YMCA training school, to coach his men. Harper's offer letter to Stagg made the expectations clear. "Knock out" the competition, Harper ordered Stagg. To get Stagg to sign on, Harper gave him a tenured faculty position, a move that—not surprisingly—outraged the rest of the faculty. The "of course what I teach is important, if perhaps misunderstood, but that . . ." motif was already in full bloom in the American Academy as the twentieth century beckoned. Still, Harper pushed the hire through. He had his man.[3]

Stagg then proceeded to create a football miracle. He assembled a team, drove his men through savagely hard practices, and played a national schedule. In 1896 Chicago defeated the University of Michigan, one of the nation's premier football programs. Before long, Stagg had commissioned the construction of things—a locker room, a stadium, and the world's biggest bass drum ("Big Bertha")—for his boys. When the big schools of the Midwest formed the Big Ten football conference, the University of Chicago got a charter membership.[4]

The University of Chicago had an innovator of the highest order in Stagg. The man experimented with vegetarianism and urged his men to avoid tobacco, alcohol, and caffeine. On the field, Stagg helped create modern football. He was among the first to huddle his players, diagram plays, and use numbers on player uniforms. While some of his achievements (e.g., the Statue of Liberty play) are noteworthy only to those very interested in football, other Stagg inventions seem to have always existed (e.g., padding the goalposts). Few coaches have had a greater impact on their sport.

Unfortunately, however, Stagg made no pretense about academics. He recruited players, not student athletes. If his football players went to class, that was fine, but it certainly wasn't mandatory. What's more, Stagg recruited and dismissed players as he saw fit. New men would show up when the team needed them, not according to any sort of academic cadence. Stagg also found it perfectly reasonable to pay recruits to pick the University of Chicago. He did so with money from a newly significant group on campus: football boosters. Here were individuals, many of them alumni of the relatively new university, who were willing to give their hard-earned money back to their school to raise its profile. Yes, it was a very specific type of giving, but nonetheless, it was a revenue stream that had not previously existed.

Over the course of his forty years at the school, Stagg created enormous promotional capital for the University of Chicago. What started with Rockefeller's money became something altogether bigger due to Stagg's football dominance. During the Stagg era, Chicago won two national championships, seven Big Ten conference championships, and a Heisman Trophy (Jay Berwanger, 1935). It built and regularly filled a fifty-thousand-seat stadium. The school's name appeared in countless newspaper stories and headlines. In a time when the football "haves" were not as far removed from the "have-nots" as today, Chicago still enjoyed being near the top of the hierarchy.[5]

Then in 1939, the school quit football altogether.

The decision came down suddenly, on Christmas Eve. The news spread quickly throughout Chicago and the college football world. One Chicago alum telegraphed the news to the *Chicago Tribune* with more than a touch of disappointment. The unanimous decision by the school's board of trustees was one that, as the alum explained, "ignores the bill of rights and sincerely flatters both Stalin and Hitler."[6]

The reasons behind the decision were fairly straightforward. The school's new leadership believed its academic mission was compromised by the inordinate attention devoted to football. Yes, the team's fortunes had trailed off in Stagg's last years, but the decision was rooted more in the future than in the past. There was little outward discussion given to the idea of sunk costs (what was to be done with a large football stadium?) or the lost traditions of Saturdays in the fall. Rather, this was a decision based on the type of university Chicago aspired to be—a world-class research university.

President Robert Maynard Hutchins, who had made his concerns about football known from the start, argued that Chicago would become a "different kind of university" by ridding itself of football; it would be a place uncompromised by "gate receipts and glory."[7]

Thus, the University of Chicago came to represent the reigning in of athletics and exaltation of pure education. Throughout the process, Chicago's leadership was a bit saccharine, a bit holier than thou, but certainly, no one could say they were not daring. A few years later, in 1954, as the commercial appeal of college sports seemed to be peaking, Hutchins published a piece in *Sports Illustrated* to ensure that the disbanded Maroons stayed disbanded. "We shall be able to disentangle sport and higher education," Hutchins wrote of the better days possibly ahead for the whole of higher education. "Students can play (or not play) as they wish; their friends may attend and applaud if they like. It will be clear that this is relaxation from higher education, not the main purpose of it. Students will come to college to study . . . the colleges and universities will be set free to be as good as they know how to be. . . . This happened at Chicago."[8]

***

Fast forward sixty-four years.

Vanderbilt University, every bit the University of Chicago's counterpart in terms of academic prestige, took its own big swing at revolutionizing college sports in 2003. It did so under the guidance of Chancellor Gordon Gee.

Throughout his career, Gee served as the president of West Virginia University (twice); the University of Colorado, Boulder; Brown University; Ohio State University (twice); and Vanderbilt University. Gee never stayed in one place for long. But at each stop, Gee, known for his bow ties and lavish fundraising operations, made splashy changes. He had an uncanny ability to rip off Band-Aids. He preferred action, whether fully vetted or not, to planning and discussion. Indeed, beneath Gee's folksy demeanor, there was a restless, renegade spirit.

Vanderbilt, however, presented a unique challenge for Gee. The university was (and is) private, rich, elite, highly selective, and a member of the most athletically obsessed group of schools (the Southeastern Conference [SEC]) in the United States. This mix of characteristics puts the school in rare company. Notre Dame, Duke, University of Southern California, and Stanford—these are among the handful of schools with the same types of resources and ambitions as Vanderbilt. They, too, chase after the brightest students and faculty and compete for championships at the highest level of NCAA Division I athletics.

Certainly, much had changed between the time of President Hutchins at Chicago, in 1939, and when Gee had arrived at Vanderbilt, at the beginning of the twenty-first century. College athletics had boomed, becoming what economists Allen Sanderson and John Siegfried call an "accidental industry."[9] It was accidental in that no one before, say, the late 1980s, envisioned that Ohio State University might someday have an athletic department budget exceeding $100 million, nor that major media companies would compete to pay billions of dollars to universities, conferences, and the NCAA for the rights to televise college athletics.

It was also "accidental" because the NCAA, after all, had spent most of the twentieth century fighting desperately to keep college sports smaller, less industrial, than it otherwise might have become.

Throughout its history, the NCAA was equal parts straightjacket, bumper rails, and fine print. The organization worked tirelessly to limit things such as television exposure, the number of coaches a school could employ, and the permissible contact hours between coaches and athletes. The NCAA restrained all manner of financial transactions. In fact, well into the 1970s, the NCAA was doing a pretty fair job limiting the money moving around in college athletics. It wasn't pure amateurism, of course, as the athletes were still compensated with scholarships, and the coaches and administrators were paid, but there was an austerity hanging over much of the enterprise. College sports *felt* somewhat restrained, even if some people were getting rich along the way.

In 1984, the Supreme Court shattered this restraint. In *NCAA v. Board of Regents of the University of Oklahoma*, the court ruled that a school—in this case, the University of Oklahoma—had the right to sell its football product to the highest television bidder. The court also found that the NCAA's policy of controlling the televising of football games, with a focus on keeping revenues down and splitting exposure fairly, violated the Sherman Antitrust Act. The NCAA was, in fact, acting as a "classic cartel."[10]

Giving athletic departments the freedom to get as much as possible, economically speaking, changed everything.

In 1980 the SEC (Vanderbilt's home conference) distributed $4.1 million in revenues gained from television, NCAA tournament, and bowl games to its member schools. From there, with the 1984 Supreme Court ruling as a major impetus, the pie grew ever larger.[11]

The following lists the revenue the SEC distributed to its members:

1980: $4.1 million
1990: $16.3 million
2000: $73.2 million
2010: $209 million
2020: $777.8 million

More money led to new buildings—stadiums and training facilities, yes, but also new athletic department administration facilities. While, in the 1970s, it was entirely possible that an athletic director might work in a space shared with a faculty or staff member unconcerned with intercollegiate athletics, the 1990s gave rise to infrastructural segregation. Increasingly, athletic administrators worked in buildings reserved just for athletics. Similarly, athletes often studied and ate and, in some cases, lived in facilities reserved only for athletes. On the issue of buildings, the 2001 Knight Commission sounded an alarm. "The building boom in college sports facilities now under way across the nation will cost well over $4 billion, with the resulting debt stretching far into the future."[12]

The divide—both physical and metaphysical—between regular students and student athletes seemed to grow each year. "Athletic departments," the *Chronicle of Higher Education* matter-of-factly reported in 2003, "especially at SEC universities, are worlds unto themselves."[13]

This trajectory unnerved Gordon Gee. So, too, did the fact that Vanderbilt struggled to compete on the scoreboard. As a result, Gee often butted heads with Vanderbilt AD Todd Turner. The two bickered constantly. Gee left one interaction with his AD so frustrated that he fumed on his way out the door, "I'm going to blow up athletics."[14]

Gee had plenty to be frustrated about. Turner was presiding over a Vanderbilt athletic department that produced neither winning football seasons nor balanced budgets—an unsustainable duo. Incompetence reigned. Two years after giving Woody Widenhofer a contract extension, for example, Turner had been forced to turn around and fire his football coach. The Commodore football team had lost eight straight SEC games. The capper was a 71–13 loss to the University of Florida.

Largely as a result of the football team's futility, athletic department fundraising had cratered. The fanbase stopped showing up. Heading into the 2003 season, Vanderbilt had just 5,244 football season ticket holders.[15]

What should an institution like Vanderbilt, which aspires to be a top-ten research university and an all-around paragon of excellence, do in the face of such incompetence?

What could Gee do?

On the one hand, Gee seemed to recognize his limits. "What do I know about college football?" he asked. "I look like Orville Redenbacher. I have no business talking about college football." On the other hand, Gee was incapable of leaving things alone. He considered the entire Vanderbilt ecosystem to be his domain. He feared no decision. To be a good university president, Gee said, required "a thick skin, a good sense of humor, and nerves like sewer pipes." Gee had all three.[16]

So on September 9, 2003, Gordon Gee disbanded Vanderbilt's athletic department. Just like that, gone.

"There is a wrong culture in athletics, and I'm declaring war on it," Gee announced. Gee's decision summarily eliminated Todd Turner's athletic director position. Thus, that argument was over. The decision moved the operations of the athletic program to the division of student life and university affairs. David Williams—Vanderbilt's vice chancellor for student affairs, its general counsel, and a faculty member in the law school—became the final voice on athletics.[17]

Gee was careful to stress that the decision did not mean Vanderbilt was tempering its athletic expectations. Nor did the school plan to move down a level in competition. No, Vanderbilt wanted to do things differently. It wanted to do things better. And it wanted to win more.

To say that the media and fans didn't quite grasp Gee's vision would be a gross understatement. ESPN explained the move as a strange rejoinder. "University to merge varsity, intramural athletics," it reported, as if the Commodores football team might now be sharing space with a sorority dodgeball squad.[18]

"Huh?" read a headline in the *Nashville Scene*. "Gordon Gee's decision to reorganize/abolish Vanderbilt's athletic department sent a resounding message to the collegiate sports world," the alternative paper said. "What the message actually said, however, is pretty much anyone's guess."[19]

Even Vanderbilt's hometown newspaper, *The Tennessean*, wasn't sure if Gee was proposing a remodel or a teardown. "Vanderbilt Scraps, Restructures Athletics Department," read the front-page headline.[20]

Rival schools piled on. Vanderbilt had always been a strange fit for the SEC. The private Nashville school had been a veritable prop plane fighting against jets. Under the new athletics plan however, mused one rival, the school would be populating its air force with hot air balloons. Another columnist for an opposing SEC newspaper wrote, "Gordon Gee last week stunned big-time college sports by declaring that Vandy's athletics department will go the way of the manual typewriter. It will disappear."[21]

Gee plunged right into the stormy waters he had stirred up. He certainly didn't want to miss the credit (or blame) for inserting Vanderbilt into the national conversation about college athletics.

Two weeks after the decision, Gee gave his full response. He penned a lengthy editorial for the *Washington Post*, which newspapers across the country picked up.

"My plan is to put the college back in college athletics," Gee began his nearly one-thousand-word manifesto. From there, he doubled down, providing declarations like these:

> *I like to win. I also like to sleep at night. But after 23 years [of] leading universities, I find it increasingly hard to do both.*
> *Clearly, the system is broken, and fixing it will require more than sideline cheering.*
> *We'll no longer need an athletic director.*
> *Many athletic departments exist as separate, almost semiautonomous fiefdoms with universities.*
> *Shifting Vanderbilt's athletics program to our division of student life and university affairs is merely a step—perhaps bold, perhaps quixotic—in a much-needed reform of intercollegiate athletics.*
> *After our announcement, I received many phone calls from college presidents who said, "You go, Gordon. Walk off the cliff, and if you succeed, we will be right behind you."*

As he finished up, Gordon returned to a more familiar script. He espoused higher graduation rates, the end of sham courses for athletes, and harsher penalties for rogue athletic programs. These were things that all university leaders parroted. Then Gee closed with a challenge: "Take a good look at the system we have created for ourselves," he wrote. "We should demand nothing less than a system in which student-athletes are an integral part of the academic institutions whose names and colors they so proudly wear on game day."[22]

You might be wondering, What happened next?

Vanderbilt went on one of the most successful athletic runs in its recent history. On the fifth anniversary of Gee's decision, the *New York Times* ran a piece declaring the grand experiment an overwhelming success. By accessing endowment funds due to the restructure, Vanderbilt had actually added sports to its intercollegiate portfolio and improved athletic facilities. For the first time in anyone's memory, Vandy athletes took on leadership roles in student government and traveled as a part of study abroad programs. The football team, especially under coach James Franklin, won more than usual and went to bowl games. The men's and women's basketball teams captured SEC championships. The baseball team became a national powerhouse. The period was, according to a self-congratulatory article in *Vanderbilt Magazine*, a complete "game changer."[23]

Gee, of course, didn't stick around for long. He left for Ohio State (again). And then he moved on to West Virginia (again).

Eventually, Gee's remake of Vanderbilt's athletics went from being viewed as shocking to normal, then from normal to passé. Increasingly, it was explained away as Vanderbilt doing Vanderbilt kinds of things. No other school followed the Commodores off the cliff.

Despite the success, however, and with Gee gone, fitting in with other NCAA schools proved to be increasingly alluring. Gradually, the Vandy athletic machine regained much of its lost fiefdom. A slow and steady retrenchment took place. In 2012, Vanderbilt's new chancellor Nicholas Zeppos asked David Williams to transition into a new, more specific role. Zeppos wanted to ensure that Vandy continued its positive momentum in athletics.

And what was the new title Zeppos had in mind for Williams?

Athletic director.

CHAPTER 9

Gallo

DAY 47. SATURDAY, SEPTEMBER 22, 2018.
BOCA RATON, FLORIDA
Getting a college soccer team from Albuquerque, New Mexico, to Boca Raton, Florida (in the Lobos' case, for a CUSA game against the Florida Atlantic University [FAU] Owls) is a byzantine undertaking. There are plane tickets, ground transportation, hotel rooms, meeting spaces, meals—the list is nearly endless. Most of these logistical tasks fall on Kelly. And not only does he need to get the team from A to B, but he also must do so in a manner that meets school, NCAA, and, most importantly, Fish's standards.

To get an OK for his traveling plan, Kelly sends the draft itinerary to an associate athletic director for compliance, an associate athletic director for sports administration, a director of compliance, a fiscal service tech, an athletic academic advisor, and an Anthony Travel representative. Fish, of course, gets a copy too. They all have to sign off. Whether this level of oversight has something to do with UNM's recent financial controversies or is simply because this outlay costs more than $15,000 is unclear. Regardless, Kelly makes the arrangements and gets the approvals. He does so with the precision, flexibility, and the good humor of a middle school principal.

As for the players, they do provide some assistance. All the underclassmen have an assigned travel duty, for example. Kelly creates a checklist for each away game, listing both the players' assigned travel duties

Chapter 9

and a list of what to pack more generally. The latter is typically basic stuff (nice clothes for dinner, a particular type of cleats, etc.), but the staff knows all too well that it's best to be specific about expectations.

In terms of travel duties, there's just so much stuff to transport. It's not football, of course, where semitrucks full of helmets and pads move college teams to their away games, but it's not a cross-country team traveling either.

For an away trip, Kelly's list of equipment includes the following:

1. Balls/pumps/needles (20 total, 2 bags of 10 balls)
2. Bibs (blue/red/yellow/green)
3. Cones (regular cones on the loop)
4. Flat discs (in a sack pack)
5. Uniform bags
6. Blood bag (extra red kit, extra white kit, extra goalkeeper kits)
7. Training gear/wet bag (big black Nike bag)
8. Sticky tactics board and markers
9. 15 foam rollers (2 bags)
10. 2 coolers

Assigning players travel duties is part of the Lobo soccer coaching philosophy. It's mundane, but it's also an opportunity to teach responsibility and shared sacrifice. It serves to keep player entitlement in check. It also means, however, that sometimes things don't arrive at the proper place and time. Freshmen tend to make freshmen-type mistakes. Fetterly, for example, on the team's first trip of the year, remembered to bring the tactics board on the trip but then forgot it in his hotel room on game day.

Fish, of course, takes such slipups seriously. No sin goes unpunished. Fish wants perfection both on the field and off. He certainly doesn't buy the idea that some mistakes are negligible ones. "Control the controllables," he says. "Don't let yourself off the hook," he preaches.

As a result of Fish's sky-high expectations and short fuse, the players and assistant coaches have a triage mentality. If a mistake or lapse can be fixed before Fish knows about it, all types of resources are deployed to make it so. This timeless us-against-the-boss camaraderie serves the team well.

The team traveled after early morning practice on Thursday. Because the team flew on American Airlines, Fish required that everyone pack a carry-on for the three-day trip. There's no use wasting precious budget dollars on baggage fees.

On Friday the team practices at FAU and meets to review the game plan. This takes just a few hours of the otherwise-unencumbered day. Finally, after a day of killing time, the Lobos take the field at FAU Soccer Stadium for a 7:00 p.m. matchup. Both teams have losing records, but with the season just at its midway point, there is still reason to hope for a turnaround. The stands are mostly empty. FAU counts the official attendance at 329, which seems generous.

The scene is all Florida: Palm trees sway over the complex fences. A soft sun fades on the horizon. The turf is green velvet. Traffic roars by on the nearby I-95 freeway. At game time the temperature is eighty-four degrees, with a healthy dose of humidity.

The Lobos play in all red—socks, shirts, and shorts. Fish wears his traditional khaki shorts and white polo while the assistants sport matching black and gray. As always, the Lobos look good when taking the field.

The announcer starts with the Lobos. "For the visitors from New Mexico . . ." He announces the players one after another. No one in the stands pays much attention. To fill in the silence, a few of the Lobos clap awkwardly for themselves.

Starting for the Lobos are Fetterly, Tom, Barrero, Dorsey, Scotty, Puig, Simon, Billy, Bailey, and Taylor.

Then something new happens. The last starter is announced for the Lobos. For the first time, freshman Erik Virgen gets the start. For Gallo, as everyone calls him, it's a dream come true. "When the National Anthem started to play," he recalls of his FAU debut, "I was like, dang, now I'm here." Indeed, he has come a long way from "the Mexican leagues" of Rose Park, Utah.

***

Chapter 9

Gallo didn't go to soccer camps as a child. He didn't have the chance to attend week-long clinics, like the one he'd helped put on in Albuquerque during his first summer as a Lobo. "I wish," he says. Instead, he learned the game on Sundays at the park. He got his first touches with siblings and cousins on the sidelines. Then he jumped into pickup games.

The Virgen family lived in Rose Park, a neighborhood in northwest Salt Lake City, Utah. Rose Park was a predominantly Hispanic enclave in the early 2000s. It featured small post–WWII homes and mature trees. The neighborhood was also home both to an active Superfund cleanup site called the Rose Park Sludge Pit. Because of its proximity to downtown, the neighborhood faced the constant threat of gentrification.

For Gallo, the most important spaces in his neighborhood were two shaggy soccer fields. "When I think about my childhood, I just remember being there," he says. Families gathered at the fields on Sundays. There was food, music, and catching up. And soccer. "Just Hispanics," Gallo says of the crowd. "Hispanic people getting together and making teams."

The soccer was informal but intense. There were no sign-ups or uniforms. Teams came together from the talent available on a given day. Games commenced for the little kids, for the teenagers, and for the men. Talent trumped age. As Gallo picked up the game, he began to play up. Sometimes he joined his older brother on the pitch and, sometimes, even the men. Though he was small, Gallo controlled the ball and saw the field. He connected the game from the middle of the field, feeding the older players who could score goals.

Gallo's father, the original Gallo, had been a semiprofessional player in Mexico. The game permeated the family household. "That's all my family does, honestly. My parents, my brothers, my cousins," Gallo says, "everybody's really into soccer." It was in these "Mexican Leagues," as he describes them with a grin, that Gallo's passion for the beautiful game was born.

When Gallo was twelve, his family moved from Utah to Tucson, Arizona. He continued to play there, but at this point, his soccer experience took a hard turn toward what has become known as the American

Youth Soccer system. Gallo moved into the world of fees, uniforms, set schedules, and strict age cutoffs.

The game, however, remained simple for Gallo. He waterbugged around the field, always moving. "Sharp on the ball . . . connect my passes, break lines, disrupt play," says Gallo of his game.

Before long, Gallo caught the eye of a Real Salt Lake Academy scout. The academy, which was affiliated with the MLS club, had recruiting rights in Utah and Arizona. Thus, even though his family had moved from one state to another, Gallo remained firmly within RSL's region.

Things progressed quickly. "I got really into it," Gallo says. "And I got scouted, and then I went to go train, and they asked me to stay." With that, Gallo went from pickup games in the park to one of the United States' most progressive soccer training academies. The club, at its Phoenix campus, provided top-tier instruction and competition. With RSL, Gallo played in events like the US Soccer Development Academy Winter Showcase, held in Bradenton, Florida, in December 2014. Gallo's play began to draw notice among the soccer set. "'Gallo' Virgen played the entire second half for the Academy Select Red," read one report from the event, "controlling the midfield in the Red team's eventual 2–1 win."[1]

When RSL opened its palatial soccer academy and high school in Herriman, Utah, in 2017, Gallo transferred back to his home state. The complex had eight outdoor fields, two indoor fields, and a stadium. The facility was designed to develop homegrown talent. It was, in many ways, about RSL building a cheap talent pool. "I can bring in a player at a lower cost at a higher quality than going and searching the world and then having to pay for a player, we can grow a player," said RSL owner Dell Loy Hansen of his investment in the academy.[2]

More than anything, Gallo has wanted to play professional soccer—that, not college, was his primary goal as he neared the end of high school. He hoped that RSL would sign him to a homegrown contract so that he could begin as a professional player right away. And, from an academic standpoint, it was clear that Gallo's priorities had been mostly on the soccer field. "Yeah, I missed *a lot* of school," he says of the academy's travel schedule. Sometimes, the U17 or U18 squad would be gone for a week at a time. "I think if I would have been at school, I would have been focused on school," he says.

As it became clear that a homegrown contract was not eminent, college coaches began to come around. Some were scared off by the hole Gallo had dug himself into academically. Fish, however, just saw potential: Here was a player who had been invited up to train with the Real Salt Lake MLS team. Here was a five-foot-seven, 150 lb. warrior who had broken bones on the field (wrist, elbow, humerus, and ankles) and returned as aggressive as ever. Here was a student of the game with a tireless motor. And here was a bilingual teenager who had successfully navigated all types of environments from the Rose Park neighborhood, to a predominantly Hispanic high school ("I knew, like, probably three or four White people"), to the Waspy Development Academy scene.

Also, it just so happened that Gallo had a best friend and RSL teammate, Glademir Mendoza, who all the college coaches wanted. What's more, Gallo and Glad—who goes by Pichu—viewed themselves as a package deal. "Wherever I go, he goes," Gallo says of their time awaiting college decisions. Get one, get them both.

Fish went to work on recruiting Gallo: calls, texts, and emails. He pointed out, among other things, that several players from RSL had played for the Lobos in recent years. Fish made the initial big pitch for the University of New Mexico.

From there, Kelly took over. Among his duties, Kelly oversees the team's academic progress. Gallo, if he were to sign with New Mexico, would need help on this front. Division I athletic departments are, among other things, clearing houses for potential enrollees. Figuring out how to get them not only into the school but also NCAA eligible so they can take the field involves a dedicated staff. And Gallo was worth the effort.

The whole process was stressful for Gallo. "The recruiting process was difficult, I think, for me," Gallo explains, "because I struggled a lot in school." Unfortunately, Gallo couldn't enjoy the prospect of being wanted and considering a new team and town without worrying that the other shoe would still drop. "It was a hard process trying to get me eligible to play college soccer," he says. But once his attention shifted entirely to college, Gallo doubled down to make grades. He made up for lost time in the classroom. He overloaded his senior class schedule to make up for lower marks. With Kelly's help, he targeted summer courses.

The fact that Kelly and the UNM coaches believed in him both as a player and as someone who could do the classroom work meant everything to Gallo. "I chose UNM," he says, "because they believed in me and trusted me."

Gallo—and Pichu—eventually signed on with UNM. They had never even visited Albuquerque or the campus, but they trusted the coaches and the soccer setup. They figured everything else would fall into place. "We knew it would be fine," Gallo says. "I had lived in Tucson. It was very similar to [Albuquerque]."

The two arrived in the heat of July to work Fish's camps. Pichu, however, arrived badly hobbled. He had torn his ACL in a late-summer club tournament. He would not play for the Lobos during the 2018 season.

Gallo, on the other hand, navigated through his academic minefield unscathed. He could play. Although quiet, Gallo jumped into the fray. "I get along with everyone," he says. "There's not one guy that I don't like on the team. I enjoy everybody's company."

***

The Lobos control the action at FAU from the start. They begin producing the signs of momentum—corner kicks and shots—within the first minutes of the contest. Passes are sharp. Taylor, in particular, playing from the left wing, produces a couple of tantalizing early crosses. Gallo, wearing his number twenty, patrols midfield.

Ten minutes into the contest, Taylor beats his man and crosses the ball. Simon is waiting. He drives the ball into the net for his first goal of the season: 1–0.

The Lobos high-five and hug. There's palpable relief at the fast start. Smelling blood, the Lobos press harder. Puig nearly scores two minutes later. The Owls do manage to counter with a good look, but Fetterly is right where he should be and scoops up the threat.

Then, with twenty-two minutes still remaining in the first half, the Lobos draw a free kick. Taylor loops a chip shot into the box, where Billy heads it past the Owl keeper: 2–0.

And just like that, on a balmy night in southeastern Florida, the Lobos are who they are supposed to be—a poised, skilled college soccer team that can impose its will on an opponent. No one is thinking of next year or the Board of Regents' decision. No one is stressing about early season losses. It's just about controlling the ball and disrupting the opponent. They are the team that Fish expects of a group of men in Cherry and Silver.

There's no work for the scorekeeper in the second half. The Owls manage some chances, but Fetterly knocks everything away. "For the first time," Champ says, "we controlled the entire game." Tom, always the master of the slide tackle, likewise turns back a handful of potential threats. The Lobos attackers lose a bit of their urgency but still generate shots and corners.

The Lobos win 2–0.

"I'm really happy to get our first shutout," Fish says after the win. "It was important to get a conference win on the road."

"We adjusted the lineup a bit," Fish continues, referencing Gallo, "and I'm happy with the result. It could have been better, but I think it's a good thing when you feel like there's still room for improvement after a win like that."[3]

Day 49. Monday September 24, 2018.
Albuquerque, New Mexico

"You're in a strange spot, but that's OK," Fish says back home, in the team's first meeting after the FAU win. "It's good to test yourself. That's life."

Mike has mixed feelings about the team's progress. "I'm glad for the result," he says several times. But the effort levels concern him. "We started off better than we ever have, but once we got that second goal, we faded away."

The next game is another big opportunity. St. Mary's College of California (SMC) comes to Albuquerque with an undefeated (9–0) record and a no. 10 national ranking. A win against the Gaels would reestablish the Lobos as a team to be watched. It would even the team's record and set the Lobos up for a second-half run. Since the SMC game is at home and at altitude, Fish is optimistic. "This place has seen a lot of big-ass wins," Fish reminds the Lobos as they head to the practice fields.

As always, Kelly leads warm-ups. After twenty minutes, he turns the guys over to Mike. "Get a sip," he reminds them, per usual. It's still hot.

The team focuses on touches and tempo. Much of the pre-SMC practice is spent working the three-team possession drill. But Billy has an objection right from the start on this day: "Kelly," he says, "every single day you've started me in the middle. [He deadpans.] And I am *not* OK with it."

The guys compete and fight. While the passes are rarely as crisp as the coaches want, the effort is good on this day. The FAU win has lightened the mood considerably.

Practice ends with Fish, again, addressing the team. He's leaving no stone unturned; his "more is more" philosophy is on full display.

"If you're a starter, be great, knowing the guy behind you really wants to play," he says. He speaks from the heart about empathy and commitment for ten minutes. While he does, Bailey, with the straps of his pinny jersey resting on his ears, slowly sidles up in front of Taylor.

With Taylor stuck between several bunched-in teammates, Bailey gradually lowers his cleated heel onto Taylor's toes. Bailey digs in—then a bit more. Taylor, however, shows nothing. Instead, he takes the challenge. He keeps eye contact with his coach.

Finally Fish finishes. Taylor lurches to an escape. Bailey's impressed with his fellow sophomore's restraint. "I've trained him to be mentally tough," Bailey concludes in a Mr. Miyagi tone, then heads back down the hill toward the locker room.

DAY 51. WEDNESDAY, SEPTEMBER 26, 2018.
ALBUQUERQUE, NEW MEXICO

After a storm that blew through yesterday, the game-time temperature is noticeably cooler for this SMC game. Finally, it's fall.

Chapter 9

Barreiro and Antoine arrive late because they have lab classes on Wednesdays. While Fish is among the handful of Lobos coaches who actually supports his players taking difficult classes even when it conflicts with soccer, the change in the pregame routine makes him nervous.

When everyone has arrived and is dressed and settled, Fish gives a last word. Today it's a question. "Who are we?" Fish asks. "That's my biggest thing."

As always, the last thing the team does before heading to the field for their game is watch a highlight video. "Hell yeah, Champ!" the boys yell as the video starts, giving credit where credit is due.

The video ends with a simple Lobo commandment: "Win at home." During Fish's seventeen-year tenure, the Lobos have always done that. He's orchestrated home-winning streaks of nineteen, fourteen, thirteen, and eleven games. The program boasts a 75 percent all-time home-winning percentage. While the UNM Soccer Complex lacks the renown of The Pit, UNM's vaunted basketball arena, the results have been similar. Visiting teams usually go home with a loss.

The players depart for the field. Once they're gone, Fish slumps into a chair. He's tired. This week he had a testy meeting with Eddie. "Almost got fired," he says. He's also clashed with other members of the athletic department. It appears that none of the actors involved in the terminal season know quite how to act.

Understandably, Fish is worried about money. After all, he's facing imminent termination. This would be enough to scare any man in his early fifties. "I wish I had tenure," he muses. "You don't get rich, but it's a good life." But mostly, it's the idea of the University of New Mexico not having a soccer program that he still can't wrap his mind around. He's still resolved not to let it happen. He plans to continue coaching this team, yes, but even more so, to keep up the political fight. "How are we going to keep up the pressure for six more weeks?" he asks, not expecting an answer.

Finally, he heads for the game.

After another shaky, off-key national anthem, the starters take the field. Fetterly is in goal for the third straight game. He tweaked his shoulder during warm-ups, but he insists it's nothing. Gallo starts again. Omar, the team's leading scorer, starts the game on the bench.

The first half is a taut, nothing-nothing affair: 0–0. The fact that the Lobos have held the Gaels, the nation's top-scoring team, without a goal is positive. Fetterly and the backline are in sync. But the offense doesn't create many chances.

The Lobos retreat to the hurdles garage at the edge of the track, which they use for their halftime talks. Since there's no bathroom, several of the starters make a detour to the fence line on their way. The players enter through a partially rolled-open garage door. They sit wearily on a couple of metal benches, waiting for Mike and Fish.

Wham!

Fish catches his head on the garage door on his way in. The guys let out a collective gasp. "Holy shit," someone says as the door continues to rattle. Momentarily stunned, Fish checks his head for blood. There's none. He rubs his head, then shakes away the cobwebs and reengages quickly.

"Take. Their. Fucking. Energy."

It's a quintessential Fish moment—a bit crazy, a lot of passion, and a resolute will.

No one expects the Gaels to fold. They're ranked no. 10 nationally for a reason. They are an experienced team that won't make mistakes, the coaches warn. Again, it will just be a moment or two. Mike tells the guys to watch for gaps during transition—SMC looks to play off turnovers. "We've got to be more disciplined, and we've got to play in their half," he says.

Despite their coaches' warning, the Lobos lapse into a defensive posture during the second half. The minutes wind down. Finally, Taylor gets more aggressive and creates some opportunities. Both teams seem to be flagging a bit as they head down the stretch. Fish and Mike yell instructions from the sidelines, often at the same time.

In the Lobo parent section, tension grows as the clock winds down. The murmurs mix hope and dread: "They haven't cracked." "They're fighting like hell." "Can they finally win one of these close games?"

No, no, they cannot.

Chapter 9

With twenty seconds left in regulation, there's a scramble in transition. Fetterly comes out. A quick interior SMC pass leads to the game winner. A tap in, bottom left: 0–1. It appears as easy as it is devastating.

Right after the ball comes out of the net, the referee sounds his whistle, ending the game.

The shock settles over the crowd and the players. There's a finality to the loss that hints at something much bigger than just one game. The chances for this team are dwindling. Eventually, everyone files out. Only a few fans and players gather at the rail.

Gallo heads for the locker room. Apparently, not all his starts will result in victories. Still, he has played well. Fetterly holds his arm as he trudges off. The rest of the players make the walk, too, mostly in silence. Finally, just one player remains: Omar. Long after the game is over, Omar stands alone on the field. He did not play in the second half.

There are no words, but Fish is a pro. He fulfills his press duties. To the awaiting *Albuquerque Journal* reporter, he simply says, "That's about as tough as it comes." Indeed.[4]

Chapter 10

Can We Stay If We Call It Fútbol?

Day 53. Friday, September 28, 2018.
Albuquerque, New Mexico
The St. Mary's College game was the first of three home games to be played over the course of eight days. Such stretches are the curse of college soccer. If this isn't hard enough, the Lobos show up to practice on Friday to find Fetterly peddling slowly on the exercise bike.

"What's wrong with you?" one of the guys asks.

"I can't get my arm above my head," says Fetterly.

"But you're playing tomorrow?" Scotty double-checks.

"No," Fetterly says.

"No?" Scotty asks, stopping in his tracks.

"I thought you said it was no big deal," Dorsey says.

There's no answer from the bike.

Fetterly felt a twinge in his shoulder as he dove for a ball during the warm-ups for the SMC game. Nothing shattering, but it's certainly painful. He shook it off and played the game, but afterward, his arm stiffened.

Fetterly has had shoulder issues before. Now an MRI reveals Fetterly has torn his labrum. He is done for the season.

It's another crippling personnel loss for the team. The number of available players has been ticking downward all season. First, multiple players left during the summer maelstrom. Then Chang and Pichu showed up to campus with injuries. Maliek was declared ineligible. Some players ended up redshirting. And now Fetterly. The options for the coaches continue to dwindle.

Perhaps sensing that more must come from fewer, Fish spends practice making the rounds. He pulls aside Ford, Omar, Billy, and Bailey. Each gets a few minutes of Fish's encouragement and exhortation. "Be better," Fish says to the whole group at the end of practice. "Make it easier on yourself, just win tomorrow."

With Fetterly out and Anthony redshirting, Ford retakes the keeper position. The coaches had considered some more nuclear options, but they collectively felt Ford had learned from his short benching.

Day 54. Saturday, September 29, 2018.
Albuquerque, New Mexico

The Lobos host Florida International University at 11:00 a.m. The game has been pushed into the morning to accommodate the evening's homecoming football game.

The early start messes with the Lobos' pregame patterns. Chicken and pasta from nearby Saggio's, right off Central Avenue, near campus, is the Lobos' go-to meal. The simple protein and carb offering is tried and true. But such a meal at 7:30 a.m. seems unreasonable, even to Fish. Instead, the team met today at the Daily Grind for a breakfast buffet. Perhaps something different is a good idea anyhow.

At game time the temperature is sixty-nine degrees. The parking lots around the soccer stadium are already filling with tailgating football fans. However, when the soccer game starts, there are only a few hundred diehard supporters in the sun-drenched bleachers. After posing for Kelly's usual right-before-kickoff photo, the starters take the field.

FIU strikes first (0–1), converting a penalty kick, but the Lobos respond quickly. First, Tom—always a threat to force the action, pushing forward from the left-back position—creates an opening and crosses the ball to Simon. With a quick maneuver, Simon scores his second goal of the season on an open net: 1–1. The senior from Belgium is often reserved and serious, but on this day, Simon celebrates with his teammates.

Then, in the twenty-ninth minute, Puig converts a header off Taylor's well-placed corner kick. The set piece conversion gives the Lobos the lead. They enter the halftime shed with the score at 2–1.

The mood is upbeat and optimistic. Football tailgating music and the smells of barbeque hang over the soccer complex.

FIU's coach is yelling at his underperforming squad.

"Don't underestimate this team for a second," Fish preaches. "They have guys who can score goals." Then Fish offers a final reminder: "The first few minutes are key." The Lobos head back to the field.

However, as has often been the case, this Lobo team seems to match each step forward with a lapse. They cannot clamp down. It takes FIU less than two minutes to tie the score: 2–2. Just a couple minutes more pass before FIU gets another: 2–3. A sense of dread sets in.

"You got to bring the energy," Billy yells from the back line. From the sidelines, Antoine is yelling at the referee in French. But it does no good. Santiago Patiño, who will be drafted third in the January MLS SuperDraft, again breaks between the Lobos back line and scores. The game ends: 4–2.

This time, it's Fish left on the field, hands on hips, as the stands empty. "Lobos upended by FIU," reads a pithy recap in *TopDrawer Soccer*.[1]

Day 56. Monday, October 1, 2018.
Albuquerque, New Mexico

With just three days until another game—this one, against Loyola Marymount University (LMU)—the coaches dig in. When the players arrive in the team meeting room at 8:30 a.m., they barely get settled in their seats before Fish starts up.

"Quit feeling sorry for yourself," Fish yells. He's livid at the slumped shoulders and downcast glances he sees in front of him. He's barely in control.

"Get the fuck out, and come back in like you're ready to go," he shouts.

The guys file out. Unclear just how far they're supposed to go, they logjam outside the door. It's not far enough. "All the way to the locker room!" comes the command. For the next seven minutes, Fish's voice echoes through the hallways of the athletic complex. Finally, the team trudges back to the meeting room to try it all over again.

"I don't want to look out and see a beaten group," Fish says, a bit softer now. He knows the pressure they're facing. But there's still a chance to make something of the season. "Be excellent today. Be excellent tomorrow."

Mike gives his scout of LMU: "Typical California team. Give them time and space, and they're pretty good."

On the practice field, the ball issue surfaces once again. Champ has found two balls and added them to the bags. So now there are forty-one balls out at practice.

This doesn't add up. Just as Fish is turning to Nick Williams, Puig jumps in. He has a theory. Maybe, he speculates, two of the balls got together during the season and had a baby or two.

"That's the answer," he concludes.

Fish considers the possibility. But, he says, if a miraculous conception did happen, there should be a size discrepancy: "They'd be little balls, like size 3s, at this point," he says. Finally, with a grin, he lets it go—for today.

The ball saga refuses to die.

With the losses piling up and the pressure of the season and semester only intensifying, Fish leans on the information he has gleaned in two decades as a coach. He points out that the players who come from stable, affluent homes seem to be handling this strange, trying season better. This makes sense—they have security in other parts of their lives. This allows space for a crazy soccer campaign.

Fish is also aware that the advice coming from the coaches is starting to splinter. Fish, on one hand, makes it clear to the players that he hopes they'll stay loyal to UNM as long as possible. His party line remains the same: There will be a miracle, and thus, there will be a Lobo soccer team next year. The assistant coaches, however, are moving toward more nuanced advice. For players with options, Kelly, Mike, and Lucas are beginning to talk about the transfer process.

The LMU game starts poorly for the Lobos. They give up a goal midway through the first half. The New Mexico attackers generate hardly any opportunities on the other end.

At halftime Mike, who almost always focuses on strategic adjustments, tries to reach his wounded team. "This is not about tactics," he says calmly, but pleading too. "Your biggest challenge is putting the last ten games behind you and focusing on this forty-five."

The guys listen. There's still life here. Immediately, the offense gets going. They get two quick shots on goal. Then two corners. Finally, Nick Taylor breaks through. Finding some space on the right wing out of transition, Taylor uses his patented, left foot dribble—dribble, tap, tap, wait . . . *shot*. He finds the bottom left corner: 1–1.

The Lobos nearly score again two minutes later. Then, however, comes the punch in the gut this team always seems to find.

Antoine—always a scrapper—scuffles with the LMU goalie. The refs see an elbow thrown. Red Card.

The Lobos have to play a man down through the rest of the regulation. In overtime, LMU gets a penalty kick. The foul comes against the steadiest of the Lobo defenders, Tom Smart. It happens just barely inside the box. But no matter, the ref calls it. LMU converts the penalty kick, and the game is over: 1–2.

***

At the first Board of Regents meeting where cutting sports was discussed, a soccer supporter showed up with a memorable sign that read, "Can we stay if we call it fútbol?" It was a brilliant turn of phrase. The sign also captured an interesting dynamic: While it's possible to be a fan of both soccer *and* football, it's rare. This is true of both individuals and institutions.[2]

A quick look at the list of Division I soccer national champions over the past twenty-five years reveals the basic soccer/football split in college athletics.

The NCAA Division I men's soccer national champions since 1995 are as follows:

CHAPTER 10

Indiana (5)	Connecticut (1)
Maryland (3)	Georgetown (1)
Stanford (3)	Marshall (1)
Virginia (3)	Notre Dame (1)
Clemson (2)	Santa Barbara (1)
North Carolina (2)	St. Johns (1)
UCLA (2)	Syracuse (1)
Akron (1)	Wake Forest (1)

On this list only Notre Dame and Clemson can be counted as football schools (and both vault far over the bar). UCLA and Stanford have had some success on the gridiron, winning five Rose Bowls each over the past century.

Otherwise, to be a soccer champion means to come from a school with a rather weak football team. Indiana, Maryland, Virginia, North Carolina, Syracuse, and Wake Forest are traditionally Big Ten and ACC football bottom dwellers. Akron, Marshall, and the University of Connecticut have FBS football programs—but just barely. Georgetown competes at the Football Championship Subdivision (FCS) level. UCSB and St. Johns quit fielding football teams in 1992 and 2002, respectively.

Neither the SEC nor the Big 12 sponsors men's college soccer. While two SEC schools (Kentucky and South Carolina) and two Big 12 schools (Central Florida and West Virginia) field men's teams, they do so adjacent to their primary athletic conferences.

Put another way, men's soccer seems to flourish at "basketball schools." This description generally fits the University of New Mexico's athletic positioning.

On New Mexico's campus throughout the fall of 2018, there have been murmurs against Bob Davie and his gridiron squad. "Perhaps it's the football team that should get cut," say the grumblers. Historically, the University of New Mexico has had just a thimble of football success, winning just over 40 percent of its games over more than a century of competition. Not since 1964 have the Lobos won a conference championship. The Lobo football squad has been involved in a litany of lopsided defeats: 94–17 to Fresno State in 1991, 69–0 to Texas Christian University (TCU) in 2010, and 72–0 to Oregon in 2011, to name a few.

The school pushed out its most successful coach, alum Rocky Long, who led the Lobos to five bowl games in the early 2000s, only to see conference rival San Diego State snatch him up. Under Long's leadership, the Aztecs became a football power in the Mountain West. In 2017, as the budget crisis intensified, Bob Davie's squad finished the season with a record of 3–9.

Not surprisingly, some onlookers have had enough. In June 2018 the *Santa Fe New Mexican* published a representative editorial arguing, "The Lobos should cut football program." In it James Barron, a *New Mexican* reporter and UNM alum, called for the university to pursue a new, football-free paradigm. "All it takes is one brave, bold soul," he wrote either naively or daringly. "Too bad that person doesn't reside at UNM."[3]

President Stokes is certainly aware of the antifootball sentiment. "Our faculty probably would have voted to cut football," she says. But Stokes also understands the landscape of American higher education. She knows that when the question involves college athletics, doubling down on football has always been a safe response. It's like answering "Jesus" in Sunday school.

What the out-with-football crowd misses is the overwhelming centrality of football within the world of NCAA Division I college athletics. Football simply dwarfs everything else. Whether one approaches college sports through the lens of budgets, cultural resonance, or historical significance, football dominates. It is and has long been, as scholar Michael Oriard puts it, "King Football" versus everything else.[4] Or as scholars Spencer Wyld and David Wyld have noted more recently, "Football is the straw that stirs the drink." The scholar duo adds, "Whether the centrality of football to athletic department operations in universities at present is 'right' or not is a topic for another day."[5]

Thus, proposals to cut football are, effectively, absurd. They equate to asking Buckingham Palace to phase out the queen's role.

Calls for cutting football may be fun to banter about, but there is almost no precedent to allow for their adoption. Since 1978, when NCAA leaders divided Division I football into the Football Championship Subdivision (FCS) and the Football Bowl Subdivision (FBS), only a handful of FBS-playing institutions have canceled their football programs altogether. And the University of New Mexico has always competed as an FBS school.[6]

This is not to say there hasn't been some attrition. The University of Vermont cut its football program in 1974, the last flagship university to do so. Several Cal State Universities cut football in the early 1990s. In 2018 the University of Idaho took the rare step of moving down from FBS to FCS in order to join a conference—the Big Sky—that allowed for more regional competition. But for the most part, universities that play football at the highest level do whatever it takes to stay a part of the football competition.

Correspondingly, it's fair to say that cutting football was never a serious possibility at UNM during the 2018 budget crisis. There was chatter: "We're not talking about the white elephant in the room," Regent Suzanne Quillen said at the July 2018 meeting, when the cuts were originally announced. "So I have to ask you, Eddie, about football. . . . Why aren't we talking about football?" But it was mostly for show. Football, even at UNM, is king.[7]

Day 60. Friday, October 5, 2018.
Birmingham, Alabama

After losing three straight at-home games, the Lobos continue their season in the heart of football country: Alabama. The team arrived late yesterday. Practice begins at noon today at the football facility of the University of Alabama, Birmingham (UAB). The day's humidity is an affront to the Lobos, who are used to the bone-dry conditions of the Southwest.

There is an irony here. UAB experienced its own athletics financial panic in 2014. That year, UAB made the controversial decision to cut its football team (along with the bowling and rifle teams) primarily for financial reasons. The move sparked outrage, so much so that the school conducted a second round of studies and evaluations. Andy Schwarz led the take-two task force.

Schwarz provided an economic analysis that tilted the argument in favor of keeping sports. Having secured more than $17 million in new donations and discovered that the cuts wouldn't quite provide the financial relief initially projected, the school reinstated its football program. The Blazers football team began play again in 2017. They did so housed in a new administrative building and with the benefit of a new indoor/outdoor practice facility.

This facility is where the Lobos practice on this sultry Friday afternoon. Goals are pushed onto the turf football field. On this front, Ford is offended. "Soccer is a game on grass," he declares. Still, the facility is top-notch.

At the end of practice, an impromptu field goal kicking contest breaks out. Puig has found a football in one corner of the complex and bangs a couple of kicks through the uprights from thirty yards.

Later, the team heads to the Birmingham Civil Rights Institute, a visit which Fish and Kelly had planned weeks in advance. Fish wants the guys to grapple with issues of social justice and racism, even as they're preparing to handle UAB's soccer team.

"I'll be respectful of you. You [be respectful] to me," the tour guide says at the door. While many members of the team certainly would have preferred an afternoon in their rooms, watching TV and passing the hours with their phones, they engage in the history of Jim Crow in the United States. They ask questions and pay attention. It's an afternoon well spent.

At one point Fish steps away to take a call from a recruit. "[It's] a top recruit," Fish says, explaining that the player had been committed to UNM but is now leaning toward Maryland. This is the second big recruit to drop off New Mexico's list in a week. The fact that there may not be an actual team or season next year does little to dampen Fish's disappointment.

For dinner, the team heads to Café Dupont—a fine-dining, "slow food" establishment that, according to *Birmingham Magazine*, sets the standard for the city's food scene. It's a far cry from the usual places haunted by traveling college athletic teams.[8] The Lobos dine there because the establishment is owned by Grayson Dupont's father.

The dinner starts with sesame-crusted ahi tuna and ends with sugar-dusted beignets. When the chef enters the restaurant's private upstairs dining room to greet his son and the rest of the Lobos, he asks, "How many of you see something on this menu you've never had?" Almost everyone's hands go up.

It's a fine evening filled with laughter and exquisite food. Conversations range far beyond soccer. At one point, Joe and Miguel exchange high fives over the fact that they both can actually write in cursive.

The guys also ponder on an alum who showed up to visit with Fish. "What position did he play?" one asks. Several other players pepper Kelly for additional information.

"Why?" Kelly finally asks.

"Because, well, he did not look like a soccer player," the group finally responds.

Indeed, being middle-aged, bald, and carrying twenty extra pounds around the middle seems miles away for these young men. It's almost inconceivable that this old guy was once one of them. Ah, youth.

The only drawback to the farm-to-table evening is the portions: They're small. And so several Lobos trek out to a Chipotle near the hotel for a second dinner a few hours after leaving Dupont's.

Finally, after two nights at the Birmingham Downtown Courtyard Marriott, it's game time. UAB enters the game winless in four CUSA contests. The Lobos also have history on their side, holding a 5–1–1 all-time record versus the Blazers.

Still, the Lobos are wobbly. There's tension as the team gets dressed in a tent beyond the field—the locker rooms at UAB's new BBVA Field are still under construction. The Lobos sit on a hill, putting on their cleats. The freeway roars beside them, with the field and Birmingham's modest skyline in front of them.

The game gets underway in the slow tentative way in which many matches start. Passes and probing. Perhaps it's an omen when Nick Taylor blows out the side of his Nike cleats (ala Zion Williamson) early in the game. "Nike owes you two hundred bucks," says one of his teammates. Taylor switches into Champ's boots.

Roughly halfway into the first period, there's an apparent handball by Bailey. The Lobos momentarily pause, waiting for the whistle. The Blazers do not. In the confusion, Gallo makes a costly error. He fails to connect a pass at the top of the eighteen-foot box. "One mistake, super uncharacteristic by Gallo," says one of the coaches when explaining the miscue. UAB scores to take a lead into halftime: 0–1.

Fish is calm at the break. "Get the first one," he urges. "The goals are going to come." Mike, on the other hand, does not address the team at all. Instead, he goes from player to player, offering quiet words of encouragement.

In the second half, nothing goes right.

Early on, Ford deflects a catchable shot right back to an attacking Blazer: 0–2. Eight minutes later, Bailey loses possession just past midfield. The stealing Blazer takes the ball and dribbles it, nearly unimpeded, to the top of the box. From there he fires it into the bottom left corner: 0–3. Then, with eight minutes left, the Blazers use a long throw-in from their own half to get the ball into the Lobos' box. From there it takes just one move for the Lobo defenders to fall away. A shot off the post caroms to a waiting white-shirted Blazer: 0–4.

The bottom has fallen out. When the whistle finally blows, signaling the end of the beat down, it's one of the worst defeats in the history of Lobo soccer.

In the tent Fish lets loose on the team for seventeen minutes following the game. One player later summarizes the tirade: "F-bomb, F-bomb, you guys gave it to them, F-bomb, F-bomb, you made too many mistakes, F-bomb, F-bomb, quit feeling sorry for yourself." At one point, Fish turns to walk away to let the team finally get changed, only to turn back and offer some additional harsh words.

The ride back to the hotel in Fish's van is tense and moody. When Ben and Elijah start a bit of chatter, Fish shuts them down.

As he's driving, Fish's phone rings. He answers it. It's an Albuquerque reporter. "I feel sorry for the guys," Fish says. "And that's not a good thing for a coach to feel."

Chapter 10

For the Birmingham kid, Grayson, the trip could hardly have gone much worse. His team was humiliated. Sure, Grayson played fifty-two minutes of the game, but the Lobos managed only one shot on goal in the contest.

Several hours after the game, Grayson sits in a Waffle House, waiting to meet up with his father. "Something has to change," he says, baffled. He suggests a more direct approach. "Sometimes you just need to lump it up there and see what happens."

But at least there's the Waffle House. While his father might be the chef at one of the city's finest restaurants, Grayson is a Southerner through and through. The Waffle House is a soothing cocoon. "Just the smell makes me feel better," he says as he orders a chocolate milk.

Day 65. Wednesday, October 10, 2018.
Albuquerque, New Mexico

In a season that is, in many ways, consumed by questions about the future, the fact is that many of the Lobos playing in 2018 were supposed to be riding the bench until 2019. This has had a major effect on the outcomes. With nine losses already, the team will at least match the worst record of a Fishbein-era team. They are keenly aware that only once under Fish has a team finished with a losing record.

"These guys were supposed to be getting experience, not playing major minutes," one coach tells me after the UAB loss. But with the end-of-the-program announcement in June, many key players departed for other teams. This left the Lobos to play many of their talented but inexperienced freshmen.

The team practices at 8:15 a.m. today. The plan calls for a scrimmage and weights. Thankfully, the pace of the season is finally slowing down. For the remaining four regular-season games, the Lobos will play only weekend matches. This allows for a week of training in between contests. It also allows the dinged-up Lobos—Simon, Barrero, and Antoine among them—extra rest and time in the training room.

As practice winds down, the losing side in the scrimmage gets increasingly chippy. Ben takes exception to Billy's constant harping. Billy accuses Ben of having a pervasive habit of dribbling to nowhere.

The two resort to some minor pushing and shoving. Bailey, nonplussed, looks on and remarks, "You can cut the tension with a butter knife out here."

At 10:30 a.m., the team reports to the meeting room, where the athletic department administration has arranged a meeting. It's time to talk about the details of the program's endgame.

"The objective here is to open up a dialogue," starts an associate athletic director. Then he plows forward. Nothing has changed. "This will be the final season of men's soccer."

Thud.

He continues, "You can transfer with no consequences." However, for those who choose to stay through the spring, scholarships will be honored. The players will also maintain access to training facilities, the sports medicine staff, and academic advising. No one, the associate AD stresses, is being pushed out.

Then comes the part that the players and coaches have been waiting for. What about exhibition games in the spring? "We will *not* be playing a spring season," the administrator says. With this, the floor is opened for questions.

The players have plenty. Three seniors—Simon, Dorsey, and Antoine—wade in first. *Why not allow the players with remaining eligibility to play the handful of exhibition games that make up college soccer's abbreviated spring schedule?* The three ask this question in several different ways, never getting an answer they like. The fact that the seniors take the offensive on an issue that doesn't affect them at all is indicative of their collective character.

The freshmen, especially those unsure about their prospects of getting an offer from another soccer program, follow up. Their questions come quickly.

"The university said we were funded through the 2018–2019 season. Why the change?

"Who will be in charge of everything?"

"Clarify. Coaches? Practices?"

"What do you benefit to cut spring games?"

"When was this decision made?"

Chapter 10

Dorsey jumps back in for the last word. "If the university doesn't benefit, why are you screwing over the athletes?" There is no ready answer. The players have dominated the exchange. They have the upper hand in part because there are some uniquely eloquent and forceful young men on the team. Fish has always targeted such individuals for his program. But their dominance is also because the administrators in the room are operating from a truly sucky script. Their job is to tell a group of athletes that they must go away. It's a thankless task.

Slowly, the players get up and trickle out. Some have class; others are simply done with the conversation.

That Fish has created so much upheaval during the fall—both for the department and the university—certainly hangs over the moment. Some on campus are simply ready for him to be gone. "There's just no way Fishbein can be around in the spring," one athletic department administrator says following the meeting.

Day 68. Saturday, October 13, 2018.
Albuquerque, New Mexico

There are still four more conference games to play. The Lobos likely need at least a win and a tie to advance to the Conference USA tournament. This is the new goal. In 2016, after a middling season, the Lobos won the conference tournament in order to advance to the NCAA tournament. So the Lobos know it can be done.

With the University of South Carolina (USC) coming to town, the Lobos have a prime opportunity to get a win. USC is winless through four games in the conference.

The USC game starts at 5:00 p.m. on October 13. It's fall break on campus, and the semester is halfway over. The pitch is showing signs of dormancy, with brownish patches creeping in throughout. The parking lot is full of buses that have come from all over the state for a band competition hosted at the university.

The team's chances of a successful season are on life support, but here's the reality made obvious by watching the team warm up: There's still joy here. The Lobos sprint and slap backs; they revel in the chance to play college soccer. A sanitized version of Drake's "Nonstop" bounces off the bleachers.

"Ninety minutes for each other," Fish says.

"Yes, sir!" the Lobos respond in unison.

The Lobos are down two of their three seniors: Antoine is serving the second of his two-game suspension for a red card. Simon has tweaked his ankle. The two circle the field in a slow jog as warm-ups are underway. Two seniors, two Europeans, and two honors students—their absence leaves only Dorsey.

The Lobos score first. Omar breaks the defense and delivers a cross. Grayson hits a one-timer home: 1–0. It's the Birmingham native's first score of the season. He celebrates by zipping through the bench line with hugs and high fives. The Lobos take the lead into halftime.

"Here's the thing for me," Fish says. "We don't lose another fifty-fifty ball. Don't let them breath."

As if a team stuck on repeat, the Lobos lose their lead at the seventy-three-minute mark. The Gamecocks use a throw-in to create a scramble: 1–1. The sense of dread is palpable in the stands—*not again*.

Fortunately, Dorsey, the last senior standing, comes to the rescue. With just a few minutes to play in regulation, he takes a cross from Taylor and heads it into the back of the net. Goal New Mexico: 2–1! Dorsey sprints for the corner with his arms lifted skyward. His face is one of sweaty joy.

This time, for once, the minutes tick off the clock like they're supposed to. Victory. Finally.

The Lobos gather at the rail. "Whew, we needed that one," Mike says wearily. Ford, who made a couple of huge saves down the stretch to preserve the win, is enveloped by his parents in a hug. His mom has tears in her eyes. "It's been a tough go," she says, faltering.

Chapter 11

The Backs-Against-the-Wall Effect

Day 70. Monday, October 15, 2018.
Indianapolis, Indiana
The cavernous glass and brick headquarters of the National Collegiate Athletic Association is located on Washington Street, just across from White River State Park and within walking distance of Lucas Oil Stadium in downtown Indianapolis. This morning, at least a handful of the nonprofit's five hundred employees on-site must be aware that a new era is beginning: the transfer portal era.

Starting at 8:00 a.m., the process of a college athlete switching schools takes on an entirely new shape. And it's about time. For decades the student athlete (to use the NCAA's ubiquitous parlance) needed to secure permission from his or her coach in order to contact other schools. This was often an awkward dance. If the coach said no, the athlete could appeal to the athletic director. If the AD said no, the athlete could appeal to a nonathletics administrator. The dean of students often filled this role. If this designee also said no, the athlete could take the process to a review board.[1]

The stunning absurdity about this process is that if the student was rejected all the way to the top—no, no, no, and no—the NCAA then designated that student as ineligible to receive an athletic scholarship at another institution. Sorry, out of luck. The student could still pick up and move his academic and athletic life elsewhere—he could still transfer (this is America after all)—but he could not accept any athletic aid at his new school.

This prior system created an enormous distortion of power, one tilted toward the coaches and institutions and away from the students.

The transfer portal is meant to give more power and control to the student considering a change in schools. The new process fits squarely into the milieu of the post-O'Bannon era of college sports. It grants more power to the athletes.

Susan Peal, NCAA director of governance led the development of a software program to make the portal idea actionable. Working with campus compliance officers and the NCAA's information technology team, Peal helped create the "NCAA Transfer Portal."[2]

While widely regarded as a step toward equity and fairness, the NCAA couldn't totally override its DNA as it lurched forward. Thus, the transfer portal has several peculiarities, including the following:

1. Students cannot actually access the portal themselves.
2. Coaches, conference personnel, and athletic department staffers can access the portal.
3. The athletic department's compliance officer serves as the point person for the portal.
4. A student must bring their request to transfer to the compliance officer.
5. Compliance officers then have two business days to enter a student's name into the portal.

There is a ready-made joke here. In essence, in its effort to empower students, the NCAA has created a tool to track students' desires and eventual movement but did not see fit to grant those same students direct access to the database. Rather than give Gen Zers access to handle such tech on their own, the NCAA made the compliance officer the hero of its Transfer Portal story.[3]

Not surprisingly, compliance officers loved the new tool right from the start. Perhaps overlooking, say, the iPhone or the heart defibrillator, one compliance officer from the University of Alaska Anchorage described the transfer portal as "probably the best use of technology [she'd] seen in a long while."[4]

Day 70. Monday, October 15, 2018.
Albuquerque, New Mexico

Albuquerque's first snowfall of the year has arrived. Just hours after the end of the city's annual Balloon Fiesta, and as the Lobos enjoy a recovery day after Saturday's much-needed win, the New Mexico skies are gray and spitting. Winter seems intent on jumping ahead in line.

The Lobos spend this cold, blustery day considering their futures. UNM's director of compliance, Eric Schultz, has helped most members of the soccer team enter their names in the transfer portal. With the portal now up and running, coaches from other programs are allowed to contact New Mexico's players to express their interest. The messages begin hitting the players @unm.edu accounts first thing today. Phone calls and texts follow. In most cases, the communication starts off with a general probe: "Hey, sorry, um . . . heard your program got cut. . . . I don't know what your plans are for the future . . ."

"Blah, blah, blah. This is what we have," says a Lobo describing the opening salvos. "This is the best conference in the country. . . . We've got the best field, and we've got this [other stuff]" is how another describes the generic pitches.

UNM's assistant coaches will play a key role in helping the Lobos navigate these waters. Many players have already given Kelly their list of potential transfer schools. Champ has been hard at work cutting film for individual players throughout the season. Additionally, Mike is reaching out to his network to help the players as well.

Fish, however, remains mostly on the sidelines in the transfer process, given his obsessive desire to save the New Mexico program. "It's just not natural to shop your players around, you know," he says. How can he, in good conscience, push players in another direction when he remains certain that they are best off in New Mexico? There is an unresolvable tension developing here.[5]

On this front, Mike has made the case to Fish that it's time to begin separating the matters at hand. He nudges Fish to consider a more nuanced position—for example, approaching it with the belief that saving the program at UNM does not mean keeping the current players. But Fish remains unconvinced.

"I think there's a good chance we probably set a record for men's soccer players on the transfer portal on the first day," Mike says. "I'm still back and forth on how I feel about the idea of the portal," he continues, "but you know, I think in this specific situation . . . it's probably a good thing for them to have an opportunity to get their information out there and get themselves looked at in a different way." He equivocates further: "But at the same time, it's tough. It's right in the middle of the season, when things are hard, and we're getting ready to play a no. 3 team in the country who's incredibly hot."

Fetterly and Omar are among the players expected to attract the most attention. Fetterly has national team experience, and Omar, as a freshman, leads the Lobos in goals scored. Indeed, on day one of the transfer-portal era, both get plenty of messages.

Fetterly in particular is ready to move on. "Nothing against Albuquerque, but I just come from a really nice area," he says, playing the role of a Texan in New Mexico to near perfection. Originally committed to the University of Virginia, Fetterly assumes that he will end up in the ACC or at another top-tier soccer school. But unlike most of the Lobos, Fetterly is acutely aware of the structural limitations working against him and the rest of soon-to-be-free-agent teammates. He knows the nuances of the NCAA and college sports better than most. Thus, he knows that moving campuses by spring 2019 will be difficult. Several coaches he's spoken with have initially expressed interest but also hesitated regarding the timeline. Their seasons are still in full swing. The coaches don't know how their own scholarship situation will work out. "Money-wise in soccer, it's not like it's basketball or football," Fetterly points out, "where there's all these scholarships. Yeah, there's only 9.9, so unless someone leaves or something, most of the good teams already have people lined up."

Omar approaches the situation with his characteristic optimism. "My plans are to transfer to a big school," he says, "into a big conference . . . so I can grow, get better, and get more exposure." He trusts that Kelly, in particular, will help with the details. However it transpires, Omar seems to be enjoying the recruiting process again. "It's definitely been on my mind. I'm always looking out for e-mails," he says.

The freshman from Seattle is among those who notice the team's shift in mentality at about this juncture. "I think that with people, the whole transferring thing and going to this school, that school . . . a lot of the players, at least half of them, they're all like, 'Oh well, [UNM] isn't really my team anymore.'"

The coaches predict that players like Tom, Gallo, Pichu, Maliek, Fetterly, Taylor, Omar, Billy, and Scotty will have plenty of options. The others? It will be tougher. "I think there's gonna be a lot of guys that are kind of caught in the middle," Fish says.

Of course, it's not just the players. Champ, Mike, and Kelly all hope to be gainfully employed next year. They prefer, all things being equal, that this employment is at the University of New Mexico, but they aren't closing off any possibilities at this point. They're quietly sorting possibilities and primping their resumes.

As for Fish, he's already received some interest. Just as the player transfer portal opens, Fish receives what he calls a "sort-of" job offer from a Midwest school. He stashes it away.

"We're not mercenaries," Fish says to the press as the transfer-portal era opens up in earnest. "We wear New Mexico across our chests. Everywhere we go, we represent an entire state and a university. And it's the thing I'm probably most proud of over the last seventeen years. . . . As long as there's Lobo soccer, and as long as I'm involved, we're going to continue to represent our state and our institution with class and dignity and pride."[6]

Day 74. Friday, October 19, 2018.
Albuquerque, New Mexico

"Where's Nick Williams?" Fish asks on this breezy morning. He is standing on the UNM practice field. It's a couple of days after the South Carolina win and just a few hours before the team leaves for Lexington, Kentucky.

Chapter 11

Fish scans the group. Nick Williams, standing squarely in the front of the group, raises his hand: "Right here." Everyone knows where this is going.

"I was down in the locker room, and I counted thirty-nine balls . . ." Fish starts.

"No. No! There are forty," Nick Williams cuts in. He's having none of this. "We can count them right now."

"Ooooh," the guys respond.

"Count them! Count them! Count them!" The chanting grows as the group picks up on the discord.

"It's a matter of eleven balls in one bag and nine in another," Nick Williams explains. He's all business. After all, his father is a lawyer. And today, young Nick Williams might as well be arguing over the location of a cache of precious jewels or the whereabouts of a gaggle of children he was charged with babysitting.

Fish pauses, then smiles. OK, he nods. Slowly, Nick Williams nods right back. There's eye contact in both directions. Finally, Fish lets it go. The guys cheer. Score one for Nick Williams.

The balls sorted out, the team runs through its shakeout practice. It is an uneventful, if chilly, workout.

Then everyone heads for the Sunport. After a quick airport lunch, the team boards its plane. Once again, to avoid unnecessary fees, it's a carry-on situation. From Albuquerque to Denver, then Denver to Louisville, and (by minivan) Louisville to Lexington, the Lobos make their CUSA journey. They arrive at their Lexington DoubleTree Suites hotel just after midnight.

Day 75. Saturday, October 20, 2018.
Lexington, Kentucky

"Get those groins big, and open them up," Kelly says during warm-ups for practice at the University of Kentucky (UK). He's talking about the aerobic stretches the team does to start every workout. Still, the request draws the expected off-color comments from the New Mexico men.

"Done and done!" someone says.

This is the Lobos' first visit of the season to an SEC school. That fact that it comes on a football Saturday (UK is facing Vanderbilt for its

The Backs-Against-the-Wall Effect

homecoming game) and that the powerhouse UK men's basketball team has an open practice scheduled provides a ready reminder once again of the pecking order in college athletics. Football tailgating has taken over the Kentucky campus. A helicopter swirls overhead. The Lobos' soccer team caravan had to pass through numerous security check points just to get to its practice field. The Wildcat marching band can be heard in the distance.

Still, the Lobos get their work in. Mike wants to focus on tempo. He's edgy today. The week of transfer uncertainty has taken its toll. As the session sags a bit, Mike pushes the team to up its work rate toward something "more realistic."

"The whole thing's not realistic," grumbles a player in the back. Later in practice, Tom and Ford bicker a bit over a defensive lapse during a routine drill. Does the blame go to the back line or the goalie? It's one of soccer's eternal, unanswerable questions.

"It's going to be a long two weeks," Fish says as he observes from the end line. He sees the discord on the field, but mostly, he's thinking ahead. On Tuesday, November 6, New Mexico voters will head to the polls. Fish is convinced that the election of Democrat Michelle Lujan Grisham—who is ahead in all the polling and who has promised to save his team—will provide the final act of salvation in this long soccer war.

After practice and film review, the Lobos head out for an Italian dinner at a hole-in-the-wall spot in Lexington. Champ, always vigilant, found it by scouring Yelp reviews. The players eat their fill and approve. They aren't the most exacting critics regarding cuisine, but none are anxious to mess with their protein and carbs ritual.

Day 76. Sunday, October 21, 2018.
Lexington, Kentucky

The Kentucky Wildcats are ranked no. 3 in the country. As a member of the SEC conference, UK has an athletic budget three times larger than New Mexico's. The Wildcats are led by J. J. Williams, who will go on to sign a Generation Adidas contract and be selected eighteenth in the 2019 MLS SuperDraft. The team plays at the gleaming Bell Soccer Complex. "This is a pro setup," Champ says as he walks out onto the field before the game. "This will do," Scotty concurs.

Chapter 11

The New Mexico–Kentucky game is set for an 11:00 a.m. kickoff on this chilly, bright Sunday morning.

"This is a great challenge," Fish says in the final minutes before the game. "Control the controllables. Make them play soccer . . . then we're better than they are."

He's concerned that everyone has the right studs in their cleats. "The field is Bermuda with over-seeded rye," he says.

"Now we're getting a bit of agronomy," Kelly whispers.

Unspoken is the fact that a win against Kentucky would go a long way toward salvaging this disappointing season. It would give the team some positive momentum heading into the conference tournament.

The Lobos take the field in their all-red kits. They look composed and even a bit regal. The guys bring a dose of New Mexico pride everywhere they go. It's forty-five degrees at game time. A thousand people, almost all in Kentucky blue, are in the stands.

With the opening whistle, the nightmare begins.

Just thirty-six seconds into the contest, Kentucky gets a good look. Ford tracks the ball and makes his first save. It's the start of a busy day for the New Mexico keeper.

The scoring summary for the first half of the match tells the story:

6:02—goal, University of Kentucky

7:43—goal, University of Kentucky

10:20—goal, University of Kentucky

16:05—goal, University of Kentucky

Less than seventeen minutes into the game, Kentucky has scored four goals: 0–4. *Four!* Each time the ball hits the back of the net, a blast of blue smoke shoots off. It envelops Ford's working area. The celebrations barely clear the air before the next one starts.

It's as if all the pressure and negativity of the season have congealed in one time and place: The Lobos back line is shattered.

Antoine, back from his suspension, gets a goal before the half ends: 1–4. His celebration is muted. Yes, it's the first goal Kentucky has given up at home all season, but it doesn't mean much in light of the four scores that came before it.

The locker room at halftime is morbid. No one can remember being down this much, this quickly. A few players offer up a curse, but mostly, it's just quiet. The players spend most of their time gazing down at their cleats.

Fish doesn't yell. "You've got to reset right now," he starts. "You're going to find out what you're about." Then there's some practical advice: "If you can't connect a pass, kick it up ahead."

This is a shocking tactical place for New Mexico to land. Fish has always preached playing possession soccer—admiring programs like Akron, UCLA, and Wake Forest. He abhors "chunk and chase" soccer. But just in case the guys missed it, he repeats himself: "If in doubt, put it in behind them."

The second half is no better. Kentucky gets two more goals. The Wildcats are a powerful team running on all cylinders. Before too long, UK's coach empties his bench. The final score is New Mexico, 1; Kentucky, 6: 1–6. It is the worst loss in Fishbein's seventeen years at the University of New Mexico, and it's the most lopsided defeat in Conference USA during the 2018 season.

The Lobo coaches and players stumble into the locker room afterward. "I can't give you guys any advice on how to handle it," Fish says afterward. "Today it sucks." His talk peters out after just a couple of minutes. There's nothing to say. "At the end of the day, there's no tactics—that's four goals in twenty minutes," he says. "Let's not let ourselves off the hook."

With that, the Lobos shower and get back into their suits. The team is headed straight for the airport in order to fly back to Albuquerque. "Make sure this place is cleaned up," Fish says as he exits the locker room.

The Lobos appear somewhat shell-shocked as they process the loss. Mostly, it seems like a bad dream.

"The worst thing ever," says Grayson.

"We were just on our heels . . ." says Ford, searching.

Chapter 11

"I can't remember that ever happening," Tom says, referring to being down four goals so quickly.

"We were just terrible," Omar concludes.

Day 78. Tuesday, October 23, 2018.
Albuquerque, New Mexico

Fish has been working on a theory throughout the season. He's shared it in bits and pieces on a number of occasions. The theory pertains to what happens when a team faces adversity—or, more broadly, when an individual finds himself with his back against the wall. Today, however, in appearing for his regularly scheduled press conference, after a week of transfer-portal talk and the Kentucky debacle, Fish shares it more fully.

"We're all led to believe that when your back is against the wall, you're gonna fight, and it's gonna be the best season ever, and they are going to come together," he says. "But in reality . . ."

In reality, uncertainty undermines effectiveness.

In reality, life's full of enough unknowns, even when things are going well.

In reality, there just aren't many Hollywood endings.

"These things," Fish says of the year and the adversity, "they ripped our hearts out a little bit."

Losing to Kentucky 1–6 is an inconceivable result. It's the equivalent of losing by sixty points in a basketball game. It just doesn't happen. But given the Lobos' context, it almost makes sense. "Last week was a pretty interesting week leading up to the game," Fish tells the small group of reporters. "On October 15, the guys could register for this NCAA transfer portal, which is new this year . . . so last week was spent [fielding] calls on players and players looking to transfer." Fish guessed that only a couple of his players had *not* entered their names in the transfer portal. "Last week Kentucky was preparing all week for our game, and our guys were preparing to go somewhere else."

Fish has gotten sucked into the portal vortex as well. He's talked to plenty of coaches interested in his players. "It's kind of stinky," he says, searching. "They'll call you . . . 'Hey, how you doing, thinking about you . . . by the way, about that guy . . . does he want to transfer?'"[7]

The Backs-Against-the-Wall Effect

As Fish sees it, this is the effect of having one's back up against the wall. The true effect. It's stinky. It's distracting. It's tiring. It's unfair. It's unrelenting. And, usually, it's *not* going to work out with a miraculous win coming out the other side. Almost always, Fish points out, Disney is *not* going to come shopping around for the story of a backs-against-the-wall situation.

Day 82. Saturday, October 27, 2018.
Albuquerque, New Mexico

It's an hour and fifteen minutes before the final home game—ever—for the New Mexico men's soccer program, and Fish is working the vacuum cleaner. Upon entering the team's meeting room on game day, Fish discovered that a recent storm had caused a leak. This leak caused a tile to drop from the roof, creating a mess. And Fish won't have it: "I don't want this place to look like a shithole."

Within a few minutes, the project has consumed most of the coaching staff. Kelly and Champ join Fish in the cleanup effort. A ceiling tile is borrowed from another part of the building. A ladder is positioned, and the tile is changed out. Vacuuming ensues. When the players arrive a few minutes later, there is no evidence that their meeting room was ever out of order. The Lobo meeting room, lined with jerseys and built out over a decade and a half of success, looks as good as ever.

"You've got to play your nuts off today," Fish tells the team. "We send off the three seniors with a win tonight." Together, the team heads up the hill one more time.

The fact that the last men's soccer game at the University of New Mexico involves a conference foe from West Virginia (the Marshall Thundering Herd) somewhat explains why soccer is on the chopping block. The union makes little sense geographically.

But back when former AD Paul Krebs secured a position in the CUSA in 2012 for Fishbein and his dominant program, the talk was all about future opportunities. "We thought our league (the Mountain Pacific Sports Federation) was holding us back," Krebs said at the time.[8]

The last home game means it's senior night too. Matt Dorsey, Simon Spangenberg, and Antoine Vial will be recognized in a pregame ceremony. Given the situation, all the Lobos are basically seniors, of course, but special attention will be paid to the actual seniors. There's Simon, the computer science major from Belgium, who is interviewing for a position at Google this week. There's Dorsey, the fifth year from Houston, who came back for one more semester of soccer and to complete an MBA. And there's Antoine, the transfer from Division II Drury University, who will graduate with honors. These three will walk through the paces of senior night.

The logistics of ceremonial send-off fall on Champ. He makes sure that the requisite flowers and plaques are ready. And he provides the information for the program.

During the week ahead of the game, Fish wants to know the details.

"Is your girlfriend coming out on the field with you?" Fish asks Antoine at practice, in front of the team.

"I'm still thinking about it," Antoine says.

"You don't have to marry her. Or you could. We'll do it right there," Fish offers.

The senior ceremony goes off without a hitch—and with no wedding. There are hugs all around. The end of a college athletic career is a momentous event.

The backstory of the evening is not lost on Marshall. Thus, instead of lining up with Marshall on one side and New Mexico on the other for the national anthem, the Marshall players intersperse themselves with the Lobos. Arms go over shoulders in both directions. It's a show of support and solidarity. A horde of youth soccer players, always a fixture at Lobo games, joins in the mix.

When losing a program like New Mexico's, the entire soccer community shares a sense of grief and apprehension. For a nonrevenue sport like soccer, with Title IX still a work in progress at many universities, there is always the threat of cutting sports.

Remember:

In 1982 there were 146 DI men's wrestling programs. In 2023 there are 77.

The Backs-Against-the-Wall Effect

In 1982 there were 181 DI men's swimming and diving programs. In 2023 there are 131.

In 1982 there were 59 DI men's gymnastics programs. In 2023 there are 12.

In 1982 there were 20 DI men's skiing programs. In 2023 there are 11.

To be clear, the overall number of teams offered for men at the Division I level has increased significantly over the past forty years. But beyond football and basketball, every sport is vulnerable when cuts need to be made.[9]

The stands are full for the program's curtain call. The night is cool at game time, in the low sixties and falling. The Lobos are in all white. Fish is wearing cherry and silver, with an old-school, slightly misshapen Lobo hat. The Sandia Mountains fade to pink and then out of sight as the lights take over.

Feeding off the energy of the largest crowd since opening night, the Lobos come out firing. They create several early chances. Less than thirty minutes in—at which point, in their last game, they had been down by four goals—Scotty pokes away a ball from Marshall in their half. Dorsey centers it to Taylor, who fires a left-footed rocket into the top right corner. Goal: 1–0!

Three minutes later, Dorsey breaks into the clear and, with Marshall's goalie charging, slips a soft grounder into the net: 2–0.

The Lobos are looking good as they enter the hurdles shed for halftime. Dorsey gets in first, and taking no chances, he raises the garage door a bit. Even still, up 2–0, Fish is amped. "Can we bring the intensity for the first ten minutes?" Fish yells. "That's my biggest thing."

Again, the Lobos cannot.

Marshall comes out strong and scores a quick goal five minutes into the second half: 2–1. This, however, seems to wake the Lobos up. As the half wears on, they generate good chance after good chance. With five minutes left, New Mexico begins to stall. Several times, Taylor dribbles the ball into the corner and shields it from Marshall, letting precious seconds tick off the clock.

Chapter 11

But then it happens. Again.

With a minute left, there's a Lobo foul just outside the box. Marshall lines up for a penalty kick. After watching his teammates jostle for position for a few seconds, Marshall's Collin Mocyunas takes matters into his own hands. He lofts a bending ball over UNM's wall and just past a diving Ford's fingertips. Goal. The game is tied: 2–2.

A collective groan is punched out of the crowd.

The game moves to overtime. This first period expires, then a second. Neither side can generate much in the way of offense. Thus, the game is recorded as a tie. It is the first of the Lobos' season and the forty-first of Fish's UNM career. It secures the Lobos' spot in the CUSA Conference tournament.

But never has a tie felt more like a loss. The Lobos had controlled the game from the start, only to give it up just as the contest expired.

Despite the less-than-perfect outcome, the scene at the rail is crowded. Players hug their various spectators. The crowd lingers in the finality of the moment. As always, the players seem to take the loss with less tumult than the coaches. The guys make plans with their loved ones and greet the dozens of youth players who cluster around them.

Fish, on the other hand, doesn't want to talk. He shoes people away—"Thanks for coming, thanks for coming"—without really making eye contact. "Unbelievable," Mike mutters as he leaves the field.

Chapter 12

Is This Purgatory? No, It's Charlotte

Day 87. Thursday, November 1, 2018.
Albuquerque, New Mexico
The team gathers on the practice field at 7:30 a.m. The sun is barely awake. Frost covers the grass. It's thirty-seven degrees. When Joe, the trainer, tries to kick a ball back toward the action, he strikes a veritable rock. "Holy crap," he says, shaking his foot. After the ups and downs of senior night on Saturday, the Lobos have spent the week readying themselves for one final push. After a rest day and then a recovery day, the team returned to practice in earnest on Tuesday.

Despite the strange circumstances, the coaches still harp on the small stuff. Sometimes. To start the week's first practice, Champ reads off a long list of items missing from the players' game-day bins—a literal laundry list of mistakes. Almost everyone is missing something: a sock, a warm-up, something. "Fix it," Champ tells the players.

But herein has been the unsolvable riddle for the coaches this season. How do you maintain a culture when everyone knows the end is in sight? How do you demand excellence in a screwed-up situation?

Or, as one coach puts it, how much can we hammer the guys on the little things when they'll all be gone next year?

So while the team has generally held it together, there have been more compromises and screwups than in past years. "It was the hardest season not only because we got cut but . . . because it was the most off-the-field bullshit I've ever been a part of," says one assistant coach. There was a night when the players went out drinking after Fish had called for an early curfew. In Tulsa several guys snuck out of the team hotel to meet up with some coeds. On a more granular level, more players have showed up late for things during this season than, perhaps, during all the rest of Fish's tenure. Even more dire, several of the players, especially later in the semester, have lost their focus in the classroom as well.

Calibrating the proper response, which would have been absolute and without question in previous years, to such slipups has flummoxed the coaches. In hindsight, they have doubts. "We didn't handle it right," Champ says. "You know, there's kind of two ways to get respect from players. Either they really like you, and people will do crazy things for people that they like and . . . believe in and want to work for. Or if you're an absolute hard ass and you crack down and you lay down the law, people will just do it because if they don't do it, they're out." With all the stresses of being a dead-man-walking team, the likeability approach was a pipe dream. And of the latter, Champ says, "We weren't hard asses."

"I think as a staff," says Kelly, "we were a little soft at times because we didn't know how to deal with this." Certainly, no one provided a handbook.

Additionally, Fish's focus on saving the program has been, in many ways, a constant blaring distraction. He's been playing the political game all along. "[The] number one priority is that there's a soccer program," Fish says.

Kelly had realized it would be this way from the start. On the day the program cuts were first announced in July 2018, Kelly came face-to-face with Fish's priorities.

"We just spent all day at camp. It's like 4:30. I'm sweating, caked in sunscreen, and I go to Fish's office. He's like, 'Yep, that's it, we're cut,'" Kelly recalls. "Fish said, day one, 'I don't care about the season. If we can save the program to be here in '19, I'm fine with that.'" There was some hyperbole here, and Fish always wants to win, but it set the tone for the season.

Now the much-anticipated election is now just a few days away. Fish is holding out hope that Santa Fe will deliver much more than just rhetoric in support of his program.

All that's left of the 2018 season is Charlotte. The Lobos are scheduled to leave for Charlotte today at 12:20 p.m. The team will play its last CUSA regular-season game against the Charlotte 49ers, on Saturday, November 3. Then the team will remain in the Queen City, at the University Hilton, for three days before beginning to play in the CUSA tournament, which Charlotte is hosting this year.

"Hopefully, we'll be gone for ten days," Fish tells the team.

On this departure morning, the team practices at the UNM practice facility, probably for the last time. "Thinking back to August days—hot," Fish says, wrapping things up. "Now it's freezing. This is the beauty of our game."

With that, the guys gather up the balls (the team has made it through the last practice with all forty) and push back the goals. They make the walk down the hill.

Day 89. Saturday, November 3, 2018.
Charlotte, North Carolina

It is damp and cool, just about what you'd expect for a November evening in North Carolina. The players are told the pregame meeting in the Charlotte stadium locker room will begin at 6:00 p.m. As always, Fish can't wait to get things started. By 5:58, he is well into his talk. On time is late in Lobo land. "Not once this season have we waited until 6:00 p.m.," Kelly says with a shake of his head and a grin.

Charlotte represents a stiff challenge for New Mexico. Coached in the style established by Jeremy Gunn, Charlotte has yet to give up a goal at home during the season. "They'll look to play a little bit, but usually, they serve it in," Mike tells the team. This direct approach, looked down upon by some soccer insiders, works in the college game.

Again, there's a bit of grass talk. "It's a big field," Fish reports. "It's over-seeded winter rye. The ball sits up." The guys nod blankly.

After debating it for the whole year, the coaches have finally altered the team's shape a bit. Instead of their usual 4–4–2 operative setup, the

Chapter 12

Lobos install a 4–5–1. Gallo is positioned in the middle to help absorb pressure. The Lobos will "play" less but be more protected as a unit.

The game plays out just as the coaches have predicted. When the ball goes into Charlotte's half of the field, it's usually one touch and then a boom out by the 49ers. Charlotte presses constantly. But the Lobos' new tactics limit the 49ers' chances. Charlotte gets lots of shots and possessions but has little effect. At half, the scoreboard reads 0–0, even if it doesn't feel like a tie. Charlotte has nine shots, while the Lobos have none.

But all the Lobos need is a chance or two.

It's more of the same in the second half. Finally, with two minutes left, the dam breaks. A Charlotte corner kick yields an opportunity. Omar tries to head the ball out of the box, but it falls to a waiting 49er. That 49er, Tommy Madden, scores his first goal of the season, deflecting the ball off a Lobo defender past Ford. It's the game winner.

"The game was perfect, exactly how we wanted to script it," says Kelly. "Except that we didn't score, and they scored in the eighty-eighth minute." The result is typical of this season. Fight, fight, fight . . . break just for a minute.

The postgame locker room is warm and pungent. And for the most part, the mood is stable. "You played your asses off," Fish says. "I'm proud of you." He repeats this last point twice more.

"I was on death's doorstep," Fish continues, "but watching you guys play tonight brought me back."

Having lost to Charlotte, the Lobos fall to the number seven seed in the CUSA Conference tournament. The Lobos' regular season record ends with four wins, eleven losses, and one tie. This record exists on a different planet than the Lobos' typical results. In fact, it's the first time the Lobos have finished the regular season with a losing record since 2003, Fish's second season.

Since travel back to Albuquerque is impractical, the Lobos settle in. As midnight approaches, the four coaches sit in the hotel lobby. Their collective attitude is a strange brew of dejection and bemusement. What more can this season bring? "Can you believe all these close losses?" Mike asks. They start planning how to use the next three days.

By the time they play their next match, the team will have stayed six consecutive nights at the business-park Hilton. It's a soccer purgatory of sorts, complete with complimentary breakfasts and afternoon practices on the Charlotte University fields.

Sunday will be a recovery day, a Sabbath for the players as they get their minds and legs right for what's ahead.

Day 91. Monday, November 5, 2018.
Charlotte, North Carolina

The days starts with a team breakfast at 9:30 a.m. and then practice at noon.

Fish spends much of the morning on the phone. He back-channels with Patty Lundstrom, the powerful chair of the New Mexico House of Representatives Appropriations and Finance Committee, and then touches base with a well-placed supporter in UNM's administration. Rumors are flying. "I can't think straight," Fish confesses. "What a mess."

The weather in Charlotte is cool and drizzly. The last of the leaves are blowing off the trees on Charlotte's wooded campus. With nowhere else to go and the hours counting down on their season (unless something changes dramatically), the Lobos practice long and hard. The guys are clearly thrilled to be out of the hotel.

As the team runs its three-team possession drill, the guys compete as vigilantly as ever. And as usual, they argue about the rules and score. Barreiro, who is turning twenty today, wants to change the end score at one point. "Hey, can we play to 5?" he asks. Kelly is incredulous. "We're not even keeping score yet," he responds.

As practice winds down, the team takes penalty kicks. In college soccer, it's often the penalty kicks that decide who moves on in the postseason. The Lobos each take their tries. Those who aren't shooting take to launching balls toward a trash can that's forty yards away. Finally, after several dozen tries, Tom dunks one. His celebration is as wild as anything anyone has seen from him all year.

Since it's Barreiro's birthday, the final act in practice is to assemble a spanking line. As Barreiro crawls through his teammate's legs as fast as possible, each Lobo lands a prodigious whack on the birthday boy's backside.

"Why do you guys love this so much?" Fish asks with a shake of the head. "It's weird."

Day 92. Tuesday, November 6, 2018.
Charlotte, North Carolina

By Tuesday the other CUSA teams have arrived at the Hilton. Breakfast is a sea of colors: blue for ODU, green for Marshall, and gold for Florida International University (FIU). The omelet bar is five deep with hungry soccer players. The players mix and mingle. "Fish is going to be pissed," Mike says. Fish prefers a decidedly old-school approach: Civility and decorum, of course, but one shouldn't fraternize with the enemy. Gen Z seems to see things differently.

The scout for tomorrow's game takes the usual form. Mike talks through the opposing team's personnel, sprinkling in anecdotes to keep it interesting. Of Old Dominion's number eleven, for example, Mike notes that he's "a great mover" and that, as a twenty-four-year-old German, "he's been around the block a bit." Next, Mike covers the shape of the opposing attack. Then Kelly handles set pieces. Video is interspersed throughout. As always, Mike asks if there are questions, which there rarely are. This scout feels somewhat more pressing because, with this game against this opponent, the Lobos face the possible end of their season for the first time this season.

Tuesday's practices on Charlotte's campus are monitored by CUSA officials. Each team gets fifty-five minutes. As the Lobos enter at 1:00 p.m., FIU exits.

Only Simon is absent. He's in the middle of a three-hour interview with Google. Recently named to the CUSA All-Academic Team (again), Simon has a 4.2 GPA and is double majoring in computer science and applied mathematics. As usual, he's in a different headspace than the rest of the team. After all, he came to UNM *because* he viewed his high-level soccer career as nearly over. When he didn't get a professional contract after giving it a few years in Europe, he shifted his attention to college. "College soccer [for me] was seen as such a perfect fit because it would be kind of a step to slowly discover something else." Thus, Simon plays soccer with a looseness that is enviable. "Soccer is not my uttermost priority," he says.

For Joe, the team's trainer, the end of the season has come with a bit of progress as well. While it probably won't get Google's attention, the Texan's prowess at kicking a soccer ball has improved noticeably. "Gravity is my nemesis," he admits. But during Tuesday's practice, he launches several balls back toward the playing field with accuracy and, well, height.

The chatter at what may be the team's final practice is similar to what's gone on all year long.

"You got time, bro."

"Yeah Tom, again."

"Good hit Omar."

"Mikey, back side."

"Antoine. Back post!"

"Love it, Puig."

This is soccer's symphony. And the Lobos enjoy this practice before the do-or-die game on a swampy field in Charlotte as much as any they've had this season.

Everyone has done their part. Kelly has been in the hotel's fitness room every day since the team arrived in North Carolina. "If we win tomorrow," he says, "it's because of me and my kicking some ass on the treadmill."

After three days at the Hilton, everyone is feeling stir-crazy. In the lobby, Barreiro asks, "Can we at least go to the mall or something?" But no one else is interested. Instead, the team walks across the corporate park, around a concrete-edged pond, for dinner. Lucas has found a pasta and protein place that meets all the requirements: It's pretty close, pretty good, and pretty cheap.

Day 92. Tuesday, November 6, 2018.
Albuquerque, New Mexico

At 10:00 p.m. Michelle Lujan Grisham emerges in front of a packed ballroom at the Hotel Albuquerque. She wears a Democrat-blue suit, a

CHAPTER 12

Zia pin on her lapel, and an Apple watch. The fifty-nine-year-old native of Los Alamos has just been declared the winner of New Mexico's gubernatorial election. The tally wasn't close, with Lujan Grisham winning 56 percent of the vote over Republican Steve Pearce's 43 percent. "Michelle's the One," reads the headline in the *Santa Fe New Mexican*.[1]

Democrats win across the board in New Mexico. After eight years under the leadership of Republican Governor Susana Martinez, the state is taking a hard-left turn. Not only will Lujan Grisham take the governor's mansion, but the Democrats will also control both the state senate and legislature.

"Gone are the days where anyone talks about New Mexico not being in first place," Lujan Grisham leads off her victory speech. "Gone!" What proceeds next is a mishmash of words from the victor. Her team can't seem to get the teleprompter working. And when they do, it's clear that Lujan Grisham had already covered her key points. "I already did this . . . I did this. I did this from memory," she mumbles at one point.[2] Finally, she wraps up.

"Let's get to work!" she concludes. U2 comes on as the crowd applauds.

The governor-elect undoubtedly has plenty on her mind. But for Fish and soccer's loyal supporters, Lujan Grisham's victory represents a turning point. In August, Lujan Grisham, filming a message with Albuquerque Mayor Tim Keller, urged UNM to reconsider its soccer decision. In September she doubled down, promising in a debate to reinstate the cut sports if elected. Then she followed up with a statement to the *Journal*—"Absolutely!"—when asked to confirm if she truly planned to intervene in Lobo athletics. Lujan Grisham, who has also pledged to radically remake the UNM Board of Regents, is a key part of Fish's long-term strategy.[3]

Of course, direct gubernatorial intervention in college athletics is not unprecedented—not nationally and certainly not in New Mexico. It was Louisiana Governor Huey Long, during the Great Depression, who intervened directly to fund LSU football and write the school's fight song, "Touchdown for LSU." Similarly, various governors of Alabama stepped in to ensure that the University of Alabama and Auburn University played each other annually. Alabama governors also, for years, required that Alabama and Auburn play some games in Birmingham's aging Legion Field.⁴

In New Mexico the political interventions have been frequent and varied. Daniel Libit, during his *NMFishbowl* heyday, had plenty to say on this topic. The former political reporter spent some ten thousand words on what he called "The Petty Politics of Loboland." In the piece, he detailed how Governors Gary Johnson, Bill Richardson, and Susan Martinez each directed funds to the Lobos and shaped coaching searches during their tenures.⁵

Bill Richardson, New Mexico's governor from 2000 to 2008, bought into Fish's vision for soccer excellence. Richardson directed more than a million dollars to the UNM's soccer program for a new soccer facility. "We have to upgrade our facilities and create the atmosphere for UNM to continue to excel," Richardson said shortly after Fishbein's Lobos advanced to the NCAA championship game.⁶

Over the years, Fish developed a blueprint for effective politicking in New Mexico. On this topic, Fish keeps his cards close to the vest. It takes a bit of probing to gain some insight to Fish's strategy.

"We raised a lot of money," Fish says of the early days.

"How do you raise money for soccer in a state like New Mexico?" I ask.

"You make yourself really an important part of the community and you meet the right people," Fish replies.

"Like who?"

"The legislature . . . and then the governor."

"Which governor?" I probe.

"Richardson. . . . After the first final four, we got a big chunk of money from the governor."

"How do you go from being a soccer coach to meeting with the governor?"

"Make a lot of phone calls and be real persistent. . . . Go find out where he's going to be, and yeah, you gotta be pretty tactful."

"And now?"

"It still works that way."

As of November 6, 2018, Fish appears to have a vocal soccer supporter in the governor-elect of New Mexico. As he says, "You gotta be pretty tactful."

Day 93. Wednesday, November 7, 2018.
Charlotte, North Carolina

The New Mexico–Old Dominion game (starting at 4:30 p.m.) is the sandwich contest. FIU and Marshall play at 2:00 p.m. Charlotte and UAB will kick off at 7:00 p.m. Kentucky, as the top seed, has a bye into the second round.

The midafternoon start means the team has another day to kill. Unable to resist, the coaches hold one final scout at noon. The guys have now heard the ODU information multiple times. Regardless of how things turn out, the guys know what they are supposed to do against this opponent.

Finally, it's time to leave for the field, and the minivans depart.

The New Mexico team gathers in a track-side tent at 3:50 p.m. Fish closes the flaps tight for privacy. "Can you bring the energy from minute one?" he asks. "It's a fresh start. Play for each other. Get the energy right to start," Fish continues.

The Lobos take the field in their New Mexico turquoise shorts and shirts. They wear red socks. Ford is in all black. The stands are practically empty, which seems about right, given that the two teams on this North Carolina pitch are from New Mexico and Virginia and it's a Wednesday afternoon.

The whole complex is eerily quiet. UNM will record attendance for the game as zero (which, given that Kelly's mother, Dorsey's parents, and I were there, seems harsh).

The Monarchs take charge right from the start, forcing Ford to make his first save two minutes into the contest. ODU maintains a constant forward pressure.

Given the sparse crowd, much of what's said on the field reverberates up the bleachers. When one of the referees pulls Puig aside for a talking-to, Bailey's objection to the interaction is heard by everyone.

"It's not about you, ref," Bailey yells.

"Well, it's not about him either," the referee gives right back.

The Lobos' defense is vulnerable, but it doesn't break. Time after time, Tom pushes the action away from the goal and back up the sidelines. Unfortunately for the Lobos, the ball rarely goes very deep into the ODU half. As halftime approaches, the Lobos have generated just two shots on goal, neither requiring much effort from ODU's keeper to save. Still, the bend-but-don't-break strategy gives the Lobos time to make some chances of their own.

The first half ends 0–0. Ford has five saves. With the temperature dropping quickly, Kelly works to keep the guys loose.

The second half is a repeat of the first one. ODU creates all the chances, and the Lobos remain on their heels. Five minutes into the second period, Antoine goes down. He lets out a scream. An ODU player immediately plays the ball out of bounds to give the Lobos a minute. The stadium, if possible, becomes even more quiet. After several minutes on the field, Antoine is helped to the sidelines with a pulled hamstring.

Even with Antoine sidelined, the Lobos' energy is good. "It'll click. . . . This could be the fairytale ending everybody's been waiting for," Kelly thinks.

Then, just like that, ODU figures out how to convert all these chances into actual goals. At 54:52, ODU's Niko Klosterhalfen, near midfield, with his back to the Lobos' goal, delivers a through ball to a streaking teammate. Billy and Barreiro can't recover. It's a goal for ODU: 0–1.

Less than a minute later, the Monarchs strike again. "That was fast," the ODU Twitter feed reports. The Monarchs lead 0–2.[7]

For a team that entered the season with its back against the wall, the time has come to finally rise up and use all of these adversities and challenges to find some sort of greatness deep within their soccer-playing cores.

But this isn't Hollywood.

Down by two goals with the clock winding down on a disappointing season, the Lobos grasp for anything.

"Come on, boys!" Grayson yells from the bench.

"Let's get one, come on!" screams Kelly.

Chapter 12

Antoine works with Joe to see if his taped leg will allow for a few more minutes of college soccer.

With fifteen minutes left in the game, the Monarchs score again. A Lobos defender errs badly on a cross not more than five feet in front of his goal, tapping the ball to a waiting attacker who fires a point-blank shot. Ford blocks it but can't get to the rebound. Another nearby Monarch finishes it off: 0–3.

With ten minutes left, ODU has twenty-six shots to UNM's four. Ford has ten saves. With the final minutes winding down, Dorsey, the fifth-year senior, subs back in.

On a breakaway, the Monarchs score one more: 0–4.

Then, finally, mercifully, the game ends.

And so the season, finally, mercifully, ends.

On paper at least, it appears that the Lobos closed their season with a whimper. A blowout loss in the first round of the conference tournament.

Only twice during the first sixteen years of Fish's reign at UNM has his team lost by four goals or more. Now, with the ODU loss added to those against Kentucky and UAB, it's happened three times in a little more than a month.

But given the swirls and the tumult, this blowout loss feels different. There was effort and intent, and now, there's a bit of peace. Kelly, Mike, Fish, and Champ all head out on the field as soon as the action is over. The coaches hug their players. The players hug each other. Handshakes and weary smiles abound. Antoine can barely move; Billy and Simon each take an arm and help the injured Frenchman toward the team van.

Once clear of the field, there are some tears. Gallo and Miguel, two freshmen who played major minutes and formed a close bond off the field, share a long hug. The team piles back into the minivans for the short ride to the Hilton.

Back at the hotel, the team gathers in a ballroom once again. It takes an hour to determine on which flights everyone will depart in the morning. As if trying to will something into happening, Kelly had made no plans to travel home after the first round of the tournament. Anthony, the freshman keeper, gets the first pick of flights because his sister is playing in the New Mexico state soccer tournament tomorrow.

With all the logistics sorted, there's no business left. No more practices or games for the players. There is no more recruiting or planning for the coaches—just an uncertain future.

With pizza boxes at his right and left and his flat-brimmed hat in his hands, Fish searches for the right words.

"I don't know what to say, " he starts, shifting in his seat. "I don't think another college team has been asked to deal with what we did." Then he apologizes for not keeping his word in terms of the promises he made when recruiting these guys—namely, to get them to graduation—and for his coaching during the season. It was not his best year, he says. His focus, he continues, had to be on saving the program first.

Some of the guys meet his gaze, others look anywhere else. Taylor and Ford twist their empty water bottles into knots.

Fish thanks the seniors. It's a strong trio. Matt is graduating in December. "On to the real world," Fish says. A job and marriage await him. "Probably have a kid by this time next year," Fish jokes. Antoine, too, will graduate in a few weeks. He is headed for grad school. "No real world yet," Fish jabs. As for Simon, he will do another semester at UNM, and then Fish says, "Probably has like six more years of school." As different as they are, each of the three played an important role this season. When they came to campus years ago, no one could have imagined how strangely their final season would play out. Fish thanks them again.

After fifteen minutes, things run out of steam. Fish asks that the players give him two more weeks before they make any final decisions to transfer. Hopefully, something will be worked out by then.

"Proud is a funny word," Fish finishes. "We didn't get the results, but I'm as proud of this group as any in my twenty-seven years."

CHAPTER 13

Saved by the Bill

DAY 163. WEDNESDAY, JANUARY 16, 2019.
LOVINGTON, NEW MEXICO
Up and down. Up and down. Up and down. The motion is steady and consistent. It betrays no strain or effort. Watch it long enough, and you'll come to doubt that there's much going on at all.

This is it? This is what's changing everything in New Mexico?

The setting is dusty. The nearby town of Lovington doesn't have much to offer regarding hospitality. Lea County, of which Lovington is the seat, is mostly scrub brush and desert, although it does have the distinction of making up both an eastern and northern border of Texas. Thus, it sits in the crook of West Texas's massive, backwards L.

Lea County has a population of about seventy thousand, although serious growth seems like it might just be on the way.

From a sports standpoint, Lea County is football country. Hobbs High School has a storied rivalry with Clovis High School. To the west, Carlsbad and Artesia High Schools take their annual gridiron grudge match equally seriously. Friday night lights means something here, in southeast New Mexico, that the residents of Albuquerque or Santa Fe don't really understand.

Politically, there may not be a more conservative place in the state of New Mexico than Lea County. Its residents vote Republican by heavy,

CHAPTER 13

heavy margins. In November's election, for example, Michelle Lujan Grisham picked up just 22 percent of the county's vote.

But above all else, it's about the up and down here, which is, on this and every day, the movement of an oil-pump jack. At the start of 2019, Lea County is home to fifty-five such rigs.

This particular one is surrounded by a cattle fence. It's all black but for some white lettering. At its base, the desert is piling up, fighting back against this hostile intrusion. Lea County's location, sitting squarely in the Permian Basin, makes all of this possible. With the fracking technology that came online a decade ago, New Mexico's side of the basin, known as the Delaware Basin, has boomed. At the start of 2019, Lea is the nation's third-highest oil-producing county. New Mexico, likewise, is the third-highest oil-producing state in the United States. And it has no. 2 North Dakota in its crosshairs.[1]

The *Albuquerque Journal* reports, "Southeastern New Mexico is riding a monster wave of oil production, with output flooding into an all-time record of 250 million barrels in 2018. The good-news gusher means more money for state government, which is already enjoying a record $1.2 billion surplus going into the new fiscal year."[2]

DAY 163. WEDNESDAY, JANUARY 16, 2019.
SANTA FE, NEW MEXICO

Because of what's going on in Lea County (and Eddy and a couple of others), the legislators in Santa Fe are all mulling over this question on this opening day of the annual sixty-day session (January 16–March 16): How many billions in "new money" will there be? This is the economic context as the New Mexico legislature opens its 2019 session today. Oil money is gushing into the state. Governor Lujan Grisham could not have asked for a better opening hand. House Appropriations and Finance Chairwoman Patty Lundstrom certainly knows that the state has more money than it rightly knows how to spend. And it's because of this bounty from the taxes and fees on oil and gas extraction that there's a real chance the legislators might spend state money on something like restoring UNM's soccer team.[3]

Day 171. Thursday, January 24, 2019.
Santa Fe, New Mexico

Chairwoman Patricia Lundstrom, the indefatigable politician from Gallup, introduces House Bill (HB) 320. The bill wastes few words, as it's barely two pages long. But what it lacks in length, it more than makes up for in powerful backers. At the top of the short bill are the names Patricia Lundstrom, Javier Martinez, Antonio Maestas, Sheryl Williams Stapleton, and Brian Egolf. It would be difficult to gather a group of five more powerful and connected New Mexico politicians on one piece of paper. Lundstrom is the chair of the House Appropriations and Finance Committee. Representatives Martinez, Maestas, and Stapleton are longtime legislators. Brian Egolf is the Speaker of the House. All are Democrats.

The bill is direct. It promises two things: increased oversight of the UNM Athletic Department and $2 million to reinstate men's soccer and the other cut sports.

This is it. *This is it!*

This is what Fish has been waiting for. It's what the other backers of the save-soccer cause have been hoping beyond hope would transpire. Lundstrom, seemingly agitated about this matter since she was cut off by Regent Doughty back in August, has delivered.

Not surprisingly, HB 320 attracts far more attention than most of the hundreds of bills being bantered about at the capital.

"Saved by the Bill," crows the *Daily Lobo* (UNM's student newspaper) shortly after Lundstrom announces the measure.[4]

"House Leaders Offer $2M to Save UNM Soccer," the *Albuquerque Journal* writes.[5]

Soccer America chimes in: "Fight to Save New Mexico Men's Soccer Team Gains Support from Legislature."[6]

Fish celebrates on Twitter. "The State of New Mexico loves and supports Lobo Soccer.... WE LOVE NEW MEXICO and love impacting the youth of our State. Looks like we have the money to RE-INSTATE LOBO SOCCER. LETS DO IT!"[7]

***

CHAPTER 13

HB 320 is the culmination of a political effort spearheaded by Fish over the past year. Don't miss what this soccer coach has done: He has orchestrated one of the most aggressive campaigns ever in support of a college athletics program.

Consider again the political theater that Fish managed to arrange on his team's behalf.

On July 24, 2018, Democrat politicians, led by Patty Lundstrom, held a press conference promising to reverse the cuts. Moe Maestas ended the events by saying, "There will be Division I Men's soccer in 2019."[8]

On August 8, 2018, Attorney General Hector Balderas ordered the Board of Regents to meet again. The official reason was the Open Meetings Act, but the technicality belied a deeper warning. The move forced the Regents, President Stokes, and Eddie Nuñez to hold a painful redo of the sports-cutting meeting.

On August 16, 2018, Albuquerque Mayor Tim Keller and Michelle Lujan Grisham, then the Democratic candidate for governor, ahead of the second Board of Regents meeting, filmed a Facebook statement of support for UNM soccer. "We are investing in soccer. . . . We're going to have soccer at Isotopes Park at the professional level, we should probably have it across the street at UNM stadium," Keller said. "We have to have it," Lujan Grisham agreed.[9]

On August 17, 2018, Keller doubled down. Standing with a collection of local politicians, Keller had a press conference titled "the Importance of UNM Lobo Men's Soccer." Keller made the case for, at the very least, postponing the decision.

On September 14, 2018, as the Lobos were mired in their losing-home stand, Michelle Lujan Grisham pledged directly to save soccer. "It's outrageous," she said in a gubernatorial forum hosted by the NAACP. "I will work immediately with the Legislature to provide whatever oversight and investment we need to immediately restore those programs."[10]

On October 2, 2018, Fish, working with the support staff of some of the politicians who had come out as pro-soccer, provided his own editorial to the *Journal*. "I applaud elected officials for standing up for what's right and committing to find common-sense solutions that New Mexicans can get behind," he wrote.[11]

On November 14, 2018, Brian Egolf, Speaker of the House, waited just one week after the election to declare his soccer plans. "Restoring the UNM Men's Soccer program is a priority for the House going into the legislative session," he told the press.[12]

The mayor of Albuquerque. The New Mexico attorney general. The Speaker of the House. The chairwoman of the House Appropriations and Finance Committee. The governor of the state of New Mexico. Suppose you were trying to change something in New Mexico. Can you think of a group of five individuals you'd rather have on your side? I doubt it.

Each of these leaders promised support for men's soccer leading up to the 2019 legislative session.

Day 175. Monday, January 28, 2019.
Santa Fe, New Mexico

Speaker Egolf, standing in the Santa Fe Roundhouse (so called because the Santa Fe capitol is, indeed, round), is barking into his cell phone. It's week three of the legislative session.

"You heard me. *Nothing* gets done until we fund the soccer team."

Egolf hangs up. He smiles at the bystanders watching his performance. The thing is, there was no one on the other side of the call. Instead, Egolf's bit of theater is a joke about the blowback he's already receiving for making soccer a legislative priority. Humor is probably as good a weapon as any in this fight.[13]

Today is "UNM Day" at the roundhouse. It's a chance for university administrators, faculty, and students to push their causes with New Mexico's legislators. The halls are jammed with cherry and silver. Fish has sent Nick Williams, Anthony, and Ford to make the case for soccer's survival. The three players shake hands and share their case like seasoned lobbyists. They give interviews to the press and visit as many legislators as possible. "I grew up wanting to be a Lobo," Ford tells anyone who will listen.[14]

The days leading up to this moment have been increasingly tense.

Following the announcement of HB 320, UNM officials immediately provided a clear response: "UNM has not initiated a request for funding to reinstate any discontinued sports offerings," Cinnamon Blair, UNM's spokeswoman, said. The response was curt and flat, not the typical thank-you that follows news of new funding sources provided by Santa Fe. It's basically Stokes saying, *Yeah, um . . . no,* to Lundstrom.[15]

Concerns from the press about meddling are increasing as well. While coverage of the men's soccer saga had been largely sympathetic to Fish and his team's cause since July, the possibility of doling out state funds seems to be hitting the public as a rubber-meets-the-road moment. Not everyone is comfortable with the Santa Fe legislators picking and choosing which university athletic programs should receive special funding.

Editorials are once again flying back and forth.

"Democrats meddle where they don't belong—the soccer field," writes a *Santa Fe New Mexican* columnist as HB 320 gained steam. "That's right. In a state filled with poverty, a collegiate soccer program is a priority for House Democrats. In a state where 1 in 4 kids doesn't finish high school, a few sports teams at UNM are a matter of importance for legislators."[16]

Increasingly, it appears that the legislators will need to thread a political needle. Yes, there had been easy political points to be won by speaking out about the injustice of cutting sports. "Save soccer!" had been a guaranteed applause line for the past eight months. Everyone knew this. But in early 2019, as the legislative session gets underway, the rhetoric is trickier. Defying the state's flagship university seems riskier. One can almost see it on the legislators' faces as they interact with UNM folks. *Perhaps Stokes and Nuñez actually knew what they were doing when they made those cuts?*

And there is another oddity added to the mix as well. It's difficult to bring it up without sounding judgmental, but here goes. New Mexico's legislators are a bunch of part-timers. They are not professionals. New Mexico has the nation's last remaining unpaid legislature. Thus, no one here is drawing a salary. What's more, state representatives do not even have permanent staff members for their offices.

As one group pushing to modernize the legislature says, "It's primarily wealthy or retired candidates who can afford to mount a campaign and have the time . . . and means to serve in an unpaid post." Dr. Mike Rocca, a political scientist at the University of New Mexico, points to the inherent "asymmetry" of the system. Armed with more time, more resources, and more knowledge, full-time lobbyists and bureaucrats often run over the elected officials.[17]

A fair number of lawyers view their service in Santa Fe as an outgrowth of their practice. Brian Egolf, Javier Martinez, and Moe Maestas all have JDs. Regardless of their day jobs and instead of drawing a salary (in New York, it would be $142,000; in Wisconsin, $55,141), New Mexico's senators and representatives are paid a fee of $163 per diem to cover expenses during the sixty-day session.

This creates a unique governing environment. It also creates a seasonal housing crunch in Santa Fe. "I've either stayed with friends or in a hotel, and it's just couch surfing a lot of times," says one rep from Las Cruces. These are the politicians working not only to decide what to do about UNM's athletic cuts but also, in 2018, on a $7 billion general-fund-spending bill. These are the "citizen legislators," as Lundstrom says, that greet the university's contingent on UNM day.[18]

Day 176. Tuesday, January 29, 2019.
Santa Fe, New Mexico

The Republicans are now an afterthought in New Mexico politics. Susana Martinez is gone, and the Democrats have comfortable margins in both chambers of government. Still, one Republican has figured out a way to break through in the soccer debate.

Mark Moores is introducing Senate Bill (SB) 409 today. It's a devilish piece of counterlegislation. Exactly why Moores, who played football for UNM and earned two degrees (a BS in political science and an MBA) at the university, is so perturbed about HB 320 is unclear.

Moores's bill-drafting process appears to have been simple. Apparently, Moores cut the text of HB 320 and pasted it into a new document. Then he worked his find and replace keys. Everywhere the text said the "University of New Mexico," Moore substituted the words with "New Mexico State." That's it. Hello, SB 409.

If Lundstrom and the Democrats want to give $2 million to Albuquerque to restore soccer, skiing, and beach volleyball, then Moores wants the same for Las Cruces. Call it a gift from an old Lobo to a future generation of New Mexico State University (NMSU) Aggies. The fact that the NMSU has never had these sports before is inconsequential. "I think it's inappropriate for the Legislature to micromanage, pontificate, pander and make a decision that the presidents and regents had to make, and jump into a decision for political reasons," Moores says.[19]

Even though Moores's bill has no chance of going anywhere, SB 409 wins the press war in New Mexico for a few days.

Day 186. Friday, February 8, 2019.
Albuquerque, New Mexico

As the legislative session heats up, a legal shot is fired across the bow. After investigating the case for more than a year, Hector Balderas and the Office of the Attorney General announces charges against former UNM AD Paul Krebs. Balderas files the criminal complaint today in the second judicial district courthouse in downtown Albuquerque. For Krebs—and for UNM's athletic department—the potential shoe has now dropped. The circle of doom has been closed. Contentious regents meetings, declining attendance at the Pit, and difficult budgets are one thing; the possibility of jail time is quite another.[20]

In the criminal complaint, the state essentially accuses Krebs of misusing public funds and then covering this up. At the center of it all is a donor golf trip to Scotland in 2015.

Here's the story the complaint lays out: Krebs wanted to offer UNM's wealthiest donors the opportunity to take part in a Lobo-infused golf trip to Scotland. Such trips, which carried a nearly $10,000 price tag per person, had been overwhelmingly successful at other athletic departments around the country. Therefore, UNM put down a $50,000 deposit with Anthony Travel and began making its invites. The problem was, however, that despite their initial promises, not enough of UNM's biggest donors ended up buying the packages. This left Krebs in a bind. And so as the trip approached, Krebs decided to invite along several longtime donors—gratis. After all, the department was already on the hook for the money. Thus, as Krebs would later explain, the thinking was that the resources spent on the trip would eventually yield significant donations from the invited individuals.[21]

The trip happened. Krebs; Craig Neal, the head basketball coach; and twenty-one others golfed at Scotland's famed Old Course and a handful of other championship links courses. The group stayed in luxury hotels and toured castles. It was, as Krebs said, a once-in-a-lifetime trip.

Nearly two years later, as the athletic department continued to struggle with its budget, the trip became a political nightmare. Larry Barker, a local evening news legend, picked up on the story. After two months of digging, Barker reported on May 2, 2017. "There's a dark secret behind that golfing holiday two years ago," Barker told his KRQE audience. From there a press frenzy ensued. Daniel Libit, using the Inspection of Public Records Act (IPRA), quickly obtained and posted Krebs's emails and phone records for the public to see. "Who Has Paul Krebs Been Calling?" headlined a *NMFishbowl* story.[22]

Krebs panicked. And, according to Libit, he found "the stupidest way to deal with the scrutiny."[23] To cover his tracks, Krebs deleted emails and texts. He instructed several of his subordinates to do the same. The indexes used to fund the free trips were strangely labeled to reflect a men's basketball tournament in Ireland. As this was transpiring, Krebs just so happened to be overseeing the *first* attempt at cutting sports to balance the athletic department budget. Skiing was on the spring 2017 chopping block.

Then came the closest thing to a Nixonian move in the entire mess. Krebs wrote a $25,000 check to cover what he now acknowledged was a past mistake. He wanted to make it right or make it go away—probably both. But instead of making this donation directly, Krebs had his check delivered to the UNM Foundation. The foundation was told it was receiving a check from an "anonymous donor" who wanted to help put the Scotland controversy behind the athletic department.

But, of course, it was Krebs. The fact that he later went back and requested a tax receipt made his trail even easier to follow.

Long after the fact, the Office of Attorney General, with most of the spade work done by Barker and Libit, eventually caught up. The complaint now filed charges Krebs with fraud, making a false public voucher,

CHAPTER 13

tampering with evidence, money laundering, and criminal solicitation. If found guilty of all charges, Krebs faces more than a decade in jail.

The legal charges dominate headlines in New Mexico. National outlets pick up the story as well. As for Daniel Libit, he lists the story under the "Crime and Punishment" section of *NMFishbowl*.[24]

DAY 187. SATURDAY, FEBRUARY 9, 2018.
SANTA FE, NEW MEXICO

Room 307 at the state capitol is the venue for a final showdown between Chairwoman Patty Lundstrom and President Garnett Stokes. It really boils down to these two at this point. Fish and Eddie are just secondary actors. Lundstrom has offered up HB 320. The president's office has politely but firmly rejected the money.

On this Saturday morning, Chairwoman Lundstrom is flanked by the majority of the House Appropriations and Finance Committee. Representatives Javier Martinez and Moe Maestas are present as well. Both have been leading the battle to reinstate soccer from the start.

President Stokes has her own posse. Eddie joins the president at the small testifiers' table. So, too, does Terry Babbitt, the president's chief of staff, and UNM CFO Nicole Dopson. None of UNM's Board of Regents have made the trip to Santa Fe for the hearing.

The room is a celebration of wood paneling, all of it honey in color.

Lundstrom has called this committee meeting for 8:30 a.m. on a Saturday. The agenda calls for a discussion of higher education athletics funding. The day and time are somewhat unusual, but not entirely, given the compressed schedule of the legislators. And Lundstrom picked Saturday for a reason. "The way the day is going to work," Lundstrom starts, "is we're going to be here until we hear everybody." The chairwoman is at the center of the half crescent dais. A state seal hangs just above her head. "The reason we scheduled this today is we wanted to give people an opportunity to speak," she says.[25]

To start, the committee hears a report from the staff of the Legislative Finance Committee. There are ten university athletic programs in the state of New Mexico. The state provides a direct appropriation of $13.7 million annually toward these sports programs, with the bulk of this funding going to the state's two NCAA Division I schools, NMSU and UNM.

The committee then hears from the smaller schools: New Mexico Highlands University, Western New Mexico University, Eastern New Mexico University, and so forth. These schools have their own needs. For example, Highlands currently hopes to hire a full-time bus driver for its teams during these flush times.

New Mexico State goes next. Mario Moccia, the athletic director, reports that the school has the minimum number of NCAA-mandated sports, sixteen. Moccia further reports that NMSU has its Title IX house in order. Female athletes make up 53 percent of NMSU's athletes. This mirrors the school's student body as a whole. *Take that, Lobos.*

UNM goes last.

President Stokes opens with a statement. It's been less than a year since Stokes took over at UNM. "Athletics has loomed pretty large," she says.

Over the next sixteen minutes, Stokes again lays out the case for why UNM must cut sports: the budget, Title IX, the connection to the Mountain West Conference, and the fact that the university simply has too many sports. She says that the choice really came down to soccer and baseball. One large men's team had to go. "We were going to be slammed for either choice," she says. The fact that soccer competed outside the Mountain West and that its schedule required so much travel carried the day, she summarizes.

"These are the choices we made," she says. "And there are very, very difficult choices."

Eddie follows. "As you've heard, we've had some challenges," he starts. He follows the same script. He struggles mightily with the formalities of the setting, stumbling repeatedly over addressing Madam Chairman over here and Representative So-and-So over there.

Finally, after more than twenty minutes, Lundstrom cuts in. She wants to know why the university is requesting $4.1 million in funding for athletics. This is $1.5 million more than it received last year. "Just so I'm clear," Lundstrom says. "Requesting $4.1 is for . . . that's for what?" Stokes and Eddie respond that it will go to student-athlete support services. They dance around the implied question. No, the extra money will not be used to restore men's soccer.

"Are you in compliance, right now, with Title IX?" Lundstrom asks.

"No, not now," Eddie responds. He's operating in a gray area here. While there has been no notification (from the NCAA or Department of Education) that the school is out of bounds, the athletics department is taking a newly strict approach to their compliance via Title IX prong 2. Unless it builds a beach volleyball facility ASAP, the department and its consultants have decided, the school is now out of compliance.

"We will be *in* compliance once these teams are no longer at the University of New Mexico," Eddie continues.

Lundstrom opens the discussion to other legislators: "Who has questions?"

The first flurry comes from Javier Martinez. What about football? Martinez brings up budgetary and scoreboard metrics. "Football seems to be losing on the field and financially," he says. Yet football has escaped the budget scalpel. "So, why are we punishing those student athletes who have actually succeeded?" Martinez asks.

"Our football program actually generates revenue for our athletic department," Stokes replies. This, too, is a relatively new interpretation from the athletic department.

Martinez ends his questioning with requests for the numbers: How much, his questions probe, does it cost exactly to run these programs? How much will be saved by cutting the soccer program? And when exactly did these programs start in the first place?

There is a shuffling of papers at the testifying table. Twelve seconds of awkward silence follow as the questions hang in the air.

Finally, the UNM group settles on a savings of $9,800 by cutting beach volleyball.

And what about the savings on the other sports? On the longevity of the programs? There's more shuffling and whispering.

Strangely, the UNM group cannot come up with the $605,630—or even a figure in the same ballpark. Nothing.

Eddie finally wades in, clearly rattled. "Uh, Rep . . . Uh . . . Excuse me, uh . . . Chair, uh . . . Madam Chair, Representative Martinez, I'll have to get you that as well. . . . I don't want to just throw out a number."

Martinez accepts the deferral graciously. He knows that the transference of information is secondary in today's proceedings. "I don't question your intent. Not at all," Martinez wraps up. "I do question the decisions that were made by *bad* administrators."

The Q and A goes on for the next hour. There are moments of high debate, as well as moments of petty triviality. "You're being really selfish in what you're doing here," says one agitated legislator. President Stokes brushes it off. She answers what she can. She lets alone what she can't. She's a seasoned defender of higher education. "We can't do everything that everyone wants from us," she says at one point.

Before opening the proceedings to the public for comments, Lundstrom gives the floor to Moe Maestas. He's not a member of this committee, but he's been along for this ride since the beginning. Maestas points out that the legislature is trying to forge a partnership, that there's a way forward for everyone. "If 320 passes," he says, "that's a commitment from this committee and this statehouse to UNM and Aggie athletics into the future." Presumably, Maestas meant *Lobo* athletics instead of Aggie athletics. This is the type of slip that so often infuriates New Mexico sports fans as they watch national coverage. To see it here, in this context, is a strange slap in the face.

Eventually, Lundstrom seizes control. She has already delayed a full-throated debate of HB 320. She promises that there will be a separate hearing on the bill.

"You're very emphatic, Dr. Stokes, when [you] talk about how painful this decision was, so I'm going to ask you point blank: 'Why did UNM refuse to work with me last July?' I'd like to understand why, when I went [to] your Board of Regents meeting and had the independent meetings with you to offer support, why UNM refused to work with me." Lundstrom looks out over her reading glasses. Her left hand is suspended in midair as the questions hang. "I am the appropriations chairman, for goodness sake! And if it's a resource issue, wouldn't I be the appropriate one to work with? If it's so painful?"

These questions, too, hang for a few seconds.

Stokes starts slowly. "Chair Lundstrom, last summer, I recognized that you wanted to help," Stokes says. "You and the others that did the press conference really wanted to help us," she continues. But the ask was simply too big. The stakes were too high.

Here, Stokes switches into a different gear. She's one politician talking to another. President Stokes has her own constituencies to worry about, she explains. And as she addresses Lundstrom's questions, she lays out her quandary. As a new president, Stokes had to make inroads throughout campus. She mentions the staff and the faculty and the behemoth across Lomas—the UNM Health Sciences Center. Athletics might have been noisy, but it was far from the most important group Stokes had to win over.

The amount of funding to prop up athletics was, Stokes explains, too great for a quick fix. This couldn't be a handshake, good-old-boys (even if the two charges were women) exchange. "I couldn't work this deal out with you," she says, "without truly alienating the people at our institution." This is the crux of the matter. The intervention by Lundstrom would have invalidated a university budget process involving dozens of people. These are people whose job is, well, to help construct the budget. As a new president, Stokes simply wouldn't burn those bridges.

Lundstrom remains unconvinced. When Stokes mentions cuts to academic funding at the university, Lundstrom wants specifics. "We'll have to get back to you with that information," the president says.

Things begin to peter out. Lundstrom mentions the criminal complaint against Paul Krebs filed on Friday. "This is a black eye, of course, for all of us," Lundstrom says with a touch of resignation.

In closing, Lundstrom stresses that she doesn't buy the idea that she should butt out. "I can tell you without question that as long as general fund money is appropriated, the New Mexico legislature will have oversight." Perhaps what's necessary is a constitutional amendment to make this oversight relationship clearer, Lundstrom says.

What's more, Lundstrom continues—she's on a roll again—she sees the August Board of Regents meeting that initially decided in favor of cuts as a sham: "I thought it was a weak attempt at trying to convince people of what you were already going to do."

Finally, there is no more runway left on which to land this plane. "We get the per diem of $161 per day to be here," Lundstrom says. "As long as I'm chairwoman, we will have oversight."

With that, she opens the floor for public comment. The ski lobby makes its case. Fish, who might well have created an entirely different environment in room 307, is not present. He's back in his hometown of Cincinnati, caring for his ailing mother. Greg Williams, accompanied by Nick Williams (sans his forty balls), makes soccer's case. Greg points out, with a lawyer's precision, that the new plan will *not* make UNM Title IX compliant, and he again raises the matter of the disputed savings calculations. While his points are razor sharp, it's unclear who the jury is at this point.

Day 221. Friday, March 15, 2019.
Santa Fe, New Mexico

Today is the Ides of March. I'm not sure what that means, but it feels worth pointing out.

In the statehouse the hour is late when the negotiating committee representing both chambers emerges. The group is led by Lundstrom, and it has finally agreed on a reconciliation of the competing state Senate and House budget bills. The group has finished its work just in time. The legislative session ends at noon tomorrow.

The *Santa Fe New Mexican* proclaims the compromise achieved by the committee with front-page coverage: "The New Mexico Senate and House of Representatives appeared to have an agreement on a $7 billion state budget late Friday after ironing out difference over pay for educators, funding for roads *and college athletics*."[26] There it is, one more time.

After the testy exchange between Lundstrom and Stokes on Saturday, February 9, Lundstrom moved on to a different tact. She, as well as her like-minded colleagues, took the spirit of HB 320 and inserted it directly in the House's General Appropriation Act, HB 2.

Buried on page 133 of the document, in the University of New Mexico appropriation section, is this text:

> *The general fund appropriation to the athletics department of the university of New Mexico* is contingent on *the reinstatement of national collegiate athletic association sports for the women's ski team, women's beach volleyball team, men's ski team and men's soccer team.*[27]

If the university wanted its athletics money, it would have to reinstate the sports. Period.

During the reconciliation process with the Senate today, however, the language changes dramatically. The new language reads as follows:

The general fund appropriation to the athletics department of the university of New Mexico may be used for *the reinstatement of the national collegiate athletic association sports women's ski team, women's beach volleyball team, men's ski team, and men's soccer team.*[28]

From "is contingent on" to "may be used for"—so few words but such a radical shift in meaning.

While the legislature ends up giving the UNM Athletics Department more funds than ever in the 2019 budget (not quite the $4.1 million it asked for, but still more), it does not provide the strings-attached $2 million that HB 320 had conjured up six weeks before.

Despite her promises on the stump, Lujan Grisham does not weigh in on the matter.

Not surprisingly, Fish does not accept this as politicians simply being politicians. He's not about to let them off the hook. "I'm never going to say, 'Oh well, they're politicians.' That's bullshit," he says. "Then they're not very good politicians. That's what I would say."

But that's it. *That's it.*

The season is over. The team has dispersed. And now the politicians have made their compromises.

Day 1. Friday, March 22, 2019.
Albuquerque, New Mexico

Despite all that has happened, it's not until I get a text from Fish a few days later that I realize it's finally done: "Hope all is good. Pretty rough days here. Would be great to catch up soon. Is it OK to list you as a reference for two coaching jobs? Thanks and talk soon."

Afterword

Everyone left.

College soccer players play soccer. Thus, University of New Mexico's pledge to honor the scholarships of the men's soccer team members through graduation held little appeal. News of the Lobos finding new positions and new schools slowly trickled out. Nick Taylor and Matt Puig did not return to Albuquerque for the spring 2019 semester. Taylor chose Southern Methodist University (SMU); Puig signed on with Creighton.

In January Mike accepted an assistant coach position with the New Mexico United of the USL. The expansion team played its games in front of league-leading crowds just across the street from where Mike had coached and played with the Lobos.

In March, Champ, who paid his bills while volunteering on Fish's staff by coaching a club team and working summer camps, took a full-time assistant position with the North Carolina State Wolfpack.

Those players who could turn professional did so. Scotty ("Mel Gibson") signed a professional contract back home in Scotland. Gallo signed with the USL League One Tucson FC.

Finding a good spot for everyone became the sole remaining mission for Fish and Kelly as the spring progressed. "That's all we did," Fish says. But if it was Fish's mission, as always, it was Kelly carrying out the details. "Kelly almost single-handedly made sure every single player was placed," Fish told the *Journal*. "I give him all the credit. He was unreal."[1]

All of the starters with remaining eligibility went to strong DI programs:

Afterword

Ford: University of California, Irvine
Bailey, Billy, and Nick Williams: UNLV
Grayson: UAB
Puig: Creighton University
Nick Taylor: SMU
Nick Barreiro: Grand Canyon University
Omar: California State University, Northridge
Tom: Akron University
Miguel: Northern Illinois University
Alex Fetterly: Virginia Commonwealth University

For those who redshirted or played only sparingly, the process was a bit more difficult. But most of them also found places to continue their soccer and educational journeys.[2]

Kelly, after finding everyone new schools and then taking a sabbatical of sorts to wander America's soccer landscape, resurfaced at the University of Dayton as an assistant coach.

Fish, of course, was the last one out the door. On his final day, June 29, 2019, the *Albuquerque Journal* showed up to mark the occasion. "Fishbein Closes the Door on UNM Career," read the headline. Accompanying the piece was a picture of Fish literally closing the door on his empty, cleaned-out office. It was done.[3]

What came next for the old ball coach?

For starters, he acquired a new wardrobe. After years of his daily garb dominated by cherry and silver, Fish made a fashion 180. "I never wear that stuff," he says. On one of his last days on UNM's payroll, Fish took a big garbage bag of his Lobo gear out to his car. On his way home, he stopped and gave it to a homeless man. "I'll never forget it," he says.

Beyond deciding what to wear, however, Fish's pathway forward was hardly a pathway at all. The first months were disorienting. "It was a complete daze," Fish says. "I just remember kind of trying to put a smile on my face."

Afterword

In the fall of 2019, he volunteered as an assistant coach for his daughter's high school team. That was, he says, "one of the greatest things ever." Wearing a green Albuquerque High hat perched atop his head, Fish roamed the field with a freedom he hadn't known in years. For once, around a soccer team, he wasn't in charge.[4]

The long-term mission, however, proved challenging to find. In 2019, Fish earned his commercial real estate license. But he never really had his heart in it. "It dawned on me pretty quickly that wasn't what I wanted to do," he says.

Next, he tried consulting. Some bit contracts with coaches and teams about leadership proved to be interesting but ultimately unsatisfying. When COVID-19 hit, Fish was already ready to look elsewhere. After all, at heart, he was a builder and a decider much more than a consultant.

Finally, something interesting opened up. Fish met—in the way he always managed to meet interesting people—a billionaire determined to build a world-class soccer training facility in India. Girish Mathrubootham, the cofounder of Freshworks software company, was willing to spend whatever it took to move the soccer needle in his home country. Upon their meeting, Fish and Girish immediately hit it off.

In February 2022 Fish moved to Chennai, India, to take the lead in developing FC Madras. "I'd say a similar project in the United States," Fish told the *Albuquerque Journal*, "would probably be close to 80 to 100 million. It's 20 acres, it's residential. It's got a school, business offices, a stick-lighted stadium, lighted practice fields, an indoor swimming pool."[5]

In total, Fish spent fifteen months in India. When he was done, the program was operational. The first classes of potential Indian soccer (called football, of course) stars had been selected and were off and running. The challenge had been an intense one. "Setting up a scouting plan for the whole country was quite a feat," Fish says of his responsibility to find the best young soccer players in a country of more than a billion people. The experience was also an intensely lonely one. Fish's wife remained in Albuquerque, working in the Albuquerque Public Schools system. His daughters had gone off to college. The isolation wasn't sustainable. Still, when he returned home to Albuquerque for good in April

Afterword

2023, Fish had reason to feel it had been worth the sacrifice, as he had once again been a part of building something meaningful. "We left it set up for incredible success," he says.[6]

Once back home, the same challenge reappeared. What was he to do next? "I guess I thought there would be more value associated [with] what I was a part of," he says of his India work. But the phone continued not to ring.

Fast forward to August 2024. It's now been nearly six years since UNM shuttered the Lobo men's soccer program. Sitting at the Michael Thomas coffee shop just a couple of miles from UNM's campus, Fish is clear about what made his Lobo role so special. "It was creating pathways," he says. That was the magic. Seeing a young man through to a college degree, to a career no one in his family could imagine, to a better sense of himself, or, yes, for a few, to professional soccer—that was what fueled Fish. That's what made the UNM soccer program so meaningful. That's what has made moving on so difficult.

"I've never gotten on track," Fish says, now fifty-eight, of his post-UNM life. "You wonder about it . . . you want to have confidence in yourself that something will come out, but there is another reality, man. . . . That might be it."

"That's a hard one to swallow. That that might be it in terms of your big job, finding something you're passionate about."

He sits in a trance for a minute. Silence. Stewing. Intensity. Fish is still Fish.

"I don't know. I hope," he says finally. "But man, it was, like, a perfect job in a community that you loved, to do something that you love each day."

***

As for the UNM Athletic Department, life returned to normal—sort of. State funding for the program grew steadily as the oil boom in New Mexico continued. In 2018, UNM received $2.6 million in state funding for athletics; in 2023, it received $6.7 million. Additionally, more money flowed from the main campus to the athletic department. What's more,

Eddie overhauled the athletic department's fundraising arm, the Lobo Club, to bring in record giving. Overall, the UNM Athletic Department increased its revenues from $42 million to $48 million.[7]

This did not bring an end to budgetary sleights of hand. These continued. In the midst of cutting sports in 2018, the annual debt obligation payments for the $60 million renovation of The Pit were quietly shifted from athletics to the main campus. The university promised to pay the $1.7 million annual payments moving forward.

Of the pesky $4.7 million accumulated deficit (the number had varied over the years depending on the particular accountant involved), which had driven the crisis to cut sports, New Mexico leaders simply made it disappear when no one was looking. It happened as the state was shut down during the COVID-19 crisis. The *Journal* caught it and offered the following muted report:

> *A little more than two years ago, two major tactics were used in response to persistent financial problems by University of New Mexico athletics: The department was placed on a decade-long repayment plan for its seven-figure deficit, and four sports were cut. The sports—men's soccer, women's beach volleyball, and men's and women's skiing—are long gone. But quietly over the spring and summer, university and state higher education officials agreed that athletics money won't be used to correct the books.*[8]

With New Mexico schools still shuttered amid some of the most extreme COVID-19 policies in the United States, few New Mexicans could muster much of a response, understandably. But—poof!—gone was the all-troubling deficit.

None of these measures really solved UNM's Title IX puzzle. From a financial perspective especially, the athletic department remains in jeopardy. While roster padding helped somewhat with proportionality compliance (UNM reported a duplicated head count of 109 female participants in indoor and outdoor track), the outlay of scholarship money has remained heavily skewed toward male athletes. In its 2023 report to the NCAA, UNM reported awarding roughly 60 percent of its athletic scholarship dollars to men. This 60/40 athletic scholarship ratio not only varies significantly from the school's participant proportion (49 percent of UNM student athletes are male; 51 percent are female), it also is nearly *the inverse* of the gender breakdown of students enrolled at UNM (males make up 42 percent of the total student population). Thus, Greg Williams's persistent refrain from 2018—*This doesn't actually fix Title IX problems*—still rings true. So far, no one has cared to bring it up again.[9]

As for Paul Krebs, the AD at the start of this tumultuous era, he won complete exoneration. "Scotland-gate" eventually ran out of steam. In the summer of 2023, a jury found Krebs not guilty on all criminal counts. The trial itself had all the makings of a sham. After charging Krebs in February 2019, amid local headlines and hoopla over the debate about UNM athletics and cutting men's soccer, Attorney General Balderas let the case linger. The charges were eventually reduced from six down to two.[10]

At trial Krebs's lawyer called just one witness in defense of his client: Paul Krebs. The prosecution called more than a dozen witnesses, most of whom seemed to help Krebs more than the state. On the last day of the four-day trial, the lead prosecutor could not get his PowerPoint to work for his closing argument. His apology—"Sorry, I seem to have a case of sticky buttons"—was a fitting end to the ordeal. The jury deliberated for just a few hours before clearing Krebs on all counts. A jury survey by the judge revealed that the decision was unanimous.

The outcome, like the trial itself, received national attention. Much of that attention came from the fact that Krebs's case was only the second in recent memory that an AD had been put on trial for alleged crimes committed on the job. Before Krebs's clumsy fundraising junket came under legal scrutiny, a much more serious issue had been at hand in Pennsylvania. The previous trial, in 2017, involved Tim Curley, the Penn State AD on watch when the Jerry Sandusky abuse tragedy had unfolded. Unlike Curley, Krebs won.

That the Krebs case went to trial at all seems to have been the prosecution's biggest mistake.

"This was not a good case," said one college athletics expert shortly after the not guilty verdict came. "This was not a story about a bad-acting athletic director who stole money from a public institution. This was a story and has always been a story about transparency or the lack of transparency."[11]

Who was the college athletic expert who said this? Daniel Libit.

Regardless, the toll for Krebs was crippling.

"A nightmare," he says of his six-year legal odyssey, a year after his acquittal. "Cost me in legal fees, *a lot* of money. Cost in reputational damage . . ." he trails off. There's not really a number here. Even more damaging has been the fact that throughout the process, Krebs's health declined precipitously. The stress was toxic. As his lawyers maneuvered in the court system, Krebs battled thyroid cancer. When I saw Krebs a year after his verdict, he had good energy, and the cancer was in remission, but he understandably looked worn down.

Krebs still lives in Albuquerque. He plays golf five days a week. While the courses in Albuquerque can't compare to those in Scotland, Krebs isn't complaining. His wife, Marjorie, continues to teach at the University of New Mexico. "I have worked hard not to be bitter," he says. "Life deals everybody blows. Everybody has shit in their lives. What I dealt with, other people have had to deal with a lot worse. You deal with it, and you move on. I still root for New Mexico."

If Krebs's trial in the summer of 2023 closed the door on a difficult period for the University of New Mexico and its athletic department, a couple of subsequent moves locked that door and turned the deadbolt.

Eddie Nuñez, who had presided over Lobo athletics for seven tumultuous years, finally did what everyone had always expected him to do. He left for a bigger job. He became the AD for the University of Houston, a Big 12 school, on August 21, 2024.

He got out just in time. In September 2024 five schools announced they were leaving the Mountain West Conference for the newly reconstituted Pac-12 Conference. New Mexico, seemingly caught flat-footed during this particular bout of realignment chaos, was not among them. Thus, the conference that had been such a key part of UNM's decision making as it considered cuts in 2018 was left crippled moving forward. Such is loyalty in college sports.

Afterword

***

The fall of 2018 was a blizzard of politics, meetings, promises, practices, games, and travel. I attended everything—or, at least, almost everything. On many days I found myself rushing from the soccer complex, still sweaty from pacing around at practice and chasing down balls in the glaring sun, to the main campus just in time for the class I was supposed to teach. Other days, things moved in the other direction; I would duck out of a curriculum meeting on main campus to get to a scout in the team room. The season was busy and invigorating. It sometimes overwhelmed me, but it never ceased to fascinate me.

Then everything stopped. A quiet emptiness replaced the cacophony Fish had worked so hard to create.

I sat down to write this book in the spring of 2019. Much of what you've read, especially the day-by-day accounts of the team, was composed then. As I wrote, I looked back over my notes and interviews. I looked through the hundreds of pictures I had taken. I watched film of the games. Everything was fresh. I could still feel the passions of the season. I could still hear Fish's voice. I could still smell the pungent halftime shed. I could see the players' faces. I still cringed at the low points and smiled with many of the good memories. The whole thing was all still alive.

However, I could not figure out the point of the story. What did it all mean? Was there some sort of lesson to be gleaned from the experience? Not all stories have points, of course. But still.

Obviously, the Lobos—and the politicians and leaders of New Mexico—eliminated any possibility of a feel-good resolution. The 2018 season was difficult. The team lost many more games than it won, some by embarrassingly lopsided scores. After the games stopped, the players dispersed to other colleges. The assistant coaches left for new jobs. Then, despite a flurry of bluster and bloviating, the politicians did nothing. Soccer remained cut, and Fish did not immediately make his next move.

Who would want to read that story?

No one, I presumed. Definitely no one, my agent confirmed. And so, I published a few stories on the season for *TopDrawer Soccer* and, essentially, put the manuscript in a drawer. What more could I do with this tale anyhow?

Several years passed. I went to work on other projects. But I could never quite quit the Lobos story entirely. I kept in touch with the key characters off and on. I cheered from afar and then closer when I could as the players had new successes. On a cold December night in 2023, for example, I watched from the stands in Louisville, Kentucky, as Mike warmed up his team (he's an assistant coach at Notre Dame now) at the NCAA College Cup. His work with the Irish reminded me of how he had put the Lobos through their pregame paces.

I also watched as the college athletic timeline got elongated by COVID-19. Amazingly, it wasn't until November 2023 that the final former Lobos played their last collegiate soccer games. Peter Chang, Maleik Howell, and Ben Shepherd, three of the redshirts of 2018, had stretched out their college careers as long as possible. They took advantage of new rights and opportunities for athletes. They wore out the transfer portal. Ben, for example, went from UNM (2018) to Regis (2019) to UMass (2020–2021) to Fordham (2022), then back to Regis (2023).

More broadly, I looked on with amazement as college athletics underwent several generations of change in just a few years. Since the Lobos' final season in 2018, name, image, and likeness (NIL) dollars began to flow directly to athletes. The transfer portal (as Ben demonstrated) led to unprecedented athlete movement. When the NCAA subsequently stripped away all requirements to sit out a year of competition after moving, even more players transferred. Conference realignment broke up century-old alliances. Scholarship and roster limits came under intense scrutiny. The House decision, still unfinalized at the time of this writing, made direct payment to athletes from universities a near certainty.

American soccer rumbled through change as well. The Development Academy system—long the plan to produce elite-level talent and the pathway by which many of the 2018 Lobos made it to New Mexico—was summarily dismantled in 2020. "It is with profound sadness," read the letter that went out on April 15, 2020, "that we have made the determination to end the operation of the US Soccer Development Academy, effective immediately."[12] The following day, April 16, Major League Soccer announced the formation of MLS Next, giving America's top professional league a larger role in youth development.

For college soccer, the body blows kept on coming. Conference USA (the conference in which the Lobos played) decided to stop sponsoring men's soccer following the 2021 season. As for the college game more broadly, the twenty-first-century model championed by Sasho Cirovski and others failed to gain traction. The NCAA tabled the proposal again, in 2022. While news of the USSF partnering with the Big Ten and ACC to pilot a year-round college soccer league surfaced in early 2025, substantial change remains elusive. Thus, the college season remains a condensed one, although changes to substitution and overtime rules have brought the game slightly more in line with international standards.[13]

It was finally at this juncture, with plenty of distance from the 2018 season itself, that I began to gain some new perspective.

Even if it wasn't simple or tidy, the Lobos' story mattered.

In 2018, Fishbein and his Lobos had been on the leading edge of a period of revolutionary change. What happened to this soccer team from the University of New Mexico was part of something much bigger. It was part of the struggle over funding and higher education, over teams and Title IX, and over athletes' rights and athletes' opportunities. It was part of a reckoning regarding how we pay for college sports. It was also part of a dark era for American men's soccer. Thus, in a way, the Lobos were just a casualty of these dynamics.

But that's not the whole of it. Strip away the system changes and flaws. Strip away the idiosyncratic debates about college athletics. Strip away questions about America as a soccer nation. All these years later, what's most clear to me is that the Lobo soccer team mattered to a group of people and a place. It changed the lives of many of the players and coaches who were a part of it. It served the state of New Mexico well. The program wasn't perfect—Jeremy Fishbein certainly wasn't perfect—but Lobo soccer fostered hope, belonging, and excellence in a place that has often struggled to see such virtues in itself. That mattered.

Afterword

Lastly, there was the struggle itself. Faced with losing his team, Fish, joined by a band of loyal soccer supporters, fought with everything he had to reverse the decision. Told by his bosses to go quietly into the night, Fish said no. Instead, he worked and scrapped. Fish confronted every adversary. He left no possible avenue of escape unexplored. He called in every favor. In many ways, the struggle for survival mirrored what had made the program successful for so many years: *Don't let yourself off the hook. Control the controllable. Play your nuts off.*

In the end, of course, the struggle to save Lobo soccer failed. But the fight was nonetheless inspiring.

That final season of 2018 was, I'd say, a beautiful shame.

Acknowledgments

This book would not exist were it not for Jeremy Fishbein's decision to give me unfettered access to his program during its terminal season. He let me in, even as he was going through the greatest crisis of his professional life. I thank you, Jeremy, for trusting me with that access. Likewise, Mike, Kelly, and Champ said yes when I asked. These three plucky men went so far out of their way to make me feel welcome during the 2018 season—and to share and explain their world—that it makes me misty-eyed to this day to recount their generosity and good humor. Thank you. Similarly, the Lobo players' willingness to let me tag along, sit in during team meetings, and take up a backseat in a minivan on road trips was beyond accommodating. They engaged with me and humored me far beyond what was required. Thank you, gentlemen! In sum, during this stressful period, the coaches and players of Lobo soccer gave me the gift of allowing me to observe their unfolding story. I hope I have done that story justice in this retelling.

To the dozens and dozens of people who agreed to interviews for this book—from those in the soccer universe, to President Stokes and members of the UNM Administration, to experts in the worlds of youth sports and college athletics—I give my sincere thanks. I learned so much from our conversations.

To those colleagues and friends and family members who read drafts as I wrote ("Wait, you're writing a book about college soccer?"), I appreciate your willingness to provide feedback. You saved me from many a pothole; those that I still hit are my fault alone.

My editor Christen Karniski deserves special mention. That she saw some potential in this work—a book about a disbanding team in a remote outpost that didn't end up winning much of anything—defies easy explanation. Perhaps it just took a former soccer player to see what I was after! Regardless, Christen, I thank you for this opportunity and your support.

Lastly, let me try one last time to properly thank my wife and kids for their support and thoughtfulness throughout this book project/midlife crisis. Who else would have been so understanding when their husband needed to travel to Tulsa and Birmingham for soccer games? Who else would put up with attending another game at the ol' UNM stadium while Dad takes notes and scurries off to the locker room during halftime? Who else could put up with so much discussion of lost soccer balls and athletic budgets at the dinner table? No one, I presume. To Carter, Tyler, and Kate, thank you! I am so proud of each of you. And I am grateful that while I'm supposed to be investing in and raising you all (at least, I think that is what a dad is supposed to be doing), you gave me the gift of engaging in a passion project of mine.

To my wife, Rachael, there are no words that are enough. Your support and your enthusiasm for this project have been unwavering. That we can talk at length about the accounting methods of athletic departments is the stuff of marital bliss. Truly. I hope you know that your support for me as a writer and as a man still trying to find his way serves as the cornerstone for everything I do. Thank you. I love you.

Notes

Prologue

1. Carly Bolwing, "New Mexico Population Projections: An Aging Population and Minimal Growth," *UNM Newsroom*, June 6, 2024, https://news.unm.edu/news/new-mexico-population-projections-an-aging-population-and-minimal-growth#:~:text=; New Mexico Economic Development Department, "Census Data, New Mexico Population," EDD, accessed June 2024, https://edd.newmexico.gov/site-selection/census-data/; UNM, "New Census Data Shows New Mexicans Are Getting Older," *UNM Newsroom*, May 25, 2023, https://news.unm.edu/news/new-census-data-shows-new-mexicans-are-getting-older.

2. Journal Editorial Board, "Editorial: NM Is Leading All Right, on the Lists of Bad Things," *Albuquerque Journal*, March 4, 2024, https://www.abqjournal.com/opinion/article_473dd786-d809-11ee-a4b6-17d1ee55393c.html.

3. Adam McCann, "Best States to Live In," Wallet Hub, published August 12, 2024, https://wallethub.com/edu/best-states-to-live-in/62617. There are too many of these lists/articles to share here. Plus, as a New Mexican, I object to the constant reporting on these lists. It's important to have clear-eyed information, yes. But not the self-flogging. So what follows is a sampling. Google away if you want more. Jayme Sileo, "Wages in New Mexico Flatline, Employment Sees Uptick," *Albuquerque Business Journal*, May 7, 2024; KRQE, "Study: New Mexico Ranked as Worst Place to Live," August 14, 2023, https://www.krqe.com/news/new-mexico/study-ranks-new-mexico-as-worst-state-to-live-in/; Justina Grant and Cayla Montoya-Manzo, "New Mexico Ranked Worst in Nation for Child Poverty," *New Mexico News Port*, December 5, 2017.

4. Unless otherwise identified, quotes in the prologue and throughout the book are from interviews with the author.

5. At the time of this writing, promises have been extended to ease the most troubling of these slights: the lack of an In-N-Out in New Mexico. I'll believe it when I finally order my first double-double in the Land of Enchantment. See Julie Littman, "In-N-Out to Open First New Mexico Restaurant in 2027," Restaurant Dive, published November 9, 2023, https://www.restaurantdive.com/news/in-n-out-expanding-new-mexico-2027/699352/.

Notes

6. Waste Isolation Pilot Plant, "The Nation's Only Deep Geologic Repository for Nuclear Waste," WIPP, accessed July 2024, https://www.wipp.energy.gov/.

7. Albuquerque International Balloon Fiesta, "FAQs," Balloon Fiesta, accessed August 2024, https://balloonfiesta.com/FAQs.

8. Leanna Teresa Martinez and Torres, "Manito: Examining and Deconstructing New Mexico's Tri-Cultural Myth," *New Mexico Humanities Council* (blog), May 30, 2021, https://newmexicohumanities.org/category/blog-pasa-por-aqui/tri-cultural-myth/.

9. V. B. Price, *A City at the End of the World* (University of New Mexico Press, 1992), xi.

10. Andy Lyman, "Meet the Man Peering into the UNM 'Fishbowl' 10,000 Words at a Time," *New Mexico Political Report*, March 13, 2017.

11. Daniel Libit, "The Capitol of Gay-Marriage Gridlock," *The New Republic*, April 1, 2013; Daniel Libit, "The Man Who Discovered Susana Martinez Could Also Be Her Downfall," *National Journal*, November 23, 2014.

12. This site has since been removed. I worked from a screenshot taken in 2023.

13. Marc Tracy, "The Blogger Who Became One University's Scold," *New York Times*, October 20, 2017.

14. Daniel Libit, "Did UNM Ever Really Believe in WisePies?" *NMFishbowl*, accessed November 2024, https://nmfishbowl.com/2016/11/18/did-unm-ever-really-believe-in-wisepies.

15. Charles Pierce, "How It Ends: The Last Gasp of Amateurism in an Oakland Courthouse," *Grantland*, June 20, 2014, https://grantland.com/features/ncaa-amateurism-lawsuit-mark-emmert/.

16. O'Bannon v. NCAA, No. 14-16601, 2015 WL 5712106 (9th Cir. 2015).

17. John Ruiz's LifeWallet company became an early leader in the NIL space, offering deals to most of the University of Miami's football and basketball players. As of 2024, that move has seemed unsustainable for LifeWallet. See Myron Medcalf, "'Substantial Doubt' Over Company of Miami Booster John Ruiz," *ESPN*, August 16, 2024, https://www.espn.com/college-sports/story/_/id/40884354/substantial-doubt-company-miami-booster-john-ruiz; J. Brady McCollough, *Los Angeles Times*, July 1, 2021, https://www.latimes.com/sports/story/2021-07-01/how-southern-california-helped-launch-ncaa-nil-revolution.

18. "NCAA v. Alston," *Harvard Law Review* 135, no. 1 (November 2023), https://harvardlawreview.org/print/vol-135/ncaa-v-alston/.

19. Michelle Brutlag Hosick, "New Transfer Rule Eliminates Permission-to-Contact Process," NCAA, published June 13, 2018, https://www.ncaa.org/news/2018/6/13/new-transfer-rule-eliminates-permission-to-contact-process.aspx.

20. GAO, "College Athletics: Education Should Improve Its Title IX Enforcement Efforts," U.S. Government Accountability Office, published April 9, 2024, https://www.gao.gov/products/gao-24-105994; Kenny Jacobs, Lindsay Schnell, Rachel Axon, Steve Berkowitz, Dan Wolken, and Nancy Armour, "College

Sports, Title IX, and the Dark Illusion of Gender Equity," *USA Today*, December 15, 2022.

21. Jeremy Bauer-Wolf, "A 'Retro' Title IX Lawsuit," *Inside Higher Ed*, June 26, 2018, https://www.insidehighered.com/news/2018/06/29/eastern-michigan-sued-sports-equity-title-ix-lawsuit .

CHAPTER 1

1. New Mexico Lobos, "Lobo Men's Soccer Facilities," posted August 25, 2015, 3 min., 28 sec., by Lobo Films, YouTube, https://www.youtube.com/watch?v=UDmY2ydPy3M.

2. Jessica Dyer and Geoff Grammer, "AG: UNM Vote to Cut Sports Unlawful," *Albuquerque Journal*, August 9, 2018.

3. Fort Lewis College, "Hall of Fame," Go Sky Hawks, accessed November 2024, https://goskyhawks.com/honors/hall-of-fame/jeremy-fishbein/32.

4. Go Lobos, "Jeremy Fishbein," University of New Mexico, accessed November 2024, https://golobos.com/coach/jeremy-fishbein/.

5. Matt Baker, "Timeline of Investigations, Suspensions and Allegations Involving Jameis Winston," *Tampa Bay Times*, June 21, 2018, https://www.tampabay.com/blogs/bucs/2018/06/21/timeline-of-investigations-suspensions-and-allegations-involving-jameis-winston/; Susana Svrluga, "U. Missouri President, Chancellor Resign Over Handling of Racial Incidents," *Washington Post*, November 9, 2015, https://www.washingtonpost.com/news/grade-point/wp/2015/11/09/missouris-student-government-calls-for-university-presidents-removal/.

6. It is not all that unusual for a university to have an athletic team (or teams) that competes outside of the school's primary athletic conference. Of New Mexico's Mountain West peers, for example, University of Nevada, Los Angeles (UNLV) competes in men's soccer in the WAC, San Diego State competes in women's water polo in the Golden Coast Conference, and Wyoming competes in men's wrestling in the Big 12, just to name a few.

7. Attempts to interview Patty Lundstrom for this book went unanswered.

8. Jay Mason, "Gallup and Soccer," *The Gallup Journey: The Free Community Magazine*, November 2013; Boderra Joe, "Sammy C's Hosts 'Lobo Meet and Greet' in Downtown Gallup," *Gallup Sun*, March 23, 2018, https://gallupsun.com/index.php?option=com_content&id=11308:sammy-cs-hosts-lobo-meet-a-greet-in-downtown-gallup&Itemid=606.

CHAPTER 2

1. These statistics come from the *UNM FY 2019 NCAA Report*. The participant ratio noted in the text is the unduplicated count. In terms of athletic scholarships (Athletic Aid Equivalencies, in NCAA parlance), 144 go to UNM male athletes and 102 to female athletes. See University of New Mexico, *UNM FY 2019 NCAA Report*

(NCAA Membership Financial Reporting System, 2019), https://athleticscontracts.unm.edu/ncaa-financial-reports/fy-19---ncaa-report.pdf.

2. Helen Grant Consulting, "University of New Mexico Title IX Assessment and Summary," in UNM, *Athletics Department Review Supporting Documents* (University of New Mexico, 2018), 163–203. https://president.unm.edu/documents/archived-documents/athletics/2018/athletics-department-review-supporting-documentation.pdf.

3. U.S. Department of Education, "Clarification of Intercollegiate Athletics Policy Guidance: The Three Part Test," January 16, 1996, https://www.ed.gov/laws-and-policy/higher-education-laws-and-policy/higher-education-policy/clarification-of-intercollegiate-athletics-policy-guidance-the-three-part-test.

4. U.S. Department of Education, "Clarification of Intercollegiate Athletics Policy Guidance."

5. U.S. Department of Education, "Clarification of Intercollegiate Athletics Policy Guidance."

6. Laura Simon, Shannon T. Dieringer, Elizabeth Wanless, Rebecca M. Tyner, and Lawrence W. Judge, "Title IX Proportionality Prong: Compliance of Division I FBS Universities," *The Journal of SPORT* 3, no. 2 (2014), 183–202, https://doi.org/10.21038/sprt.2014.0322.

7. There is a long, sordid history of program cuts being made under the guise of Title IX diligence. See Ellen J. Staurowsky, Kevin Murray, Matthew Puzio, and John Quagliariello, "Revisiting James Madison University: A Case Analysis of Program Restructuring Following So Called 'Title IX' Cuts," *Journal of Intercollegiate Sport* 6, no. 1 (2013): 6, 96–119, https://doi.org/10.1123/jis.6.1.96.

8. Gregory P. Williams to Sara Cliffe and Eddie Nuñez, August 22, 2018.

9. University of New Mexico, "Men's Soccer Pre-Season Presser," posted August 22, 2018, by UNM Lobos, YouTube, 22 min., 24 sec., https://www.youtube.com/watch?app=desktop&v=XTMaaBaaW7M.

10. Cameron Goeldner, "Men's Soccer: UNM Defeats Seattle 4–2 in Season Opener," *Daily Lobo*, August 26, 2018.

11. Nick Patterson, "Arlington Alum a 'Ruthless' Competitor for Seattle Men's Soccer," *HeraldNet*, August 13, 2018, https://www.heraldnet.com/sports/arlington-alum-a-ruthless-competitor-for-seattle-mens-soccer/.

12. Goeldner, "Men's Soccer: UNM Defeats Seattle."

13. Glen Rosales, "Fans Give Lobo Soccer a Feel-Good Moment, and Vice Versa," *Albuquerque Journal*, August 24, 2018.

CHAPTER 3

1. These statistics are from Project Play, "2023 National State of Play," Aspen Institute, accessed October 2024, https://projectplay.org/state-of-play-2023-introduction. While participation numbers can vary significantly, the Aspen Institute has emerged as a leader in analyzing youth sports. See also Project Play,

Notes

"Don't Retire Kid," Aspen Institute, accessed July 2024, https://projectplay.org/dont-retire-kid; WinterGreen Research, *Youth Team, League, and Tournament Market Shares, Strategies and Forecasts, Worldwide, 2022 to 2028* (WinterGreen Research, 2022).

2. Beau Dure, "How US Soccer Can Begin to Fix Its Broken Youth System," *FourFourTwo*, June 19, 2018.

3. Les Carpenter, "'It's Only Working for the White Kids': American Soccer's Diversity Problem," *The Guardian*, June 1, 2016.

4. Revenue figures from ProPublica Nonprofit Explorer, "Alexandria Soccer Inc. Association," ProPublica, accessed August 2024, https://projects.propublica.org/nonprofits/organizations/540902413.

5. Bill Pennington, "Expectations Lose to Reality of Sports Scholarships," *New York Times*, March 10, 2008, https://www.nytimes.com/2008/03/10/sports/10scholarships.html.

6. NCAA, *NCAA Sports Sponsorship and Participation Rates Report* (NCAA, 2023).

7. Richard Stevens, "Threat from the West," *Albuquerque Tribune*, July 18, 2002.

8. Richard Stevens, "Bandidos Make Mark for N.M. and Loyalty," *Albuquerque Tribune*, July 1, 2002.

9. Edgar Thompson, "Best Footwork Forward," *Albuquerque Tribune*, July 19, 2001.

10. Harold Smith, "A Final Run," *Albuquerque Journal*, June 21, 2001; Edgar Thompson, "Both Duke City Entrants at Youth Soccer Championships Settle for Third," *Albuquerque Journal*, July 28, 2001.

11. Jeff Rowland, "Hall of Honor 2018," YouTube, accessed August 2023, https://www.youtube.com/watch?v=s4IZdhs2s0M.

12. Strangely, the 2001 Lobos, with Fishbein as the associate head coach, went 7–12–2 and failed to win a single conference game. Yet they won the MSPF conference tournament, thereby advancing to the NCAA tournament for the first time in school history.

13. Glen Rosales, "Home-Bred and Chile-Fed," *Albuquerque Journal*, November 23, 2002.

14. Rosales, "Home-Bred and Chile-Fed."

15. 505 was, until 2007, the area code for the entire state of New Mexico; Glen Rosales, "Lack of Respect Stings the Lobos," *Albuquerque Journal*, November 16, 2004; Morgan Quitno, "Results of the 2004 Smartest State Award," Morgan Quitno Press, accessed November 2024, http://www.statestats.com/edpri04.htm.

16. Glen Rosales, "Lobos in Final Four," *Albuquerque Journal*, December 3, 2005.

17. Rowland, "Hall of Honor 2018."

18. Noah Seligman, "Huskies Too Strong for Lobos," *Albuquerque Journal*, August 28, 2018.

Chapter 4

1. University of New Mexico, "9-4-2018 Press Luncheon—Men's Soccer," posted September 4, 2018, by New Mexico Lobos, YouTube, 16 min., 11 sec., https://www.youtube.com/watch?v=OVQqxuiXPwI&t=48s.

Chapter 5

1. Taylor Branch, "The Shame of College Sports," *The Atlantic*, October 15, 2011.

2. Branch, "The Shame of College Sports." Branch's work joined a short list of articles and books that shifted public perceptions of college sports over the last thirty years. See Walter Byers, *Unsportsmanlike Conduct: Exploiting College Athletes* (University of Michigan Press, 1995); Andrew Schwarz and Daniel A. Rascher, "Neither Reasonable nor Necessary: 'Amateurism' in Big-Time College Sports," *Antitrust Magazine*, Spring 2000; Daniel Libit, "The Scandal Beat," *Columbia Journalism Review*, September 11, 2011; Jeff Benedict and Armen Keteyian, *The System: The Glory and Scandal of Big-Time College Football* (Anchor Books, 2013); Jay M. Smith and Mary Willingham, *Cheated: The UNC Scandal, the Education of Athletes, and the Future of Big-Time College Sports* (Potomac Books, 2015); Joe Nocera and Ben Strauss, *Indentured: The Inside Story of the Rebellion Against the NCAA* (Portfolio, 2016).

3. College Soccer News Staff, "Decision to Drop Men's Soccer Program at New Mexico Warrants Further Consideration," *College Soccer News*, July 23, 2018, https://www.collegesoccernews.com/index.php/articles/1176-decision-to-drop-men-s-soccer-program-at-new-mexico-warrants-further-consideration.

4. All coaches' survey quotes in this chapter are drawn from NCAA, *2016 Men's and Women's Soccer Rules Survey Report* (NCAA, 2017).

5. Megan Ryan, "As U.S. Sits Out Soccer World Cup, Poor Player Development Is Blamed," *Minnesota Star-Tribune*, June 11, 2018, https://www.startribune.com/as-u-s-sits-out-soccer-world-cup-poor-player-development-is-blamed/485052331.

6. Tisha Thompson, "Is College Soccer Too Much of a Risk for Rising U.S. Talent?," ESPN, published March 22, 2018, http://www.espn.com/sports/soccer/story/_/id/22869596/2018-world-cup-college-soccer-too-much-risk-rising-us-talent.

7. Steven Goff, "For College Soccer, an Overdue Experiment to Match the Sport's Global Standards," *Washington Post*, April 22, 2018, https://www.washingtonpost.com/news/soccer-insider/wp/2018/04/22/for-college-soccer-an-overdue-experiment-to-match-the-sports-global-standards/.

8. NCAA, *Soccer, 2018 and 2019 Rules* (NCAA, 2018), 40–43; Goff, "For College Soccer."

9. *Ted Lasso*, season 1, episode 10, "The Hope That Kills You," written by Jason Sudeikis, Bill Lawrence, and Brendan Hunt, directed by M. J. Delaney, aired October 2, 2020, on Apple TV+.

10. Oliver Roeder, "In 126 Years, English Football Has Seen 13,475 Nil-Nil Draws," FiveThirtyEight, published October 3, 2014, https://fivethirtyeight.com/features/in-126-years-english-football-has-seen-13475-nil-nil-draws/.

11. NCAA, *Soccer, 2018 and 2019 Rules*.

12. NCAA, *2016 Men's and Women's Soccer Rules*.

13. NCAA, *Soccer: 2018 and 2019 Rules*.

14. Matthew Doyle, "Armchair Analyst: Future of the College Game? Here's the Take from the MLS Combine," MLSSoccer.com, published January 10, 2016, https://www.mlssoccer.com/news/armchair-analyst-future-college-game-heres-take-mls-combine; Charles Boehm, "'Stuck in Neutral': College Soccer Still Grappling with Uncertain Future," *FourFourTwo*, September 23, 2016.

15. NCAA, *2016 Men's and Women's Soccer Rules*.

16. Staff, "Div. I Men's College Coaches Propose Academic Year Season Model," *Soccer Wire*, August 23, 2016, https://www.soccerwire.com/news/nscaa-div-i-college-mens-coaches-propose-academic-year-season-model/; Tom Hindle, "The Origins of The 21st Century Model," *TopDrawer Soccer*, April 5, 2022, https://www.topdrawersoccer.com/college-soccer-articles/the-origins-of-the-21st-century-model_aid50684.

17. NSCAA, *NSCAA DI Men Propose Academic Year Season Model* (NSCAA, 2016); Chris Rael, "NSCAA College Coaches Academic Year Model," *Soccer Today*, August 29, 2016, https://www.soccertoday.com/nscaa-college-coaches-academic-year-model/?cn-reloaded=1.

18. Paul Kennedy, "MLS SuperDraft: Teams Pass on 21 of 43 Picks in Third and Fourth Rounds," *Soccer America*, January 15, 2019, https://www.socceramerica.com/mls-superdraft-less-relevant-but-still-productive/.

19. Kennedy, "MLS SuperDraft."

Chapter 6

1. Attempts to interview Eddie Nuñez for this book went unanswered. See Brooks Kubena, "LSU Athletics Brought in $145 Million," *The Advocate* (Baton Rouge, LA), January 31, 2019; Eddie Nuñez, LSU Sports, accessed July 2024, https://lsusports.net/sports/ad/roster/player/eddie-Nuñez/; Geoff Grammer, host, Interview with Eddie Nuñez, *Talking Grammer Podcast*, October 23, 2023, episode 67, https://soundcloud.com/geoff-grammer/ep-67-unm-athletic-director-eddie-Nuñez-tg-10323.

2. Mike Adams, Interview with Eddie Nuñez, *Mike Adams 2.0*, January 14, 2022, https://podcasters.spotify.com/pod/show/team-broadcasting/episodes/UNM-Director-of-Athletics-Eddie-Nuñez-joins-Mike-Adams-e1cv64s; Steve Gorten, "Warm Emotions in Tough Matchup," *Miami Herald*, February 1, 1998.

3. Chris Harry, "Little-Known Reserves Spark UF to Victory," *Orlando Sentinel*, February 4, 1997; Gorten, "Warm Emotions in Tough Matchup."

4. Gorten, "Warm Emotions in Tough Matchup."

Notes

5. KOAT, "New Mexico Athletic Director Pledges Integrity, Transparency," Eddie Nuñez Introductory Press Conference, posted September 8, 2017, YouTube, 28 min., 42 sec., https://www.youtube.com/watch?v=5_xtEeXTTG8&t=594s.

6. Geoff Grammer, interview with Eddie Nuñez, *Talking Grammer Podcast*.

7. Geoff Grammer, interview with Eddie Nuñez, *Talking Grammer Podcast*.

8. Matt Brown, a college sports insider whose *Extra Points with Matt Brown* is a must-read for industry leaders, captured this mindset in a 2021 newsletter title, "We Need to Stop Talking about Athletic Department 'Profits.'" Brown explained, "College sports IS a business. But they don't follow the same accounting rules businesses use. And focusing on 'profits' can lead to some incorrect conclusions." See Matt Brown, "We Need to Stop Talking about Athletic Department 'Profits,'" *Extra Points with Matt Brown*, March 1, 2021, https://extrapoints.substack.com/p/we-need-to-stop-talking-about-athletic.

9. Cedric Dempsey, NCAA president, spoke on the matter: "In 1978, the membership of Division I agreed that departments of athletics should be financially self-supporting. To meet that goal, many institutions were forced to reduce spending and increase revenue." Many other programs simply didn't meet the goal. See Kay Hawes, "The NCAA News Archive 2002," NCAA, published December 9, 2002, https://ncaanewsarchive.s3.amazonaws.com/2002/Association-wide/panel-on-athletics-opportunity-hears-heated-debate-in-final-town-hall-event----12-9-02.html; NCAA Division I Board of Directors, "Division I Membership—Division I Membership Requirements—Philosophy Statement—Self-Sufficiency of Athletics Program," NCAA LSDBi, published August 1, 2008, https://web3.ncaa.org/lsdbi/search/proposalView?id=2180.

10. The New Mexican, "UNM Ices Ski Team Over Budget Problems," *Santa Fe New Mexican*, April 14, 2017; The President's Office, "Athletics Department Review Supporting Documentation," University of New Mexico, August 15, 2018, 328, https://president.unm.edu/documents/archived-documents/athletics/2018/athletics-department-review-supporting-documentation.pdf. UNM would report its grant-in-aid cost for fiscal year 2018 as $8.15 million to the NCAA, but during the budget crisis discussion of the spring 2018 numbers, UNM would use the number $5.8 million for the same line item, thus reflecting the NCAA distortion built into the process.

11. *Santa Fe New Mexican*, April 14, 2017.

12. Minutes of the Regular Meeting of the Board of Regents of the University of New Mexico, May 11, 2017, https://regents.unm.edu/meetings/minutes/2017/bor-minutes-2017-05-11.pdf.

13. Richard F. Taylor, "Jerome Lee Nicholson," *Accounting Historians Notebook* 2, no. 1 (1979).

14. Kristi Dosh, *Saturday Millionaires: How Winning Football Builds Winning Colleges* (Wiley, 2013); Aaron Gordon, "Here's How the NCAA's Black Magic Accounting Turns Profit into Loss," *Vice*, April 23, 2015, https://www.vice.com/en

/article/heres-how-the-ncaas-black-magic-accounting-turns-profit-into-loss/; Jason Kirk, "College Athletic Departments Aren't Necessarily as Broke as You Think," SB Nation, published June 6, 2014, https://www.sbnation.com/college-football/2014/6/6/5783394/college-sports-profits-money-schools-revenues-subsidies/comment/238340431; Andy Schwarz, "How Athletic Departments (and the Media) Fudge the Cost of Scholarships," *Deadspin*, May 2, 2013, https://deadspin.com/how-athletic-departments-and-the-media-fudge-the-cost-1570827027/.

15. For a sampling of this debate, see Heather J. Lawrence, Liz Wanless, and E. Ann Gabriel, "Applying Activity-Based Costing to Intercollegiate Athletics," *Sports Innovation Journal* 1 (2020): 81–105; V. A. Matheson, D. J. O'Connor, and J. H. Herberger, "The Bottom Line: Accounting for revenues and Expenditures in Intercollegiate Athletics," *International Journal of Sport Finance* 7, no. 1 (2012): 30–45; H. J. Lawrence, E. A. Gabriel, and L. E. Tuttle, "Leveling the Playing Field: Creating Transparency and Consistency in Accounting for Division I College Athletics," *Journal of Intercollegiate Sport* 3 (2010): 366–81, https://doi.org/10.1123/jis.3.2.366.

16. Lawrence, Wanless, and Gabriel, "Applying Activity-Based Costing." See also Lawrence, Gabriel, and Tuttle, "Leveling the Playing Field," 366–81.

17. The President's Office, "University of New Mexico Department of Athletics Analysis and Review," accessed June 2024, https://president.unm.edu/documents/archived-documents/athletics/2018/unm-athletics-analysis-and-review.pdf.

18. The President's Office, "Athletics Department Review Supporting Documentation," accessed June 2024, https://president.unm.edu/documents/archived-documents/athletics/2018/athletics-department-review-supporting-documentation.pdf, 36–39, 141–44, 424.

19. The President's Office, "Athletics Department Review Supporting Documentation," 36–39, 141–44.

20. Sam Haas, "Keep All Sports; Deficit's Not Real," editorial, *Albuquerque Journal*, June 24, 2018.

21. Andy Schwarz, "Case Study: New Mexico Miscalculates 'Savings' from Cutting Scholarships," *Sportsgeekonomics*, August 28, 2018, https://sportsgeekonomics.tumblr.com/post/177486890583/case-study-new-mexico-miscalculates-savings.

22. Schwarz, "Case Study: New Mexico Miscalculates 'Savings.'"

23. The President's Office, "Updated: Athletic Department Supporting Documentation," University of New Mexico, published 2018, https://president.unm.edu/documents/archived-documents/athletics/2018/updated-athletic-department-supporting-documentation.pdf; Tony Strati and Jason Hix, "UNM Sports Cuts Based on Seriously Flawed Analysis," op-ed, *Albuquerque Journal*, November 14, 2018.

24. Andrew Schwarz, Letter to Whom It May Concern (UNM), October 25, 2018.

25. Andrew Schwarz, Letter to Whom It May Concern (UNM), October 25, 2018.

CHAPTER 7

1. NCAA, *Men's Soccer Attendance Records* (NCAA, 2018), http://fs.ncaa.org/Docs/stats/m_soccer_RB/2019/2018attendance.pdf.

2. Will Webber, "Coach Steps Out of Line, Possibly Saving His Team," *Santa Fe New Mexican*, April 21, 2018, https://www.santafenewmexican.com/opinion/local_columns/coach-steps-out-of-line-possibly-saving-his-team/article_7a95a51b-59e1-5dd2-b2fd-70c3f592fba5.html.

3. Mayor Tim Keller, "With any complex decision, it's important to consider not just the choice at hand but when the decision should be made," Facebook, August 16, 2018, https://www.facebook.com/MayorKeller/videos/1960869867306912/.

4. Minutes of the Regular Meeting of the Board of Regents of the University of New Mexico, September 11, 2018, https://regents.unm.edu/meetings/minutes/2018/bor-minutes-2018-09-11.pdf; Jessica Dyer, "Regent Says Faculty Should Share the Heat," *Albuquerque Journal*, September 12, 2018.

5. "Lujan Grisham Earns Red Card for UNM Pandering," editorial, *Albuquerque Journal*, September 21, 2018; Geoff Grammer, "Candidates Decry UNM Cutting Four Sports," *Albuquerque Journal*, September 19, 2018; Michelle Lujan Grisham (@Michelle4NM), "The next governor will have a unique opportunity to appoint regents for our university. As governor, I'll put students first and push for transparent budgeting and restore the programs cut at UNM. #nmpol #NMGovDebate," Twitter, September 14, 2018, https://x.com/Michelle4NM/status/1040780539072933888.

6. "Lujan Grisham Earns Red Card, *Albuquerque Journal*; Grammer, "Candidates Decry UNM"; Lujan Grisham (@Michelle4NM), "The next governor."

7. "Lujan Grisham Earns Red Card, *Albuquerque Journal*; Grammer, "Candidates Decry UNM"; Lujan Grisham (@Michelle4NM), "The next governor."

8. "Lujan Grisham Earns Red Card, *Albuquerque Journal*; Grammer, "Candidates Decry UNM"; Lujan Grisham (@Michelle4NM), "The next governor."

9. Chron Staff, "Local Resident Is in the Business of Scaring People with Success of ScreamWorld," *Houston Chronicle*, October 22, 2013, https://www.chron.com/neighborhood/spring/news/article/local-resident-is-in-the-business-of-scaring-4917380.php; Ana Gonzalez, "ScreamWorld's Final Night Is This Friday the 13th. What You Need to Know Before Their Doors Close for Good," *KPRC Houston*, March 10, 2022, https://www.click2houston.com/features/2020/03/11/screamworlds-final-night-is-this-friday-the-13th-what-you-need-to-know-before-their-doors-close-for-good/.

10. Glen Rosales, "Grey's Spark Not Enough for Lobos," *Albuquerque Journal*, September 16, 2018.

11. "Lujan Grisham Earns Red Card," *Albuquerque Journal*.

Chapter 8

1. Jared Shanker, "Jameis Winston to Sit Whole Game," ESPN, published September 19, 2014, https://www.espn.com/college-football/story/_/id/11555354/jameis-winston-florida-state-seminoles-banned-entire-game-vs-clemson-tigers.

2. Office of the President, "William Rainey Harper, 1891–1906," University of Chicago, accessed November 2024, https://president.uchicago.edu/en/about-the-office/history/william-rainey-harper.

3. University of Chicago, "Physical Culture and Athletics," UChicago Library, accessed May 2024, https://www.lib.uchicago.edu/collex/exhibits/university-chicago-centennial-catalogues/life-quads-centennial-view-student-experience-university-chicago/physical-culture-and-athletics/.

4. The Big Ten was originally known as the Western Conference. See Leo Vernor, "Brains over Brawn: How Football Found Its Place at UChicago," *Chicago Maroon*, September 19, 2023. https://chicagomaroon.com/39731/grey-city/brains-over-brawn-how-football-found-its-place-at-uchicago/.

5. Robin Lester, *Stagg's University: The Rise, Decline, and Fall of Big-Time Football at Chicago* (University of Illinois Press, 1995).

6. Chuck Culpepper, "In 1939, the University of Chicago Made One of College Football's Boldest Plays: I Quit," *Washington Post*, August 23, 2019, https://www.washingtonpost.com/sports/2019/08/23/university-chicago-made-one-college-footballs-boldest-plays-it-quit/.

7. Robert Hutchins, "Gate Receipts and Glory," *Saturday Evening Post*, December 3, 1938.

8. Robert Hutchins, "College Football Is an Infernal Nuisance," *Sports Illustrated*, October 18, 1954.

9. Allen Sanderson and John Seigfried, "Why American Universities Sponsor Commercial Sports," *Milken Institute Review*, July 31, 2018, https://www.milkenreview.org/articles/why-american-universities-sponsor-commercial-sports.

10. Thomas Scully, "NCAA v. Board of Regents of the University of Oklahoma: The NCAA's Television Plan Is Sacked by the Sherman Act," *Catholic University Law Review* 34, no. 3 (Spring 1985), https://scholarship.law.edu/lawreview/vol34/iss3/13.

11. SEC Release, "2004–2005 SEC Revenue Distribution," UGA Sports, published June 3, 2005, https://uga.rivals.com/news/2004-2005-sec-revenue-distribution; Associated Press, "SEC Revenue Jumps 58 Percent," *New York Times*, June 5, 2010, https://www.nytimes.com/2010/06/05/sports/ncaafootball/05sportsbriefs-sec.html.

12. Knight Foundation, *A Call to Action: Reconnecting College Sports and Higher Education* (Commission on Intercollegiate Athletics, 2001).

13. Welch Suggs, "Vanderbilt U. Radically Reorganizes Athletics Department," *Chronicle of Higher Education*, September 19, 2003.

14. Associated Press, "Elimination of Athletic Department Spurs Success at Vanderbilt," *New York Times*, September 6, 2008.
15. "Turner's Highs and Lows," *The Tennessean*, September 10, 2003.
16. Staff Writer, "Gee Backs Off Football Remarks," *Columbus Dispatch*, December 1, 2010; Gordon Gee, "Standing on the Shoulders of Giants," *HuffPost*, October 19, 2012, https://www.huffpost.com/entry/standing-on-the-shoulders_b_1988818.
17. Amber McDowell, "Vandy to Eliminate Athletic Department, Seek Reforms," *Knoxville News Sentinel*, September 10, 2003.
18. ESPN, "University to Merge Varsity, Intramural Athletics," College Sports, published September 9, 2003, https://www.espn.com/ncaa/news/2003/0909/1612563.html.
19. Randy Horick, "Huh?," *Nashville Scene*, September 18, 2003.
20. Michael Cass, "Vanderbilt Restructures, Scraps Athletics Department," *The Tennessean*, September 10, 2003.
21. Wendell Barnhouse, "Heard the One About Vandy's Latest Move," *Fort Worth Star-Telegram*, September 12, 2003; Mark Story, "UK's Todd Chose a Safe and Smart Path to Reform," *Lexington Herald-Leader*, September 14, 2003.
22. Gordon Gee, "My Plan to Put the College Back in College Sports," *Washington Post*, September 20, 2003.
23. Associated Press, "Elimination of Athletic Department"; Rod Williamson, "Game Changer," *Vanderbilt Magazine*, May 7, 2013.

Chapter 9

1. Josh Rubin, "Academy Soccer Recap: RSL-AZ Goes Undefeated at 2014 Winter Showcase," Grande Sports World, last updated 2023, https://www.grandesports.com/2014/12/07/academy-soccer-recap-rsl-az-goes-undefeated-2014-winter-showcase/.
2. Peter Rosen, "Dreams Are Soaring for New Utah Soccer Academy," KSL.com, posted September 7, 2017, https://www.ksl.com/article/45718304/dreams-are-soaring-for-new-utah-soccer-academy.
3. UNM Lobos, Press Release, UNM Athletics, September 22, 2018.
4. "Gaels Get the Game-Winner Late," *Albuquerque Journal*, September 27, 2018.

Chapter 10

1. "Lobos Upended by FIU on Saturday," *TopDrawer Soccer*, September 29, 2018, https://www.topdrawersoccer.com/college-soccer-articles/lobos-upended-by-fiu-on-saturday_aid45012.
2. Geoff Grammer, "Some Question Why Football Escaped Scrutiny," *Albuquerque Journal*, July 20, 2018.

Notes

3. James Barron, "Lobos Should Cut Football Program," *Santa Fe New Mexican*, June 24, 2018.

4. Michael Oriard, *King Football: Sport and Spectacle in the Golden Age of Radio and Newsreels, Movies and Magazines, the Weekly and Daily Press* (University of North Carolina Press, 2004).

5. Spencer D. Wyld and David C. Wyld, "College Football's Bottom-Line Impact: Exploring the Relationship of Football Performance on Athletic Finances for Division I Institutions Today," *The Sport Journal*, July 2021.

6. Until 2006 the two divisions were known as Division I and Division I-AA.

7. Grammer, "Some Question Why Football."

8. Café Dupont, "Home," accessed July 2024, https://www.cafedupont.net/; Susan Swagler, "Café Dupont Continues to Define Downtown Birmingham's Food Scene Years After Opening," *Birmingham Magazine*, January 2016, https://www.al.com/bhammag/2016/01/cafe_dupont.html.

Chapter 11

1. Michelle Brutlag Hosick, "New Transfer Rule Eliminates Permission-to-Contact Process," NCAA, published June 13, 2018, https://www.ncaa.org/news/2018/6/13/new-transfer-rule-eliminates-permission-to-contact-process.aspx#:~:text=The%20rule%20change%20ends%20the,restrictive%20than%20the%20national%20rule; Rick Allen, "NCAA Transfer Rule Changes Effective October 15," *The Informed Athlete*, published September 27, 2018, https://informedathlete.com/ncaa-transfer-rule-changes-effective-october-15th/.

2. Greg Johnson, "What the NCAA Transfer Portal Is . . . and What It Isn't," NCAA, published October 8, 2019, https://www.ncaa.org/news/2023/2/8/media-center-what-the-ncaa-transfer-portal-is-and-what-it-isn-t.

3. NCAA, "Transfer Portal: Users Guide," PowerPoint slides, October 2018, https://ncaa.s3.amazonaws.com/files/apps/transfer/DII_TransferPortal_UserGuide.pdf.

4. Johnson, "What the NCAA Transfer Portal Is."

5. University of New Mexico, "Jeremy Fishbein Press Luncheon—Men's Soccer," posted October 23, 2018, by UNM Lobos, YouTube, 15 min., 29 sec., https://www.youtube.com/watch?v=GuHEs2-UsMM.

6. Steve Virgen, "Misery for Lobo Men, Joy for the Women," *Albuquerque Journal*, October 26, 2018; University of New Mexico, "Jeremy Fishbein Press Luncheon."

7. University of New Mexico, "Jeremy Fishbein Press Luncheon."

8. Ed Johnson, "UNM Men's Soccer Will Change Leagues," *Albuquerque Journal*, September 5, 2012.

9. Numbers from NCAA, *NCAA Sports Sponsorship and Participation Rates Report* (NCAA, 2023), 105, https://ncaaorg.s3.amazonaws.com/research/sportpart/2023RES_SportsSponsorshipParticipationRatesReport.pdf.

NOTES

CHAPTER 12

1. Tripp Stelnicki, "Michelle's the One for New Mexico," *Santa Fe New Mexican*, November 7, 2018.
2. Stelnicki, "Michelle's the One for New Mexico."
3. Geoff Grammer, "Candidates Decry UNM Cutting Four Sports," *Albuquerque Journal*, September 19, 2018.
4. Robert Mann, *Kingfish U: Huey Long and LSU* (LSU Press, 2023); Van Allen Plexico and John Ringer, *First Time Ever: The Untold Story of How Auburn First Brought Undefeated Alabama to Jordan-Hare Stadium—and Beat Them* (White Rocket Books, 2023).
5. Daniel Libit, "The Petty Politics of Loboland," *NMFishbowl*, September 5, 2017, https://nmfishbowl.com/2017/09/05/the-petty-politics-of-loboland/.
6. Rick Wright, "Governor Promises Money to UNM," *Albuquerque Journal*, January 29, 2006.
7. ODU Men's Soccer (@ODUMensSoccer), "That was fast . . . Niko Klosterhalfen knocks one in right after assisting Wilschrey second before! ODU takes 2-0 lead with 34 minutes left to play. ODU2/UNM 0. #ODUSports #Monarchs," Twitter (now X), November 7, 2018, 4:03 p.m., https://x.com/ODUMensSoccer/status/1060306835989782533.

CHAPTER 13

1. In 2021, New Mexico passed North Dakota to become the nation's second highest oil producing state. Adrian Hedden, "Oil and Gas Leaders Look to Future in Permian Basin," *Carlsbad Current-Argus*, September 13, 2019; Adrian Hedden, "Oil, Gas Lead Revenue Growth in New Mexico," *Carlsbad Current-Argus*, December 11, 2019.
2. Kevin Robinson-Avila, "Boom Expected to Continue, Pump Dollars into State for Years," *Albuquerque Journal*, March 13, 2019.
3. Common Cause New Mexico and New Mexico Ethics Watch, "The New Mexico Oil and Gas Industry and Its Allies: Oceans of Oil, Oceans of Influence," Common Cause, published March 2020, https://www.commoncause.org/new-mexico/resources/the-new-mexico-oil-and-gas-industry-and-its-allies-oceans-of-oil-oceans-of-influence/.
4. Kyle Land, Cameron Goeldneer, and Danielle Prokop, "Saved by the Ball: House Dems Push to Reinstate Sports," *Daily Lobo*, January 25, 2019.
5. Dan McKay, Geoff Grammer, and Dan Boyd, "Dem Leaders Move to Save UNM Sports," *Albuquerque Journal*, January 26, 2019.
6. Staff, "Fight to Save New Mexico Men's Soccer Team Gains Support from Legislature," *Soccer America*, January 29, 2019.
7. Jeremy Fishbein (@CoachFishINDIA; Previously @LoboCoachFish), "The State of New Mexico loves and supports Lobo Soccer. . . . WE LOVE NEW

MEXICO and love impacting the youth of our State. Looks like we have the money to RE-INSTATE LOBO SOCCER. LETS DO IT!" Twitter (now X), January 25, 2019, 6:14 p.m., https://x.com/CoachFishINDIA/status/1088968441535459328.

8. Geoff Grammer, "Politicos Say Cuts Bad for UNM," *Albuquerque Journal*, July 24, 2018.

9. Geoff Grammer, "AG to UNM: Reconsider the Process," *Albuquerque Journal*, August 10, 2018; Mayor Tim Keller, "With any complex decision, it's important to consider not just the choice at hand but when the decision should be made," Facebook, August 16, 2018, https://www.facebook.com/MayorKeller/videos/1960869867306912/; One Albuquerque Media GOV TV 16, "Mayor Keller Underlines Importance of UNM Lobo Men's Soccer," Internet Archive, published August 23, 2018, https://archive.org/details/gtv16nm-Mayor_Keller_Underlines_Importance_of_UNM_Lobo_Men_s_Soccer.

10. "Lujan Grisham Earns Red Card for Pandering," editorial, *Albuquerque Journal*, September 21, 2018.

11. Jeremy Fishbein, "NM Leaders Right to Speak Up About Athletics," *Albuquerque Journal*, October 2, 2018.

12. Walt Rubel, "Dems Will Boot Golden Chance If Priorities Are Wrong," *Las Cruces Sun-News*, November 18, 2018.

13. "Legislative Roundup," *Santa Fe New Mexican*, January 29, 2019.

14. Dan McKay, "Capitol Notebook," *Albuquerque Journal*, January 29, 2019.

15. Dan McKay, Geoff Grammer, and Dan Boyd, "Dem Leaders Move to Save Sports," *Albuquerque Journal*, January 26, 2019.

16. Milan Simonich, "Democrats Meddle Where They Don't Belong," *Santa Fe New Mexican*, January 24, 2019.

17. Common Cause New Mexico, "Modernize the New Mexico Legislature," Common Cause, accessed November 2024, https://www.commoncause.org/new-mexico/our-work/protect-the-constitution-courts-other-democracy-reforms/modernize-the-nm-legislature/; Retake our Democracy, "12 10 Michael Rocca UNM Poli Sci Prof," interview, posted December 10, 2022, YouTube, 58 min. 22 sec., https://youtube.com/watch?v=r2R_XiWZlvU&t=5s. See also, Timothy Krebs and Michael Rocca, "A Report on Legislative Professionalism for the State of New Mexico," November 2022, https://polisci.unm.edu/people/faculty/profile/legis-modernization.pdf; Michael J. Rocca, Timothy B. Krebs, and Dylan McArthur, "The Consequences of Legislative Professionalism in U.S. State Legislatures: A Review." *State and Local Government Review*, (2023) 55(3), 235–58. https://doi.org/10.1177/0160323X231167614

18. NM House Appropriations and Finance Committee, February 9, 2019, video of committee meeting, 4 hrs., 43 min., https://sg001-harmony.sliq.net/00293/Harmony/en/PowerBrowser/PowerBrowserV2/20190209/-1/62070; Rachel Knapp, "Where Do State Lawmakers Stay During the Legislative Session," KRQE

News, posted January 3, 2020, https://www.krqe.com/news/politics-government/where-do-state-lawmakers-stay-during-the-legislative-session/.

19. Steve Knight, "Bill's Message to Lawmakers: Don't Meddle," *Albuquerque Journal*, January 31, 2019.

20. State of New Mexico v. Paul Robert Krebs, D 0202 CR 2019 0369 (2019); see https://nmfishbowl.com/wp-content/uploads/2022/01/7310a-krebs-unredacted-redacted_redacted.pdf.

21. Daniel Libit, "Booster Golf Trip Puts Ex-College AD on Trial in Rare Prosecution," *Sportico*, July 14, 2023.

22. Larry Barker, "UNM Sends Lobo Execs on Golf Junket at Public Expense," *KRQE*, May 2, 2017, https://www.krqe.com/news/larry-barker/unm-sends-lobo-execs-on-golf-junket-at-public-expense/; Daniel Libit, "Who Has Paul Krebs Been Calling?" *NMFishbowl*, May 24, 2017, https://nmfishbowl.com/2017/05/24/who-has-paul-krebs-been-calling/.

23. Libit, "Who Has Paul Krebs Been Calling?"

24. AP, "New Mexico AD Resigning Amid Improper Spending Scandal," *Sports Illustrated*, June 5, 2017; https://nmfishbowl.com/category/crime-and-punishment/.

25. NM House Appropriations and Finance Committee, February 9, 2019, video of committee meeting, 4 hrs., 43 min., https://sg001-harmony.sliq.net/00293/Harmony/en/PowerBrowser/PowerBrowserV2/20190209/-1/62070.

26. Andrew Oxford, "House Reaches Tentative Budget Deal," *Santa Fe New Mexican*, March 16, 2019.

27. Patricia Lundstrom, House Appropriations and Finance Committee Substitute for House Bills 2 and 3, 54th Legislature, State of New Mexico, First Session, 2019, https://www.nmlegis.gov/Sessions/19%20Regular/bills/house/HB0002AFS.pdf; emphasis on *is contingent* added for clarity.

28. Patricia Lundstrom, General Appropriation Act of 2019, 54th Legislature, State of New Mexico, https://www.nmlegis.gov/Sessions/19%20Regular/final/HB0002.pdf; emphasis on *may be used for* added for clarity.

Afterword

1. Glen Rosales, "End of an Era," *Albuquerque Journal*, June 30, 2019.

2. Jeremy Fishbein, "Lobo Soccer Recap (Fall 2018–Spring 2019)," May 2019, document circulated via email to Lobo Soccer supporters. Document on player placement included in appendix.

3. Rosales, "End of an Era."

4. Quote from interview with the author. On the ABQ High Season, see James Yodice, "Still Kicking," *Albuquerque Journal*, October 22, 2019.

5. Rick Wright, "Fish Back on the Pitch, Working in India," *Albuquerque Journal*, October 23, 2022.

6. Rick Wright, "Fishbein Returns, Happier and More at Peace," *Albuquerque Journal*, April 30, 2023.

NOTES

7. UNM, *FY 2018 NCAA Report* (University of New Mexico, 2019), https://athleticscontracts.unm.edu/ncaa-financial-reports/fy18---ncaa-report.pdf; UNM, *FY 2023 NCAA Report* (University of New Mexico, 2024), https://athleticscontracts.unm.edu/ncaa-financial-reports/fy23-ncaa-report.pdf.

8. Ryan Boetel, "Lobo Athletics Off the Hook for Paying Deficit," *Albuquerque Journal*, October 27, 2020.

9. Title IX, Component II requires that schools provide athlete scholarships proportional to their participation rates, which are, of course, supposed to mirror their institutional demographics. This becomes complicated by the NCAA's allowance of duplicated headcounts. UNM in 2023, for example, had 202 female student athletes, but they were counted as 274 participants due to competing in sports such as indoor track, outdoor track, and cross country. See UNM, *FY 2023 NCAA Report* (University of New Mexico, 2024), https://athleticscontracts.unm.edu/ncaa-financial-reports/fy23-ncaa-report.pdf.

10. Olivier Uyttebrouck, "AG Drops All But Two Charges Ahead of Trial of Former UNM Athletic Director," *Albuquerque Journal*, June 25, 2023.

11. Bob Clark, host, *The Bob Clark Podcast*, podcast, "Krebs Verdict," Daniel Libit, guest, RSS Feed, July 24, 2023, https://omny.fm/shows/the-bob-clark-podcast/krebs-verdict.

12. Staff, "US Soccer Officially Announces the Immediate Closure of the Development Academy," *SoccerWire*, April 15, 2020.

13. Proponents of the twenty-first century model continue to advocate for its adoption. In 2023 the Soccer Coaches Association resubmitted the twenty-first century model proposal to the NCAA's Student Athlete Experience Committee (SAEC). The SAEC, however, voted against it. As of January 2024, the Division I Men's Soccer Committee planned to "review next steps for progress in the area of playing and practice season." See NCAA, *Report of the NCAA Division I Men's Soccer Committee, January 29–30, 2024 Meeting* (NCAA, 2024), https://ncaaorg.s3.amazonaws.com/championships/sports/soccer/d1/men/Jan2024D1MSO_AnnualReport.pdf.

Index

Albuquerque, New Mexico: development, xviii, 96; outside perceptions of, xviii, xx, 158; schools, xx, 14, 45; topography, xix, 38, 133

Albuquerque Journal, xviii, xxv, 4, 33, 43–45, 62, 89, 94, 105, 109, 138, 144, 172, 184, 185, 200, 201

Altman, Kelly, 28, 57, 61, 107, 108, 112, 135, 147, 148, 159, 160, 162, 165, 171; assistant coach role, 3, 4, 19, 23, 24, 55, 98, 127, 132, 133, 179, 189; coaching philosophy, 170, 172–75; pre-UNM career, 21, 22; transfer process, 157, 199–200

Balderas, Hector, xxv, 4, 186, 190, 204

Bandidos, FC, 7, 37–40, 43

Barreiro, Nick, 9, 28, 30, 31, 48, 56, 57, 62, 70, 78, 98, 103, 136, 173, 175, 179, 200

Champenois, Lucas (Champ), 3, 55, 56, 61, 70, 77, 99, 112, 113, 149, 157, 159, 161, 165, 180; assistant coach role, 19–21, 106–8, 136, 142, 166,
169, 199; coaching philosophy, 67–68, 170

Cirovski, Sasho, 7, 71, 75, 76, 208

Conference USA, 12, 76, 93, 106, 127, 148, 160, 163, 165, 171, 208; tournament, 152, 168, 172, 176–80

Division I soccer tournament, 1, 7, 16, 41, 43–46, 97, 101, 152, 177, 207

Dorsey, Matt, 9, 19, 30, 31, 70, 78, 79, 103, 129, 139, 151–53, 165–67, 178, 180, 181

Dupont, Grayson, 9, 148–50, 153, 163, 179, 200

Fetterly, Alex, 3, 28, 62, 67, 69, 106–8, 111, 112, 128, 129, 133–40, 158, 159, 200

Fishbein, Jeremy (Fish), 4, 16, 17, 30, 61, 63, 68, 74, 78, 79, 97, 102, 104, 111–13, 136–38, 141, 150, 208, 209; coaching, 1, 2, 5, 20–24, 40–45, 59–60, 99, 107, 116, 127–29, 135, 141–43, 147–49, 152, 153, 160, 165–70, 172, 174, 178–81; grassmanship, 20, 21, 162, 171; media interviews, 29, 57, 109,

134, 149; political involvement, 24, 61, 67, 69, 99, 105, 152, 161, 173, 176–78, 185–87; post-UNM, 198–202; pre-UNM, 6–7; recruiting, 39–41, 132, 147; tactics, 163; transfer portal, 157–59, 164, 165

Gee, Gordon, 120–26
Graczyk, Mike, 32, 57, 99, 102, 104, 134, 135, 137, 153, 168, 172, 180; coaching, 4, 21, 27, 30, 51, 55, 61, 62, 67–71, 108, 112, 143, 149, 161, 171, 174; playing career, 44–46; post-UNM, 199, 207; transfer portal, 142, 157–59
Grey, Omar, 9, 28, 31–33, 53, 55–62, 71, 74, 102, 108, 113, 137, 38, 140, 153, 158, 159, 164, 172, 175, 200

Johnson, Gary, xviii, 99, 177
Jones, Billy, 10, 17, 19, 28, 30, 31, 57, 70, 78, 98, 102, 129, 134, 135, 140, 141, 150, 159, 179, 180, 200

Keller, Tim, xxv, 99, 100, 176, 186
Krebs, Paul, xxii–xv, 90, 91, 165, 190–92, 196, 204, 205

Letherman, Bailey, 9, 17, 28, 31, 70, 111, 129, 135, 140, 149, 151, 178, 200

Libit, Daniel, xx–xxv, 89, 90, 191, 205; *NMFishbowl*, xxi, xxiv, xxv, 177, 191, 192
Lobos Men's Soccer Program: facilities, 3, 51, 60, 111, 171; history, 1, 7, 8, 43–45, 136; NCAA championship appearance, 45–46; outreach/camps, xxxv, 9, 11, 13, 32, 85; rules, 1, 2, 53, 173, 174; style of play, 48, 66, 150, 163, 171, 172; travel, 53–55, 61, 89, 96, 127, 160, 180. *See also* individual players and coaches
Lujan Grisham, Michelle, 69, 112, 161; election, 175, 176, 184, 186; soccer advocacy, 99, 100, 104, 105, 109, 198
Lundstrom, Patricia, 12–14, 173, 184–89, 192–97

Major League Soccer (MLS), xxv, 1, 7, 66, 74, 75, 131, 132, 205; SuperDraft, 67, 76, 77, 141, 161
Mountain West Conference, 12, 14, 94, 145, 193, 205

National Collegiate Athletic Association (NCAA), xxiv, 6, 8, 22, 62, 65, 82, 91, 94, 117, 121, 127; athlete compensation, xxii, 207; athletic scholarships, 26, 37, 86–90, 203; College

Cup (*see* Division I soccer tournament); compliance, 9, 52, 132, 155; Division I soccer tournament, 1, 7, 16, 41, 43–46, 97, 101, 152, 177, 207; evolution, xvii, 121, 122, 126; financial reporting, 84–90, 93; football, 143–46; ideal of self-sufficiency, 84–90, 93; soccer reform, 66, 67, 72–76, 208; sport sponsorship, 11, 166–67, 193, 194; transfer process, xxii, 8, 155, 156, 158, 164, 207

New Mexico: oil production, 13, 184, 185, 202; outside perceptions of, xxii–xix, 44; people of, xix; politics, 12–14, 105, 176, 184–90, 192–98; state budget, 12, 184, 197–98; state legislature, 12–14, 105, 176, 184–90, 192–97. *See also* Tim Keller; Michelle Lujan Grisham; Patricia Lundstrom

NMFishbowl, xxi, xxiv, xxv, 177, 191, 192

Nuñez, Eddie, xxv, 11–14, 47, 84, 89, 90, 94, 99, 100, 114, 117, 136, 146, 186, 188, 192–94, 203, 205; pre-UNM, 81–83

Parker, Ford, 3, 10, 14, 19, 26–32, 57, 62, 66–68, 70, 71, 77–79, 86, 103–8, 112, 140, 147, 149, 153, 161–63, 168, 172, 178, 179–81, 187, 200

Puig, Matt, 9, 31–33, 46, 57, 62, 69, 70, 78, 98, 102, 104, 112, 129, 133, 141, 142, 147, 175, 178, 199, 200

Real Salt Lake, 8, 9, 77, 131, 132
Rowland, Jeff, 40–48

Schwarz, Andy, 85–89, 92, 95, 147

Scott, Aaron, 10, 19, 30–32, 57, 70, 79, 98, 108, 109, 129, 139, 159, 161, 167, 199

Smart, Tom, 10, 19, 28–32, 70, 71, 73, 102, 104, 107, 108, 111, 116, 124, 134, 138–40, 143, 159, 161, 164, 173, 175, 179, 200

Spangenberg, Simon, 10, 19, 29–31, 48, 57, 67, 69, 70, 74, 102, 104, 129, 133, 140, 150, 151, 153, 165, 166, 174, 175, 180, 181

Stokes, Garnett, xxv, 10, 11, 89, 90, 94, 113, 116, 117, 145, 186, 188, 192–97; pre-UNM, 114, 115

Taylor, Nick, 9, 30, 31, 49, 57, 62, 70, 78, 79, 102, 129, 133–135, 137, 141, 143, 148, 149, 153, 167, 181, 199, 200

Title IX, xxiii, xxiv, 12–14, 24–27, 84, 105, 116, 117, 166, 193, 194, 197, 203, 204, 208

Index

Transfer portal. *See under* National Collegiate Athletic Association (NCAA)

United States Soccer Development Academy (USSDA), 8, 9, 66, 106, 131, 132, 207, 208

United States Soccer Federation, 36, 66

University of Chicago, 117–20

University of New Mexico; athletic department and budget, xx, xxiv, xxv, 11, 12, 20, 24, 33, 47, 81, 83–93, 100, 116, 117, 132, 136, 145, 151, 152, 156, 185, 190, 191, 194, 202–5, 212; board of regents, 1, 4, 5, 9–11, 14, 24, 61, 84, 91, 100, 109, 115, 134, 143, 176, 186, 192, 195, 196; enrollment, 24, 25, 86; investigations, xxv, 83, 84, 89; ski teams, 15, 26, 90–92, 189, 191, 197, 198, 203

Vial, Antoine, 10, 19, 30, 31, 33, 48, 53, 57, 58, 62, 69, 70, 102, 103, 104, 136, 141, 143, 150, 151, 153, 162, 165, 166, 175, 179, 180, 181

Virgen, Erik (Gallo), 19, 28, 54, 55, 71, 112, 127–38, 149, 159, 172, 180, 199

Williams, Nick, 9, 28, 58–61, 68, 97, 142, 159, 160, 187, 197, 200

Youth soccer, 35–37, 74, 76, 131, 166, 168, 185, 208

About the Author

Ryan Swanson is a professor in the Honors College at the University of New Mexico. The author of numerous books and articles about sports in America, Ryan also continues to play in an old-man basketball league at noon several days a week. Ryan and his wife, Rachael, live with their teenagers—Carter, Tyler, and Kate—in Corrales, New Mexico.